Charlotte Smith:
Romanticism, poetry
and the
culture of gender

MANCHESTER
UNIVERSITY PRESS

Jacqueline M. Labbe

Charlotte Smith:
Romanticism, poetry
and the
culture of gender

Manchester University Press
Manchester and New York
distributed exclusively in the USA by Palgrave

Published by Manchester University Press
Oxford Road, Manchester M13 9NR, UK
and Room 400, 175 Fifth Avenue, New York, NY 10010, USA
www.manchesteruniversitypress.co.uk

Distributed exclusively in the USA by
Palgrave, 175 Fifth Avenue, New York NY 10010, USA

Distributed exclusively in Canada by
UBC Press, University of British Columbia, 2029 West Mall,
Vancouver, BC, Canada V6T 1Z2

British Library Cataloguing-in-Publication Data
A catalogue record for this book is available from the British Library

Library of Congress Cataloging-in-Publication Data
A catalog record for this book is available from the Library of Congress

ISBN: 978 0 7190 8321 1 paperback

First published by Manchester University Press in hardback 2003

First digital edition produced by Lightning Source 2011

For Stuart Curran, who showed the way, and for Rod and Indie, who keep me steady.

Contents

Illustrations

Acknowledgements

Anyone who works on Charlotte Smith owes much to Stuart Curran, but I feel privileged to owe perhaps more than most; as a graduate student at the University of Pennsylvania in the early 1990s I enjoyed the great benefit of learning to read Smith under his direction. I have always found Smith fascinating: her poetry was both familiar and brand new. I can't pretend that I understood her work when I first read it, however. It has taken the better part of a decade for me to feel some confidence in saying that this is what I think it 'means', and this is because Smith's poetry works on so many levels, as I try to show in this book. I have come to feel strongly that to discuss Smith solely as a woman writer is to miss her general influence, over both men and women, during the Romantic period. For introducing me to this pivotal figure, and for giving me the tools with which to interpret her, I thank Stuart.

Versions of some chapters and parts of chapters have already appeared in print. Parts of chapters 1, 4 and 5 have appeared in two essays published by Ashgate Press. An earlier version of chapter 2 appeared as part of an essay published in *Romanticism on the Net*. A portion of chapter 5 first appeared in an essay published by Blackwell Press. I am grateful to all for permission to reprint. In addition, I thank the University of Warwick for a term's study leave which enabled me to take the book into its final stages.

I am also very grateful to the many colleagues over the years who have listened patiently to earlier versions of chapters at conferences, especially to Simon Bainbridge, Emma Clery, Philip Cox, Nora Crook, Stuart Curran, Andrea Henderson, Jane Hodson, Kari Lokke, Robert Miles, Clarissa Campbell Orr, Donelle Ruwe, Lisa Vargo, and most especially Judith Pascoe, who also read and commented on parts of this book. The input of these valued colleagues, and others too numerous to mention, has made this a stronger study. The weaknesses that remain are, of course, my own.

Finally, I owe more than I can express to my husband Rod Jones and our little girl Indie Labbe-Jones. Their patience and willingness to sacrifice a summer holiday so that I could complete this book are inspiring. My deepest thanks and love go to both of them.

Introduction

Embodying the author

Later editions of Charlotte Smith's *Elegiac Sonnets* open with a frontispiece that presents the author to her readers as embattled and weary (Plate 1). In three-quarter profile, her face turned to the left, her eyes (demurely? thoughtfully?) down, Smith's expression is resigned and set, her face lined. We see an older Smith, with the sense of passing time encapsulated in the epigraph: 'Oh! Time has changed me since you saw me last. / And heavy Hours with Time's deforming Hand / Have written Strange Defeatures on my Face.' Smith's imagery allows her readers to map the idea of writing onto the living visage: her face has been, essentially, erased and rewritten. 'Defeatures' carries with it the weight of decay, and also the burden of loss: defeat. The passage of time, as the ensuing sonnets will make clear, brings with it neither peace nor resolution. It is a deforming process; it takes things apart, unbuilds them, wrecks them. This is a particularly physical epigraph, emphasizing work and the effect of work on the body. Reading it, we are encouraged to recognize Smith as an acquaintance, as someone we know, even as it also apologizes for her unrecognizability. The date of publication – 15 May 1797 – acts as a kind of diary appointment; we have known Smith in the past, and today, 15 May, we meet her again. The interplay between picture, caption, and publisher's self-designation creates a sense of intimacy that relies on understanding the writer as a 'real' woman. Not only do we 'know' Smith, we also know that she is changed, and we even, so to speak, know her address: Cadell and Davies Strand. The frontispiece functions as Smith's calling card, ensuring that we acknowledge our previous acquaintance with the poet. This, coupled with the title-page on which her name is inscribed prominently, means we enter the world of the sonnets with a fixed idea of who the speaking 'I' is. Placing herself within the realm of gendered subjects rather than aloof from the social

1 Frontispiece, *Elegiac Sonnets* (1797).

body, Smith plays on the very personal nature of her sonnets; we willingly read the 'I' as Smith because she has asked us to do so. The author is embodied, familiar, and with a personal history known to us ('Time has changed me since you saw me last').[1]

In the *Elegiac Sonnets*, Smith moves seamlessly from the unified author figured in the volume's preliminary pages to the multiple personae that inhabit the poetry. Felicity Edholm speaks of women's self-consciousness in culture, asserting that 'a woman must continually survey herself. A woman ... is both inside and outside, both self and other' ('Mirror' 155). Smith creates a fictive situation in her sonnets wherein the speaker is both 'self', as attested by the frontispiece and title-page, and a variety of 'others'. And yet, as this book contends, she is not merely mirroring roles or collating personae; instead, she is offering a specific group of roles and personae, each following from the frontispiece body; Smith uses the sonnets to explore and, in Edholm's words, survey the selves available to women, building on the body made visible in the preliminary pages. While this means that I read Smith's work as responsive to cultural pressures, I want to go further and argue that this is not a stance open only to contemporary feminists. Smith does not simply enact or represent the pressures attendant on being a woman writer in the Romantic period; she exploits them. By this I mean that she follows through with her self-reflexive embodiment and writes poetry that relies on her readers seeing and reading her as a woman, in a variety of culturally recognizable roles. Although the Romantic idealist is often exemplified through readings of Wordsworth, and often presented as a coherent individual who stands in contrast to the fragmented and violent culture that surrounds him, I will argue in this book that Smith's personae offer, not a new version of the idealist, but its original. This means querying the accepted gendering of Romanticism as constructed through readings of Wordsworth, while also problematizing gender itself. Traditionally, the virtue of masculinity is its ability to stand up to the forces competing with it; a characteristic of femininity is its multiplicity, its shiftiness in the face of those same forces. Lurking behind the masculine lament 'what does a woman want' is the even more lamentable 'what is a woman anyway?' From a cultural point of view, the many roles woman plays sustain her fictionality: this sex which is not 'One', as Irigaray phrases it, but without her sense of gratitude. But Smith's poetry shows an engagement with gender to the point that the separating labels of 'masculine' and 'feminine' themselves come under scrutiny.

During Smith's lifetime the idea of 'gender' as such was not discussed as it is today; theories of the constructed nature of selfhood, the fictiveness of femininity and masculinity,[2] were unheard-of. And yet gender was, of course, a concern in the eighteenth century. One of the most popular forms of non-fiction writing was the conduct book; those addressed to young women sought to encourage women to develop the 'feminine' characteristics that would make them good wives and mothers: submission, decorum, propriety, personal ornamentation. Hester Chapone, Hannah More, John Gregory and James Fordyce all sought to persuade young women that the path to happiness lay through the acculturation of the characteristics of womanhood. But even as conduct books instilled the notion of 'natural' femininity – that is, the 'true' woman behaved according to conduct-book principles, and thereby proved herself to be 'true' – so too they carry the subversive suggestion that much of femininity needed to be learned, that much that constituted 'true' womanhood was more often to be found in books than in life. What happens to gender if it is cultured? How can something that is learned be 'natural'? Above all, if femininity were inherent, a marker of a 'real' woman, why did so many women require coaching? We might even speculate that the inhabitants of the eighteenth century were uneasily aware of the contradictions underlying their own insistence on 'nature'; certainly, the more subterranean problematics of sexuality suggested multiple differences rather than a simple gendered binary, since both male and female homosexuality was described in texts ranging from the fantasies of pornography to the reality of Anne Lister's diaries of lesbian love.

The mores of gender in the eighteenth century suggest less consensus than a desire that there be consensus. As Harriet Guest says, 'gender difference seems a fundamental category of eighteenth-century forms of thought'.[3] Certainly, the assurance that men and women functioned differently and hence were fit for different spheres in life allowed for the convenience of categorizing, and cataloguing, human behaviour. It also meant that when men and women produced art, it could be read accordingly to a divinely ordered script, and conclusions could be drawn as to the artist's conforming with or deviation from that script. Guest focuses on how femininity impacted the reception of women's work; this book concentrates on how Smith herself writes gender, how her poetic personae not only exemplify femininity but also inhabit – that is, wear – it. What Guest concludes is a 'contentious' and 'evasive' 'cluster of notions' (66) is exploited by Smith in ways that reveal the artifice of gender, but under a cloak of complicity that can lead even Guest to refer to her 'feminine warbling and weeping' (64).[4] It is a critical commonplace that men were endowed with the 'world' while women were assigned the 'home' (although this is a division increasingly under challenge).[5] This is what necessitates Smith's masquerade: the productions of men were given a wider latitude, and certain kinds of difference were celebrated rather than condemned. For women, gender was almost always first on the agenda, something Mary Wollstonecraft recognizes when she calls for a revolution in female manners – in other words, a freeing from the strictures of gendered behaviour.

When I suggest, then, that Smith is what I would call 'self-aware' about her use of personae and voice in her poetry, I am not asserting that she, somehow, knew what others didn't, but that her work can be seen as representative of a certain kind of thoughtful approach to the notion of selfhood and subjectivity during the period, especially that inflected by the social, sexed body. As Susan Wolfson shows in her essay 'Gendering the Soul', for Smith and her contemporaries sex and gender were intimately linked, and the sexed body was a kind of shorthand for gender itself; writers debated whether the seemingly disembodied soul didn't actually carry the imprint of the body that housed it – and, correspondingly, its gender.[6] Returning to the frontispiece of the *Sonnets*, we remember that as much as Smith appeals to her readers to overlook the ravages of time, she nonetheless points them out plainly; she sexes the body of the writer as a woman.[7] And this is how she directs her readers to understand her poems: as the work of a woman writing in the face of overwhelming sorrows and trials. In the sonnets, she appeals to her readers' familiarity with the roles women play, and writes poems accordingly: we see most often the distressed and needy woman, sometimes a romantic damsel, sometimes a devoted mother, sometimes a martyr to sensibility. In her longer poems *The Emigrants* and *Beachy Head* she writes gender less personally but no less visibly.

In part this book takes up the notion of 'Romantic theatricality' as elucidated by Judith Pascoe, since I argue that Smith performs gendered stances. In this way I also, of course, follow Judith Butler's theories that gender itself is performative. But where Butler might locate this performativity psychologically, here I take it to be much more literal. Again, the frontispiece comes in handy. We know Smith is a woman not because she says she is, but because she looks like one; she wears the right clothes. The various voices that speak the sonnets are female because we know that the writer is; the situations they are in are inflected by her femininity because we are assured of her femininity. As the case of the Chevalier d'Eon shows, for Smith and her contemporaries dress went far to assure sex and, hence, gender.[8] The Chevalier's continuing quest to 'be' a woman was communicated in the display of women's costume, even as the desire of women to be soldiers was enabled by the assumption of a soldier's uniform.[9] With her ruffled and bowed headdress and filmy collar, Smith's sexed identity is fixed.

It would be easy to stop there, at a critical conclusion I have drawn based on my reading of the implications of textual evidence. However, I have already called Smith self-aware, and it is part of my argument that the decision to include her portrait in the *Sonnets* reflects Smith's desire to enlist a kind of gendered sympathy from her readers: that, as a woman writing, with female needs, she requires a certain kind of response. She needs to be rescued. If her readers find her personae attractive enough, they will buy her poetry; her financial troubles will ease; she will live happily ever after. As a marketing strategy, this depends on her readers seeing Smith as a sexed body, unable to meet her own needs and provide her own succour. And this in turn depends on Smith's ability to promote, rather than merely represent, gender politics. Literary criticism has tended to assume that gender politics need to be uncovered, that the people of the past were simply not equipped to understand their own deep collaboration with what we now identify as constructed behaviour.[10] This has created a kind of mystique around gender: criticism uncovers and gives voice to that which has been silenced (woman) and deconstructs and questions that which has been dominant (man).

The culture of gender also affects our perceptions of the past. Consider critical responses – by this I mean by the academics of the late twentieth century – to the poetry of the Romantic period. For years we learned that Romantic poetry could adequately be understood by studying six rather disparate male poets, conveniently divided into two 'generations': Wordsworth, Coleridge and the outsider Blake; Shelley, Byron and the outsider Keats. They apparently contained within their work the sole art of value during a period of about thirty years. And that art was, in gender terms (although the gendering was invisible until the advent of feminist criticism in the 1970s), overwhelmingly masculine: it was visionary, it reified abstract notions of Truth and Beauty, it was about the Self, the quest for an establishment of the subjective 'I'; it explored the world of the Imagination; it was based in a classical exploration of the values of Reason. While important studies of eighteenth and nineteenth-century women writers began appearing from the 1970s on

– by Ellen Moers, Mary Poovey and Margaret Homans, for instance – it was in Anne Mellor's 1988 collection *Romanticism and Feminism* that Romanticists began questioning the traditional formulation of Romanticism. The most influential essay in the collection, Stuart Curran's 'The "I" Altered', signals for many the beginning of the serious study of women poets, naming more than fifteen worth studying and containing thumbnail analyses of several of the most interesting. Marlon Ross's *The Contours of Masculine Desire: Romanticism and the Rise of Women's Poetry* appeared in 1989, along with Roger Lonsdale's *Eighteenth-Century Women Poets*; both explore the work of women whose names are familiar now but brand new only a little more than a decade ago: Montague, Barbauld, Robinson, Tighe, Smith, Hemans, Landon, and so on. Finally, in 1993 Mellor published *Romanticism and Gender*, while the rest of the 1990s saw an increasing number of books and articles with 'gender' in the title. However, at this point we must ask ourselves: what emerged from these works? We now have a picture of women's writing that actually reifies gender binaries; as Curran phrased it, their work is 'occupied continually in discriminating minute objects or assembling a world out of its disjointed particulars . . . The quotidian is absolute.'[11] Ross's study situates women poets as *reactive to* masculine Romanticism, as concerned with creating an alternative feminine realm. Mellor's book argues that women writers wrote about their gendered experiences, and those who didn't were 'cross-dressing'. Each of these works contains valuable insights and argues pressing theses, and yet the picture being built up is the one still with us today: women writers are quotidian-bound, they explore the domestic, they are concerned with detail; their talent, skill and imagination are bound in their gender, as is the talent of the men. Art and body thus bind to produce gendered texts. The culture of gender – its artifice and its insidiousness – as much creates as it defines. If critics expect that a woman's writing will reflect a woman's work, then it will. Lonsdale's vast anthology creates the impression, for instance, that women in the eighteenth century wrote little besides short poems about 'feminine' concerns.

It is certainly not my intention to dismiss these or any of the groundbreaking gender studies to date, but more to ask where they have led us. There is still an impulse to study women and men writers separately, to devote books to single male authors and articles to grouped female authors: as Judith Pascoe says, to 'assume that . . . women writers share a common aesthetic' based on their sex.[12] Gender, or at least femininity, overrides all other concerns of upbringing, class, genre, style, and so on, to link women as disparate as Mary Robinson and Anna Letitia Barbauld as 'women writers' in a way that few would attempt with, say, Crabbe and Byron. The essentially undifferentiated group of 'women writers' coexists with the unexamined implication that they need gender explained to them, when perhaps what is more necessary is for critics to dispense with their own cultural biases. As Diane Long Hoeveler says, 'white, bourgeois women writers have not simply been the passive victims of male-created constructions but rather have constructed themselves . . . in their own literature'.[13] Long Hoeveler limits this self-construction to the Gothic victim, but her point carries: if (women) writers construct themselves – or rather, construct familiar versions of femininity – in their writing, then perforce the question of the construction of the gendered self is voiceable. It is no coincidence, I think, that Long Hoeveler begins her study with Charlotte Smith, a highly skilled speaker.

Long Hoeveler studies only Smith's novels; this book investigates her poetry and the apparatus of her volumes: prefaces, notes, engravings. Smith's poetry reveals the consistent development and redevelopment of the speaker's voice – the poetic persona – in a way that her novels do not. The novels dramatize certain aspects of Smith's biography, but the poetry explores interiority in a recognizably 'Romantic' way. Part of this book's thesis is that Smith's poetic development both inspires and coincides with the development of the Romantic 'I', and that this is intimately bound up with ideas of gender. As has been documented by Judith Stanton among others, Smith considered her poems to be her 'serious' work, and as such they reflect an artistry that is more deliberately structured to reflect the persona. Even as Wordsworth has long been considered to be the consummate Romantic builder of selfhood and subjectivity, so too Smith – Wordsworth's poetic predecessor and an undoubted influence on him – recognizes that poetry can be used to map aspects of the self. For Smith, this means aspects of the social self, especially those that society uses to define and contain women. Even as a sonnet, then, addresses the moon or the tides, or *The Emigrants* explores the situation of French exiles, or *Beachy Head* uses the loco-descriptive to explore British history and identity, or various songs and fables introduce children to botany, Smith reiterates a prevailing concern with culture. She creates a parade of acculturated identities, using her poetry to question the nature of the gendered self, and by extension revealing poetry's suitability to contain and represent Selfhood: the Romantic notion of individuality, but inflected by a desire to challenge social constructions of individuality. This is, of course, on the one hand a keen marketing ploy: speaking with the voice of the mother or the distressed woman allows Smith to tap into the perennial romantic appeal of such feminine types. But while Smith would have been well aware of the exploitation value of such figures, and not at all averse to using them to make her poetry more sellable, I argue that the significance of her style goes beyond its market potentials. Smith's work, I contend, demonstrates her comprehension of the culture of gender – the cultural expectation that women were feminine, that femininity and femaleness were identical. Her poetry contains both a critique and an investigation of the artificiality of socialized gender.

The Romantic culture of gender and subjectivity as developed by Smith entails an alternative model of selfhood, one that questions ideas both of Romantic 'sincerity' and Romantic 'irony', that instead devotes itself to a deconstruction – an unbuilding – of Romantic gender. In this book, I hope to complicate the ease with which gender has been assigned to bodies and to subjectivity during this period, and to open the parameters of social construction. Smith's work offers images in which conventional gender roles are contested, even as they are superficially endorsed. For this is a key point: Smith's work is not openly radical like Wollstonecraft's, but it is also not the conventional scribblings of a gentlewoman; she 'strays', as the sonnets phrase it repeatedly, and she is careful to mark the path from which she deviates. By this I mean that for Smith, writing was as much a commercial as a creative venture, and as such she had an audience to think of. For this reason, her deployments of gender are as attractive as they are subversive; when she models herself as a woman in need she is as much appealing to the chivalric impulses of her readership as she is dramatizing the alienating effects of social pressures. As Stanton's work shows, Smith's prose always made her more money than her poetry (by nearly 3 to 1), but in certain key years her poetry brought in significant earnings: 1789, the year of the fifth edition of the sonnets, published by subscription (£180); 1793, the year of *The Emigrants* (£50); 1797, the year *Elegiac Sonnets* went to two volumes (£250); and, ironically, 1807, the year of the posthumous publication of *Beachy Head* (£300). Smith's style of subjectivity is designed to attract, as Sarah Zimmerman notes in her insightful discussion of Smith's lyricism.[14] But it is simultaneously a rejection of a slavish devotion to social mores.

As I noted above, Smith's contemporaries were probably more aware of gender as a 'distinct category of social difference [related] to physical sex differences'[15] than they have been given credit for; Kathryn

Sutherland's recent article on education and conduct books establishes the late eighteenth-century impulse to inculcate gender through reading, to impose 'natural' gender and oppose 'unnatural' femininity.[16] But it is also probable that in the main her contemporaries were less exercised by this paradox than Smith. For Smith, however, the paradox of gender pointed to the contradictions of representation itself, and hence the establishment of the self. The Lacanian Symbolic – that which 'holds together relationships in patterns that relate them in particular ways', and often held to regulate an order of things by implication masculine and historically dominant – cooperates in Smith's poetic with the Imaginary – that which suspends such relationships and fuses representations.[17] She straddles multiple borders, and this brings such borders both into alignment and into question. In many ways the creation of spaces like the Symbolic and the Imaginary (or the abject or the chora) feeds into the culture of gender, since they rely so heavily on a gendered social body and a system of opposed binaries. And without wanting to challenge the viability of such categories, in this book I nonetheless approach theoretical terminology following Smith's model; that is, I make use of what's useful without subscribing wholesale to the model. Smith is flexible with and aware of gender constructions and constraints, and her work encourages a more wide-ranging approach to theory than is usually the case. Even as we understand gender partly through our engagements with different theories of gender, so too different strands of Smith's poetry call to mind multiple, and occasionally intriguingly competitive, strands of critical theory. In arguing against a monolithic approach to gender during the Romantic period, I reject a monolithic approach to theory. Instead, in investigating Smith's explorations of the paradoxes of gender and subjectivity, this book also explores the possibilities of applying theory. In practice, this means that while this book offers readings derived from, for instance, Kristeva or Cixous, or points out ways in which Smith's techniques can be seen to anticipate aspects of feminist literary theory, I do not rely on Kristeva or Cixous consistently or comprehensively. In not doing so, I hope to illustrate the ease with which Smith's poetry accepts a variety of theoretical models. Why this should be the case is a topic for another book, although I would speculate that it is connected to Smith's experimental approach to gender assignments.

Smith's engagement with gender, subjectivity and the body, then, expands the possibilities of Romantic poetry. In ways she is writing the *Bildung*, a text which, according to Marc Redfield's distillation of Gadamer, produces its own meaning.[18] But while she 'separates the subject from the Subject' (46), she also challenges the hegemony of the *Bildung* by revealing its processes and exploiting its gender mechanics; that is, she in a sense *allows* the text to produce its own meaning precisely because she seems invested in mores of gender. But simultaneously she uses gender metaphorically, to represent itself and hence show itself as representation. Lucy Newlyn writes that 'the integrity of the subject [is] placed disturbingly (but also excitingly) under question every time we write or read'.[19] Smith plays out the disturbance and the excitement; she disturbs gender boundaries each time she seems to conform to them, and she excites the Self by shaking it up. For her, subjectivity is a fluid entity; her poetry serves as her opportunity to assert this. And yet she consistently preserves the fiction of a unified Self. Unlike Mary Robinson, whose profusion of pseudonyms conveys her theatrical approach to subjectivity, Smith is apparently always the same person, as her title-pages emphasize. Changed only by time, she approaches her readers as the 'real person' her frontispiece suggests. As Arleen Dallery notes, 'woman's body is always mediated by language; the human body is a text, a sign'; when she 'writes the body' she frees herself from masculine desire and the male gaze.[20] But Smith wants it both ways: she wants to be looked at and she wants to escape visual confinement. Hence, she inflects her poetry with a representation of her body, and makes sure her readers know her as a person, a task also carried on in the many Prefaces to her poetry. She then writes poetry that emphasizes straying, exile, alienation and mystique. Further, she writes poetry that would elide subjectivity altogether, were it not for the emphasis she has placed on her self as a physical subject. In this way, Smith's creation of 'Charlotte Smith' places her authorial persona as a social being, a literary celebrity whose presence is assumed even if the poem itself offers another speaker altogether (say, Werther). Smith, like Wordsworth, writes the 'I' so convincingly (and, I would argue, deliberately so), that it can be difficult to tear one's attention away from a figure who is, ingeniously, more director than actor.

Newlyn describes women's poetry as creating 'new relations between subject and object' (236), but oddly she does not mention Smith's work. And yet Smith seems to exemplify Newlyn's argument that 'women poets' (the perpetual monolith) work with the existing system in order to 'reconfigure' it. However, Newlyn's book also carries on the kind of critical culture of gender I glossed above. The authors she studies are presented as playing out gendered relationships (hence women 'reconfigure' the masculine norm) but not as playing *with* gender. A quick

survey of Smith's stylized personae shows that she is more a player than
played; it is not difficult to divide her speakers into categories of gen-
dered subjectivities. So, for instance, we see that in her many Prefaces to
her poetry she presents the 'I' as a Woman in Need. Her iconic self-rep-
resentation in the poems allows versions of the feminine body to coexist:
we read the poet as mother, as a woman in distress, and as an ingénue-
lover. *The Emigrants* examines the place of gender when poeticizing war,
while *Beachy Head* establishes, posthumously, a poetic self who manip-
ulates public perceptions of gender and behaviour. In her poems for chil-
dren Smith combines the mother with the teacher, but the lessons she
teaches are far from conventional. The subject–object relationship is not
so much created anew, as interfused.

Smith, then, uses 'persona' as a kind of metaphor for the fracturing
of identity that a strict adherence to the idea of 'gender' requires. She
builds up, in her poetry, a proliferating Self whose intrinsic 'Self-ness' is
dependent on cultural mores of behaviour, but she also questions those
mores through more or less open challenges: for instance, when her
speaker blatantly critiques the British class system in *The Emigrants*, or
when the voice she speaks with in her supplementary material, most
especially her notes, plainly prefers her own poetical, scientific and
observational methods to those established authorities like Linnaeus,
Shakespeare and others. Smith's use of personae shows her to understand
gender as a kind of garment, and she wears that most suited to her times
and most attractive to her readers. She makes sure her readers know her
and she passes on enough information to justify her incursion into
print. She thus remains, in Mary Poovey's enduring phrasing, both a
proper lady and a woman writer. But she also embeds in her poetry a
challenge to gender and propriety, and it is this that is harder to see, pre-
cisely because of the care with which Smith establishes her embodied
subjectivity.

I sketched above a picture of Smith's deployment of gendered per-
sonae in her poems. But this is only part of the whole. What happens if
we look at the content of Smith's poetry? According to the culture of
gender, we should find a concern with the detail, the quotidian, women's
work, the domestic. As Curran notes, she 'made a virtual career out of
self-pity' ('"I"', 199); her poetry is infused with sadness and loss, need
and grief, and she returns repeatedly to her lack of a home, of succour,
of protection. In fact, she makes her sorrows plain: financial troubles,
wastrel husband, dishonest lawyers. She comports herself as a romantic
female figure, an abandoned wife, a needy but devoted mother: she

inhabits roles all consonant with proper femininity, and advertises her feminine need each time she pleads for death or gasps for assistance. In short, she plays the gender game with skill.

We could conclude that she merely displays her acculturation, her faithful reading of conduct books having had their intended effect. And yet, isn't it a little bit odd that the proper lady so openly parades her need? Is it wholly 'feminine' to tell the world about an inadequate husband? Does it conform to gender strictures that she robustly sets to work for herself and her children? And above all, is it genteel to wander deserted landscapes at night, as she does so often in her poetry? Her poems both write gender and reject it. In Sonnet LXII, 'Written on passing by moonlight through a village, while the ground was covered with snow', the speaker conducts herself in quite an unladylike fashion – that is, once we have determined the sex of the speaker, which is available from our knowledge of the author, then her gender kicks in, imposed by an audience familiar with the script. I would argue that the poem itself betrays no hint of gendering, except for the reader's expectations of who can – is permitted to – do what. But Smith invites her readers to identify the speaker with the author, and it is because she has taken so much trouble to establish herself as an embodied author that we are so comfortable reading gender into her work.

In Sonnet LXII, Smith simultaneously enacts her gender in her plea for help and her womanly despair, and rejects such a role in her wandering about.

Sonnet LXII: Written on passing by moon-light through
a village, while the ground was covered with snow

While thus I wander, cheerless and unblest,
    And find in change of place but change of pain;
In tranquil sleep the village labourers rest,
    And taste that quiet I pursue in vain!
Hush'd is the hamlet now, and faintly gleam
    The dying embers, from the casement low
Of the thatch'd cottage; while the Moon's wan beam
    Lends a new lustre to the dazzling snow.
O'er the cold waste, mid the freezing night,
    Scarce heeding whither, desolate I stray;
For me, pale Eye of Evening, thy soft light
    Leads to no happy home; *my* weary way
Ends but in sad vicissitudes of care;
I only fly from doubt – to meet despair!

Contemporary queer theory has shown us the complexities residing in a word like 'passing', while even in the eighteenth century the word 'stray', in line 10, connotes transgression. I am not, however, suggesting that Smith implies anything about sexuality; rather, I think that her diction invites us to look more closely at the speaker's purported identity. This speaker haunts a quiet village, an 'unblest' outcast, lacking the 'happy home' that is the proper sphere for the proper lady. What is the speaker hoping to 'pass' as? If we set aside the gendering that Smith insists on, and read the poem on its own terms, it could easily be called 'Wordsworthian', and thereby identified as 'Romantic' in a masculinized way. Indeed, it *is* Wordsworthian; its self-reflexivity, its inscription of the Self, its exploration of the internalized imagination all correspond to familiar moments in Wordsworth's own poetry. His fragment 'The Discharged Soldier' almost exactly replicates this scenario of an isolated speaker, a deserted public way, and a night-time wanderer (Wordsworth's poem, however, post-dates Smith's; if anything, his approach and style is 'Smithian'). What colours this poems is the tone, not of the feminine, but of the masculine. Reading it with the certain knowledge that the writer is a woman, we see it almost irresistibly as political, while Smith's readers would have seen another example of her feminine need. But if this knowledge is withheld, then the poem could as easily – indeed, perhaps more expectedly – be spoken by a man.[21] Under this rubric, Sonnet LXII is written by a woman speaking as a man speaking as a woman: in other words, 'passing'. Such layers of gendering indicate at least one of the regular paths from which the speaker 'strays'. Smith teasingly embeds in her poem a recognition of her own straying; unlike many of her other sonnets, this one has a strictly regular, Shakespearian rhyme scheme: *abab cdcd efef gg*. Even as her persona wanders from the straight path of gender, her poem sticks fast to the rules of genre: form regularizes content.

By contrast, Sonnet LXX, 'On being cautioned against walking on an headland overlooking the sea, because it was frequented by a lunatic', offers a more unsettling, even unsociable, picture.

Sonnet LXX: On being cautioned against walking on an headland
overlooking the sea, because it was frequented by a lunatic

Is there a solitary wretch who hies
  To the tall cliff, with starting pace or slow,
And, measuring, views with wild and hollow eyes
  Its distance from the waves that chide below;

Who, as the sea-borne gale with frequent sighs
  Chills his cold bed upon the mountain turf,
With coarse, half-utter'd lamentation, lies
  Murmuring sad responses to the dashing surf?
In moody sadness, on the giddy brink,
  I see him more with envy than with fear;
He has no *nice felicities* that shrink
  From giant horrors; wildly wandering here,
He seems (uncursed with reason) not to know
The depth or the duration of his woe.

The title conjures up a host of disembodied voices urging 'caution' while also offering a reason for the poem's composition: it is the result of 'being cautioned'. A headland allows for the prospect view, which, as I and other critics have argued, is a privileged place of visual power and corresponds to the social prominence afforded to masculinity. As in Sonnet LXII, the 'I' is only gendered once we know the sex of the poet; the poem itself offers no clue. Once engendering has occurred, the poem begins to challenge its own social position. Again, the speaker is out alone, moving quickly to occupy a traditionally masculine space; the male figure already there is rendered unfit because of his madness. She sets up a comparison between herself and the lunatic, which the accompanying engraving reinforces (see Plate 2): the reader is further encouraged to associate the speaker of the poem with Smith, given the visual clues. The female figure wears a headdress similar to the one Smith wears in the frontispiece, while her shawl resembles the filmy collar shown in the frontispiece. Indeed, the very presence of the engraving is significant; as I will discuss in chapter 1, of the many images of women in the *Sonnets*, this is the only one that could conceivably be viewed as Smith. Thus another subject/object fusion is presented: the lunatic is there because he doesn't know any better, and she is there because she does.

The sonnet is Petrarchan in structure: the octave constructs the lunatic, while the sestet both presents the writing self and encapsulates Smith's dismissal of gender. Balancing 'on the giddy brink', a position akin to her 'straying' from Sonnet LXII, she assumes the power and authority granted through visual mastery, *seeing* rather then *being seen*. Even as she implies that she feels what could be seen as feminine 'felicities' (Smith uses the word 'nice' to modify them, but in a footnote quotes Walpole: ''Tis delicate felicities that shrink / When rocking winds are loud'), she also asserts her possession of that most masculine of accomplishments, reason: the lunatic, 'uncursed with reason', does not

In moody Sadness on the giddy Brink
I view him more with Envy than with Fear

2 Plate accompanying 'Sonnet LXX: On being cautioned against walking on an headland'.

understand the awfulness of his situation; she, by inference 'cursed' with reason, keenly understands her own. But even as she claims reason, she rejects it as a curse rather than the blessing that distinguishes 'man' from the animals. This complex reaction to reason also forces a confrontation with the aesthetic as defined by Schiller and paraphrased by Redfield: 'the subject, having passed through sensuous determination [identification with the lunatic] and developed the autonomous power of reason [both claimed and rejected in the parenthesis], must harmonize these faculties in a moment of disinterested free play: "we must call this condition of real and active determinability the *aesthetic*"' (52 n.8). If we see the aesthetic as the field that prompts the poetic, then this sonnet functions less as an exemplar of gender politics and more as a statement of poetic drive. Despite its specific setting and an engraving that attaches material figures to the poem's actors, to disembody this poem means to recognize its literary qualities: its symbolic approach to subjectivity, its allusiveness, its meaningful structure, all of which contribute to an aesthetic of representation. And yet, because of the embodied speaker and the critical impulse to read gender, the poem is 'about' lunacy or 'about' femininity. Even the poem's structure militates against easy conclusions: as I noted, it contains a Petrarchan octave and sestet, but in rhyme scheme it approximates the three quatrains and couplet that make up the Shakespearian sonnet. Unlike Sonnet LXII, however, Sonnet LXX is anything but regular: *abab acac dede bb.* Interwoven and, in the couplet, doubling back on itself, its rhyme scheme is as deranged as the lunatic – as unbalanced as gender itself.

Not merely a performer, Charlotte Smith also directs, and in this way she exemplifies both the performative – the theatrical – nature of gender, and its use-value in a literary market increasingly populated by authors with an eye to the sale.[22] Romanticism itself must be reviewed in the light of Smith's manipulations of gender, genre and selfhood. Smith's knowing acceptance of gender roles and her self-conscious use of femininity have much to do with the marketability of her poetry; as Long Hoeveler also notes, she was well aware of the commodification of the female form. But it also forces a recognition that gender in the Romantic period was less a closed book requiring modern critical translation and more a living concern for people whose sense of subjectivity was so closely bound up with their sexed body. Smith goes beyond reflecting the public opinion that women wrote differently from men and required special handling; she makes commercial use of this assumption. She defuses the risks attendant on her publicity by insisting on the more culturally admired attributes of femininity: motherhood, wifehood, helplessness, need. The divisions between propriety and rebellion, belonging and exile, the self and society that Smith builds into her works coexist with a deliberate creation of the sorrowing woman designed to captivate the public eye. Her poetry is concerned with the very 'Romantic' idea of the nature and meaning of the Self, and moreover, in her multiple versions of the feminized 'I', with the nature and meaning of gender.

Chapter 1 will discuss Smith's prefaces and illustrations to her poetry as examples of the marketing of the Self in Need, and contrast this with the challenges to authority contained in the poems' notes. As Smith builds up an ever-more-complete picture of the sorrows under which she suffers, she in turn constructs a persona who depends on a readership ready and willing to 'rescue' her by buying her poetry. At the same time, Smith treads a fine line between selling a constructed persona and selling herself as a public woman – that is, someone whose wares are the product of her pen rather than of her body. This manipulation of the marketable self sits uneasily with the blunt and forthright voice Smith uses in her notes. The periphery, a half-invisible space, resembles the Kristevan chora and allows Smith the luxury of strength. Situated literally between the Prefaces and the Notes, the engravings are appropriately liminal in subject-matter and readability. Smith thus explores the possibilities available in the printed text.

Chapter 2 will investigate the place of motherhood in 1780s–1790s culture, linking its embryonic iconization with Smith's overt posturing in her sonnets. Structuring many of the sonnets around her dead daughter Augusta, Smith justifies her public self by creating the persona of the Good Mother – the woman who only writes because her children need support. She therefore elides her own pride in writing and desire to write and highlights instead her very proper concern with her children's welfare. The cult of motherhood that became fixed by the Victorian period finds its roots in the Romantic-period insistence on the naturalness of maternal care and grief. Smith matches her self-identified Mother with those presented in *The Emigrants*. There, motherhood stands as a symbol of general female alienation from a violently masculine culture. In both guises, the mother figures as a mask for the disenfranchised self.

In chapter 3, I balance Smith's construction of motherhood with her even more prominent picturing the woman in need. The revival of the romance and its trope of chivalry informs this discussion of Smith's persistent situating of her poetic persona as sorrowful, needy, and abandoned. Continuing the self-portrayal first built up in the Prefaces, she publicises her private sorrows, banking on the gallantry of a reading public to 'save' her. For Smith the selling of one's sorrows is as much a ploy as a realistic depiction of her *actual* needs. In both chapters 2 and 3 I will also explore the ramifications of 'disembodying' the sonnets.

Having discussed Smith's sonnet personae in the previous chapters, chapter 4 contextualizes her poetic activities by moving to her long verse-rumination on the French Revolution, *The Emigrants* (1793). It examines the place of gender when poeticizing war, and investigates Smith's movements from a feminised position of sympathy and expressiveness to a more masculine involvement with the machinery of war. In this poem, Smith takes up a more complex involvement with conventions of gender; as she concentrates on war and exile she also manoeuvres her persona dramatically, as her construction of scenarios and theatrical language suggests. In *The Emigrants*, the artificial nature of the gendered Self becomes more apparent, and Smith's embodied speaker begins her move away from the culture that she portrays as increasingly stultifying.

Chapter 5 will concentrate on *Beachy Head* (1807), Smith's answer to Wordsworth's 'Tintern Abbey'. In this poem she establishes a poetic self who manipulates public perceptions of gender and behaviour. This chapter situates Smith's most important poem in a political climate that relied on the metaphorics of the prospect view and argues for Smith's confident presentation of a self who is both feminine and masculine; in adopting either gendered position as she sees fit, Smith creates a hybrid, fluid self, and acts out the constructed nature of gendered bodies. *Beachy Head* presents its readers with a multivocal poet, and exemplifies Smith's manipulations of gender and her understanding of the expectations and requirements of her culture. Its status as posthumous and incomplete reflect and ironize Smith's poetics. And irony functions, too, in Smith's poems for children (1804–6), which I turn to briefly in the Coda. I read in her playful recastings of 'personal' sorrows and troubles as affecting the likes of bees and fish an understanding of subjectivity as constructed and fluid, which *Beachy Head* then takes up more seriously. By relating Smith's work to Wordsworth's, I conclude the book by suggesting that much of what we have learned about Romanticism from studying Wordsworth's texts is ultimately traceable, instead, to Smith's.

Gender too often becomes a critical tool that limits rather than enlarges understanding; even as we investigate its parameters and its artificiality, we reimpose its constructs on a past unable to defend itself.

Monica Wittig has said that 'in reality, as soon as there is a locutor in discourse, as soon as there is an "I", gender manifests itself . . . [E]ach time I say "I", I reorganize the world from my point of view and through abstraction I lay claim to universality'.[23] Few concepts are more abstract than gender, and few more concretely applied. Charlotte Smith's prominence and her importance as a founder of what we now call Romanticism situates her as a focal figure; her knowing manipulations of the literary market and her canny realization that 'sex' – that is, the engendered body – sells mark her as not merely a woman writer participating in what Anne Mellor has called 'Feminine Romanticism' but as a poet aware of and making use of cultural expectations. Smith complicates notions of sincerity and irony, and her poetry offers an alternative version of Romantic subjectivity. Readers were accustomed to associating their speakers – forlorn, lost, despairing – with the poet herself. She encouraged this by surrounding the poems with a print apparatus that linked author and speakers: that embodied the author as an acquaintance of the reader. A self-aware poet, she as much 'makes' Romanticism as reflects it. Charlotte Smith's poetry, from the *Elegiac Sonnets* through *The Emigrants* to *Beachy Head* and beyond, shows the re-creation of the poetic persona as a socially embodied self, responsive to and ultimately rewriting the culture which confines it. Even as her poetry cultures gender, it is the culture of gender that sustains our interpretations. Smith's poetry encourages a rethinking of our approach to Romantic gender: her shrewd appreciation of the multiplicities of femininity indicate that, in Romanticism, the subject of gender is an open one.

Notes

1 As Sarah Zimmerman also notes, 'the engraving provided a visual counterpart to the verbal self-portrait that her writings comprised. Smith was sharply aware that her continuing success was generated largely by her readers' sympathetic response to a figure of herself as elegiac poet' (50). My reading differs from Zimmerman's in the number and kind(s) of portraits Smith offers in the sonnets. See Zimmerman, 'Charlotte Smith's Letters and the Practice of Self-Presentation', *Princeton University Library Chronicle* 53 (1991): 50–77.

2 What Julia Epstein and Kristina Straub call 'the pliancy of anatomic and biological categories' (3): a particularly apt phrasing that mirrors Smith's range of gendered personae in her poems. See Epstein and Straub, 'Introduction', *Body Guards: The Cultural Politics of Gender Ambiguity* (New York: Routledge, 1991): 1–28.

3 Harriet Guest, 'Eighteenth-Century Femininity: "A Supposed Sexual Character"', in *Women and Literature in Britain 1700–1800*, ed. Vivien Jones (Cambridge: Cambridge University Press, 2000), 46–68: 47. Subsequent references will be made in the text.

4 Guest draws on a quote from George Dyer: Liberty 'weep[s] in Charlotte's melting page', from the poem 'On Liberty', 1792. In reiterating Dyer's gendered image, Guest apparently accepts it.

5 See, for instance, Anne Mellor, *Mothers of the Nation: Women's Political Writing in England, 1780–1830* (Bloomington: Indiana University Press, 2000), and the essays in *Women, Writing and the Public Sphere, 1700–1830*, eds. Elizabeth Eger, Charlotte Grant, Cliona Ò Gallchoir, and Penny Warburton (Cambridge: Cambridge University Press, 2001).

6 See Susan Wolfson, 'A Lesson in Romanticism: Gendering the Soul', *Lessons of Romanticism: A Critical Companion*, eds. Thomas Pfau and Robert F. Gleckner (Durham: Duke University Press, 1998), 349–375.

7 In a letter to her publishers, Smith reacts to the portrait as an unsatisfactory likeness: 'I very much doubt whether the faults I see in the engraving can be alterd – The face is too long . . . there is a want of spirit in the eyes . . .' This indicates her awareness that, for her readers, the portrait 'is' the artist. The letter is quoted in Zimmerman, 'Charlotte Smith's Letters', 51.

8 For a discussion of the Chevalier and 'his' cultural significance, see Gary Kates, 'The Transgendered World of the Chevalier/Chevaliere d'Eon', *Journal of Modern History* 67 (1995), 558–594.

9 See, for example, Diane Dugaw, *Warrior Women and Popular Balladry, 1650–1850* (Cambridge: Cambridge University Press, 1989).

10 In an astute phrasing, Judith Halberstam call this 'perverse presentism': we 'questio[n] in the first instance what we think we already know' only to 'mov[e] back towards the question of what we think we have found' with the goal of 'stabilizing what we think we know today'. Quoted in Ira Livingston, 'The "No-Trump Bid" on Romanticism and Gender', *Romanticism and Gender*, ed. Anne Janowitz (Cambridge: D. S. Brewer, 1998), 161–173: 163.

11 Stuart Curran, 'The "I" Altered', *Romanticism and Feminism*, ed. Anne Mellor (Bloomington: Indiana University Press, 1988), 186–207: 189, 192. Subsequent references will be made in the text.

12 Judith Pascoe, '"Unsex'd Females": Barbauld, Robinson and Smith', *The Cambridge Companion to English Literature 1740–1830*, eds. Jon Mee and Tom Keymer (Cambridge: Cambridge University Press, forthcoming 2003).

13 Diane Long Hoeveler, *Gothic Feminism: The Professionalization of Gender from Charlotte Smith to the Brontes* (Liverpool: Liverpool University Press, 1998), 4. Subsequent references will be made in the text.

14 See Zimmerman, *Romanticism, Lyricism and History* (State University of New York Press, 1999), chapter 1. Zimmerman's discussion of Smith's imagery is an important and valuable contribution to Smith studies.

15 Judith Shapiro, 'Transsexualism: Reflections on the Persistence of Gender and the Mutability of Sex', in *Body Guards*, eds. Epstein and Straub, 248–279: 271.

16 Kathryn Sutherland, 'Writing on Education and Conduct: Arguments for Female Improvement', *Women and Literature in Britain, 1700–1800*, ed. Jones, 25–45.

17 See Tamsin E. Lorraine, *Gender, Identity and the Production of Meaning* (Oxford: Westview Press, 1990).

18 Marc Redfield, 'Romanticism, *Bildung*, and the Literary Absolute', *Lessons of Romanticism*, eds. Pfau and Gleckner, 41–54: 45. Subsequent references will be made in the text.

19 Lucy Newlyn, *Reading, Writing, and Romanticism: The Anxiety of Reception* (Oxford: Oxford University Press, 2000), ix. Subsequent references will be made in the text.

20 Arleen Dallery, 'The Politics of Writing (the) Body: *Écriture Feminine*', *Gender/Body/Knowledge: Feminist Reconstructions of Being and Knowing*, eds. Alison M. Jaggar and Susan R. Bordo (New Brunswick: Rutgers University Press, 1989), 52–67: 54.

21 See Celeste Langan, *Romantic Vagrancy: Wordsworth and the Simulation of Freedom* (Cambridge: Cambridge University Press, 1995), for arguments that wandering is most frequently troped as a masculine activity.

22 See, for instance, Colin Campbell, *The Romantic Ethic and the Spirit of Modern Consumerism* (Oxford: Blackwell, 1987). I am grateful to Judith Pascoe for this reference.

23 Monica Wittig, 'The Mark of Gender', *The Poetics of Gender*, ed. Nancy K. Miller (New York: Columbia University Press, 1986), 63–73: 65, 67.

1

The possibilities of print

This chapter will explore in greater detail Smith's 'embodied' author by paying special attention to the marginal, peripheral aspects of her texts: the prefaces, notes and engravings that enliven the poetry and allow Smith to experiment with the possibilities inherent in print culture.[1] While, as succeeding chapters argue, Smith's poetic persona undergoes meaningful change as she moves from the sonnet to the more expansive blank verse of *The Emigrants* and *Beachy Head*, from the sonnets on she also uses the space incidental to the poetry to establish a voice and image that both complements the forlorn sonnet-speaker and enhances the confident blank-verse speaker. As Judith Stanton has established, Smith took great care over the layout and presentation of her texts, and it is reasonable, therefore, to read the peripheries as significant. To do so also means to utilize a methodology that sees the margins as a speaking space: does Smith anticipate, for instance, Kristeva or does Kristeva enable Smith? When Smith explores the periphery, does she do so because its marginality allows for the voicing of the socially unspeakable, and the portrayal of the socially invisible? Does Smith take the gamble that her readers will both notice and overlook that which introduces, supports, and ornaments the text?[2] For even as Smith takes part in literary tradition with her prefaces, notes and engravings, she also uses them to facilitate the embodying discussed in the Introduction. And, of course, the frontispiece to the *Sonnets* is itself peripheral to the text. This chapter will argue that Smith uses the margins to create voices and selves distinct from the poems' versions. In doing so it will also maintain that, in Smith's handling, peripheral material reveals the artificiality of sincerity: the 'authentic' becomes a pose, even as the pose is read as 'authentic'. Modern print culture mandates the loss of much of Smith's extra-textual material, or re-places it on the page, but Smith's original books function as a collective; the poetry is inevitably accompanied by a distinct Author in the Prefaces, a simultaneous Other in the notes, and a tableau vivant of femininity in the engravings.

This suggests that for Smith, poetry is as much about the actual object of the book as it is about the more rarified, and more conventionally Romantic, Imagination. Indeed, the Poet is not the abstract 'Man speaking to men' but the specific woman Mrs Charlotte Smith; as Sarah Zimmerman's research has shown, Smith's readers reacted to her with ' "sympathy," their responses . . . personal in tone'.[3] The care she takes to present herself as *herself* resonates with the development of a subjectivity that is distinctly Romantic. And yet, which self is the 'true' Self? The different parts of the texts 'speak' with different voices; the plates offer a variety of female figures (and one male child). Even in the *Sonnets* the 'I' exists in several versions, as chapters 2 and 3 discuss. Smith manipulates both subjectivity and readerly expectations of subjectivity: she is adept at maintaining a 'personal' tone even if the different personalities established clash with each other. They remain, however, true to themselves, so that the Prefatory or note voice is the same no matter the poem (or the edition). Smith uses print culture to enlarge subjectivity, to extend it beyond the poetry in a move that furthers her embodying while also taking advantage of the ramifications of textual design and conventions of printing. Thus, the more 'visible' sections of the periphery, the prefaces and engravings, cooperate with the poetry by providing the necessary personal history to justify and enhance the poetic speaker. The notes, relegated to the space beyond the poetry's conclusion, speak with a more contentious, cantankerous, and authoritative voice: need is subordinated to displays of knowledge. The plethora of 'I's show Smith's understanding of the potentialities of the printed book.

The prefaces and dedications: stating her case

Smith uses prefatory material to establish a sense of the personal with her readers. What Zimmerman calls her 'conversational, quotidian prose' (49) contrasts sharply with the more flowery and 'poetic' style she maintains in the body of the text, and this is continued in her notes, as I discuss below. But Smith's more prosaic style in the prefaces disguises the distinctly unordinary situation that she so freely reveals to her readers. Zimmerman's 'quotidian' tone functions to highlight Smith's unfortunate position as a public woman whose sorrows become more and more a matter of public record, as Smith herself ensures. Although Smith gestures towards the convention that women should be seen and not heard, the actual impact of her few phrases to this effect is weak (although they are more frequently quoted than her more forceful statements of worth). In the Preface to the sixth edition of the *Sonnets* Smith ends with the observation that she is 'well aware that for a woman – "The Post of Honor is a Private Station"', and in the Dedication to *The Emigrants* she notes that she is 'perfectly sensible, that it belongs not to a feeble and feminine hand to draw the Bow of Ulysses'.[4] Setting aside some minor and thoroughly unconvincing acknowledgements of the inferiority of her efforts,[5] these are the only two nods to her 'weakness' as a female poet in five Prefaces and two Dedications. Rather, what infuses her prefatory material is a keen awareness of the significance of her position as a writing woman, and a desire to make her troubles public. The personal tone enhances the sense that Smith experiences real trials, and strengthens the implicit appeal that she makes to her readers to rescue her from an increasingly intolerable situation. The prefatory material thus sets the scene for the sorrows expressed in the poetry, and carries on the task of embodying the poet as Smith herself.

Smith conveys the 'real' through a variety of literary affects: a heavy use of the personal pronoun, the recital of verbatim conversations between herself and unnamed friends, a frequent signing and dating that recalls the 'calling card' effect of the *Sonnets'* frontispiece. Again, this suggests the artifice underlying the ostensibly 'real', for even as Smith encourages her readers to associate the writing voice with Smith herself, she also relies on specifically textual methods to do so; as I mention above, the 'quotidian' serves to underline the outlandish nature of her troubles. The 'real' self at the centre of the text, then, masks her constructed nature by continually appealing to her readers' emotions in what becomes a developing conversation. As the prefaces accrue, they develop levels of self-justification, establishing why Smith writes, who she is, herself as Poet. The *Sonnets'* Dedication to William Hayley suggests Smith's aspirations while also showing her confidence in her work – 'I cannot deny having myself some esteem for them' – which immediately challenges the stereotype of the diffident amateur female writer. This is echoed in the Prefaces to the first, second, third, fourth and fifth editions of the poems. In modern terms, she 'owns' her poetry: 'The little Poems which are here called Sonnets, have, I believe, no very just claim to that title: but they consist of fourteen lines, and *appear to me* no improper vehicle for a single Sentiment' (3, *Poems*, emphasis added). Further, 'I can hope for readers only among the few, who, to sensibility of heart, join simplicity of taste' (3, *Poems*). 'Sensibility' and 'simplicity', both bywords for femininity, point this hope towards tradition, but Smith has in mind poetic tradition as well: her words call to mind the 'fit though few' readers that Milton aspired to, which elevates both poet and poetry while also preserving propriety. Correspondingly, she asserts her poems' therapeutic value: 'Some very melancholic moments have been beguiled by expressing in verse the sensations those moments brought' (3, *Poems*). This simultaneously identifies the sonnets as personal effusions and introduces the notion of personal sorrows. Her mentions of 'particular friends' and the 'list of so many noble, literary, and respectable names' (4, *Poems*) for the subscription edition of the *Sonnets* in 1789 furthers the sense of individuality.

Moreover, these initial short Prefaces also demonstrate Smith's responses to her reading public. When accusations of plagiarism were levelled by, among others, Anna Seward, Smith began to append notes to the poems; as the Preface to the third/fourth editions concludes, 'As a few notes were necessary, I have added them at the end. I have there quoted such lines as I have borrowed; and even where I am conscious the ideas were not my own, I have restored them to the original possessors' (4, *Poems*). This replaces the original proviso that 'readers of poetry will meet with some lines borrowed from the most popular authors, which I have used only as quotations. Where such acknowledgment is omitted, I am unconscious of the theft' (4, n., *Poems*). Given that Smith includes all her Prefaces in subsequent editions of the *Sonnets* – that is, the third edition also carries the preface to the first/second edition, and so on – such a change suggests that, rather than simply and passively allowing material to be retransmitted, she is actively choosing the information she wants her readers to have, and in this way actively directing the narrative trajectory of the prefaces. A closer look at the excised passage raises questions: if something is unknown, then how can reference to it be 'omitted'? Why the use of such a strong word as 'theft' (in the next preface she uses the word 'borrowed')? The carefully cultivated sense of immediacy and intimacy suggested by the tone of the prefaces is at odds with the equal care with which Smith creates her scenarios.

As if Smith uses the earlier, shorter prefaces to introduce herself to her readers as a sociable (the friends) and reasonable (the textual changes) woman, in the Preface to the Sixth Edition of the *Sonnets* she enlarges on the sorrows and troubles that previously were signified merely as 'melancholy moments'. For the first time the readers of the poems learn of the disputed will that has left Smith's children penniless although heirs to a fortune; Smith recounts a conversation with a friend who has advised her to enliven her sonnets with 'a more cheerful style of composition' (5, *Poems*). Smith counters this with an appeal to her friend's special knowledge of her circumstances that effectively enrols her readers as new 'friends':

> 'Alas!' replied I, 'Are grapes gathered from thorns, or figs from thistles?' Or can the *effect* cease, while the *cause* remains? *You know* that when in the Beech Woods of Hampshire, I first struck the chords of the melancholy lyre, its notes were never intended for the public ear! It was unaffected sorrows drew them forth: I wrote mournfully because I was unhappy – And I have unfortunately no reason yet, though nine years have since elapsed, to *change my tone*. The time is indeed arrived, when I have been promised by 'the Honourable Men' who, *nine years ago*, undertook to see that my family obtained the provision their grandfather designed for them, – that 'all should be well, all should be settled'. But still I am condemned to feel the 'hope delayed that maketh the heart sick'. Still to receive – not a repetition of promises indeed – but of *scorn and insult* when I apply to those gentlemen, who, though they acknowledge that all impediments to a division of the estate they have undertaken to manage, are done away – will neither tell me *when* they will proceed to divide it, or *whether they will ever do so at all*. You know the circumstances under which I have now so long been labouring; and you have done me the honor to say, that few Women could so long have contended with them.[6] With these, however, as they are some of them of a domestic and painful nature, I will not trouble the Public *now*; but while they exist in all their force, that indulgent Public must accept all I am able to achieve – 'Toujours des Chansons tristes!' (Smith's emphases, 5–6, *Poems*)

I have quoted this at length because of the levels of information and communication it exhibits. First, although addressing her friend, Smith effectively closes her self-quotations after 'thistles', so that even though the subsequent lines are ostensibly still part of the recollected conversation, they are also now addressed to her readers. This means that the readers as much as the friend are implicated with the emphasized phrase '*You know*', so that a private memory becomes public property. The repetition of 'nine years ago' with the emphasis added the second time serves to convey Smith's frustration and to remind her readers of the unfairness of the situation, while a similar effect is achieved with the emphasis on 'scorn and insult': Smith is a woman whose honour needs defending. Further, the hints and allusions to domestic troubles, and the empha-

sized '*now*', carry the flavour of more to come, which is strengthened
when in the final paragraph Smith emphatically proclaims '*I shall be
sorry*, if on some future occasion, I should feel myself compelled to detail
[the causes of my despondence] more at length . . .' Hanging in the air is
the implicit threat of exposure, but of who? Of what? It is in this context
that Smith quotes from Addison's *Cato* that 'The Post of Honor is a
Private Station', which now takes on less the resonance of a conventional
gendered disclaimer and more the force of blackmail.

Smith uses this Preface to make her sorrows public and to throw
herself on the mercy of her reading public, but she also seems to be
making a kind of private communication to readers unknown. Even,
then, as information is conveyed, mystery is built up; readers are encour-
aged simultaneously to succour Smith and wait breathlessly for the next
instalment. The Preface, both private and public, also demonstrates
Smith's determination to step into the legal arena despite her sex, and to
enlist popular support for so doing.[7] The question of exposure remains:
Smith effectively exposes both the men who are holding up resolution
of the will, and her husband, as inadequate providers. She portrays
herself as forced into the public eye, overturning the earlier prefaces'
emphasis on artistic concerns, a stance both conventionally gendered and
distinctly new. As Smith narrates it, she is both in need and willing to
talk about it.

It is not difficult to discuss Smith's depiction of her own circumstances
as proto-feminist. For instance, we need only remember her legal status
as a wife, and hence a *feme covert*, entitled to no legal autonomy or the
right to ownership.[8] However, she subverts the standard relationship
between the individual and the law when she declares herself, not herself
as wife, a litigant, and she rewrites the relationship when she engages
the attention of her reading public in an attempt to win over popular
opinion. Despite her legally 'covered' status, Smith eschews the hus-
bandly protection that is only hers in theory and reveals the compro-
mised nature of a system that lodges power in hands it makes little
attempt to control. When Smith poeticizes her legal troubles, she is
also publicizing her husband's failure to provide; she escapes censure
(although not totally) because she preserves a patina of feminine sensi-
bility and need for succour, but her impatience with a legal system that
cannot even acknowledge her separate existence challenges complacent
definitions of feminine sensibility. Smith airs her dirty laundry in a way
that is 'unfeminine', and yet proper as well: her objections to the lawsuit
and its dilatory progress are couched in terms of her family, and she

avoids the outright statement that it is her status as *wife* that most likely makes the lawyers reluctant to discuss the case with her. Nonetheless, she has succeeded in publicizing its details under her own signature, and in so doing justifies her sorrows while also subverting the legal system that would not admit the validity of her voice.[9]

The careful craft of the prefaces combines the standard 'don't mind me' stance with a style that absolutely demands notice. The technique of relaying a private conversation in order to communicate private information to a wide audience without compromising herself relies on control and restraint; the reader is put in an amenable frame of mind, ready to sympathize with the 'Authoress' (Preface to the Sixth Edition) who thus unavoidably sells her sorrows. In the very lengthy Preface to Volume II of the *Sonnets* (1797) this control deserts 'Charlotte Smith' (she does not sign her earlier Prefaces, although she does the Dedication to Hayley) as she divulges intimate details of her childrens' trials and tribulations, expounds upon her own illnesses, justifies the delay in publishing the volume, and especially castigates in the strongest terms the men preventing the resolution of the lawsuit over the will. Readers learn of the four sons 'all seeking in other climates the competence denied them in this' and of the death of 'the loveliest, the most beloved of my daughters, the darling of all her family' (7, *Poems*). Smith's 'extreme depression of spirit' is cited as contributing to the volume's delay; she devotes two long paragraphs to self-defence which is itself based on a sense of self-worth: 'what I was, what I am, [and] what I ought to be' (8, *Poems*). The Preface to the Sixth Edition hinted at scandal and information withheld; this Preface details Smith's disappointments and vexations, and when she scolds those 'ci-devant' friends who have deserted her, she pays no more than lip-service to private exchange: '[I] have never suffered them to be put under the painful necessity of avowing their dereliction in 1797, of the writer whom they affected so warmly to patronize in 1787. Ten years do indeed operate most wonderful changes in this state of existence' (11, *Poems*). The readers courted with the intimate tone of the earlier Preface are now implicitly called upon to prove themselves more reliable than such friends, and the critics whose accusations of 'querulous egotism' have stung her pride.

Even Smith's control over her language seems to have left her, as the closest she can bring herself to conventional modesty over her work are phrases like 'the many defects that may perhaps be found in it' and 'not intirely [sic] unworthy the general favor' (10, 11, *Poems*). The force of the Preface is such that when Smith ends with an acknowledgement of 'the extensive and still threatening desolation, that overspreads this country, and in some degree, every quarter of the world' (12, *Poems*), she seems to make her personal situation universal rather than subsuming it to the public woes. Indeed, in many ways this Preface presents a kind of domestic epic, with 'Charlotte Smith' the hero beset with troubles and fighting for her honour. The Preface is dated 15 May 1797, the same date as the frontispiece, which only confirms the identity of the personality that inhabits the text: she writes it as she feels it. Curran remarks on the Preface's 'angry and defensive tone' (6, note, *Poems*), and it would seem that Smith realized she had made a narrative error, for when the second edition of Volume II was published in 1800, the Preface was not included.[10] Need, and the revelation of private details for the fit though few, can be attractive, but anger and recrimination are not. Smith thus draws back to the semi-privacy of the Preface to the Sixth Edition.

After the 1792 Preface and before the 1797 Preface, Smith publishes *The Emigrants* with its Dedication to William Cowper. This acts as a kind of companion to the *Sonnets* prefaces; its status as Dedication initially turns her readers' attention from herself to Cowper, although in the very first sentence she refers to 'the heavy pressure of many sorrows', while seeming to counteract this in the next sentence with her reference to a 'feeble and feminine hand' (132). As noted above, however, this functions as little more than lip-service to a convention, as does the Dedication as a whole, for almost as soon as she touches on Cowper's genius she introduces her own. In the suppressed Preface to Volume II of the *Sonnets*, Smith describes her ci-divant friends; in this Dedication she portrays Cowper as exactly a friend, and, moreover, one who recognizes her value:

> A Dedication usually consists of praises and of apologies; *my* praise can add nothing to the unanimous and loud applause of your country. She regards you with pride, as one of the few, who, at the present period, rescue her from the imputation of having degenerated in Poetical talents; but in the form of Apology, I should have much to say, if I again dared to plead the pressure of evils, aggravated by their long continuance, as an excuse for the defects of this attempt. (132–133, *Poems*)

Smith performs an interesting grammatical move in this passage. She first declares what a Dedication is, and that she will not be doing one. She then conflates herself and her country with the pronoun 'She' in the second sentence; the logical referent is 'your country', but as the sentence progresses 'she' transforms into the Poet, 'rescued' by Cowper. The sentence ends with a return to the 'I' and another veiled threat to tell all she knows. Cowper is successfully recast as Smith's friend and gallant, while Smith herself assumes the central role of Poet putatively held by Cowper himself. Cowper thus moves from Poet to Man even as Smith moves herself from Woman to Poet. Cowper does not reappear as Poet (though he does as Philanthropist) until the last sentence of the Dedication, where Smith lauds his 'exquisite Poem . . . in which you have honoured Liberty' and links it to liberal politics by citing Charles James Fox's quotation of *The Task* in Parliament. Her Dedicatee seems to function more as a reflection of Smith's poetical talents than as her master.

Further, the 'decidedly political overtones' Curran sees in the Dedication's conclusion (134, note) make their first appearance half-way through the piece. Having hinted at her on-going sorrows (and in this way again potentially 'hooked' her audience), Smith takes the risk of using distinctly politicized diction when she asks to 'vindicate' herself from faults of poetic design. Wollstonecraft's highly controversial *Vindication of the Rights of Woman* was published in 1792, the year before *The Emigrants*. Smith, who later knew Wollstonecraft, Godwin and Joseph Johnson,[11] could not but be aware of the force of such a word in 1793.[12] Similarly, she ends this paragraph by appealing to 'every liberal mind', another contentious phrasing. Smith shows her understanding of the political force of her words in the poem itself, where footnotes offer a running commentary, as the last section of this chapter will discuss. Here, she packs statement and counterstatement into a text that is clearly less Dedication and more Vindication. When Smith next describes the 'undistinguishing multitude' and makes it clear she refers to 'the body of the English', politics, the preserve of her male peers, has invaded the heart of her Dedication. Viscount St Cyres, for instance, can only accept what he labels Smith's 'irresponsible treason' by colouring her opinions as 'miracle[s] of feminine logic': 'Charlotte herself took a very high line, and loudly asserted her right to preach irresponsible treason as long as she chose.'[13] Even, then, as he marvels that 'Mrs Smith was not prosecuted for sedition' he portrays her as too silly to be listened to, let alone be taken seriously, a reaction matched by her contemporaries, as chapter 4 will discuss. Smith here uses her personal oppression to introduce the notion of general political repression, and even offers an outright defence of Liberty and of the Revolution itself, but balances it with her characteristic personal pleading that works so well to mask her political leanings. The need expressed in this and the other prefaces outweighs the assertion; even a Dedication to a poem as politically timely as *The*

Emigrants does more to flesh out 'Charlotte Smith' than to enter the political arena. Smith says just as much as she wants to, and no more; the unfocussed energy of the suppressed Preface is here tightly under control. Allusion, hints, the half-spoken and the gradual unfolding of sorrows and trials mean that Smith simultaneously advertises her need and deplores doing so.

Although I would agree with Elizabeth Harries that 'Smith seems to see herself both as a woman, with all the implied exclusions and culturally enforced behaviors, and as a potential participant in the current political discourse' (470–71), I would also argue that if we read the prefaces to the poetry we see a different developmental line than if we include the prefaces to the novels. Smith seems to see poetry as a more authentic, and certainly more respectable, form of writing than novels. At the same time she plays with authenticity and sincerity, experimenting with the potentialities of voice and persona-construction, as subsequent chapters will make clear. In the prefaces, she writes a seemingly unmediated prose that suggests to her readers the 'real', but she also writes for effect and for result: she wants to win readers. The unmediated is always already a pose; the added details that suggest authenticity (signatures, dates) are a kind of temporal costume dressing the persona who introduces her poems, and who sets their scene of composition as itself unmediated and spontaneous.

The plates: ornament or testament?

The undertones of artifice in the prefaces are matched in more overt ways by the engravings that ornament the *Sonnets*. Where the prefaces depend on offering versions of reality, the plates shows versions of the ideal: ideal feminine types whose representations both enhance the sorrowing 'female' voice of the sonnets and challenge it. The sonnets are apparently spoken by the Smith we know from the prefaces, and the frontispiece has given her a face and a past. And yet the plates do not carry on depicting 'Smith', but rather mainly show a parade of beauties, a physical perfection that the frontispiece and its epigram have already admitted is beyond the sorrowful Smith. Like a series of models showing off clothes that will later have to be made over to fit a more everyday body, the plates narrate a fiction of feminine attractiveness that pleases the eye but confuses the issue of authenticity insisted on by the prefaces. If the woman in need in the text is Charlotte Smith, then how can she also be a young ingénue, a fashionable damsel, an exile, etc? Do the plates merely ornament, or do they testify to the complexities of selfhood the poems, against readerly expectation, contrive to exhibit?

There are nine plates in the *Sonnets*, five in Volume I and four in Volume II. They illustrate 'Sonnet IV: To the Moon', 'Sonnet XII: Written on the Sea Shore. – October, 1784', 'Sonnet XXVI: To the River Arun', 'Sonnet XXXVI', and 'Elegy'; and 'Sonnet LXX: On Being Cautioned Against Walking on an Headland Overlooking the Sea, Because it was Frequented by a Lunatic', 'The Female Exile', 'The Forest Boy', and 'Ode to the Poppy'.[14] All but the plate for 'Sonnet XXVI' illustrate a female figure, and only the plate to 'Sonnet LXX' could be said to represent 'Smith'. The plates to Volume I bear the date '1 January 1789' and the publisher 'T. Cadell, Strand', while of those to Volume II the first two are dated '15 May 1797' and the last two are missing the date.[15] They are published by Cadell and Davies, Strand. For those readers with fresh new copies of Volumes I and II, of course, 15 May 1797 is the date of the frontispiece and the suppressed Preface. The two volumes compress eight years (1789 to 1797) to a single encounter; time has both passed and stood still. The artists and engravers for the plates feature the great (The Countess of Bessborough, J[ames] Heath, Thomas Stothard, R[ichard] Corbould) and the less-great (Milton, Neagle, Thornthwaite, none of whom feature in Arthur Hind's comprehensive *A History of Engraving and Etching*[16]). The pictures themselves are all drawn from the work of Corbould, Stothard and the Countess,[17] while the engraving is left mainly to the lesser-known Milton, Neagle and Thornthwaite (Heath engraves the plates for 'Elegy', 'Sonnet LXX', and 'The Forest Boy'). This suggests the status of the ornamental in the sonnets; the art is drawn from respected sources. According to Zimmerman, Smith 'was closely involved with the production of her volumes and provided instructions for the plates commissioned' (44); this suggests that Smith's responsibilities as 'author' extend to the artwork, at the least its deployment in the text.

If the frontispiece shows the 'real' Smith, the plates show who she wants her readers to see, embodiments of attractive womanhood. The plate for 'Sonnet IV: To the Moon'[18] (Plate 3) figures the speaker as a stylish ingénue, devotee of the moon which shines from the upper left of the plate. The woman is dressed simply in white, with flowers in her hair, and the plate quotes the line 'Queen of the Silver Bow', encouraging the conflation of the Moon and the figure. The poem makes it clear that the Queen is the moon itself: 'Queen of the silver bow! – by thy pale beam, / Alone and pensive, I delight to stray' (1–2), but the

3 Plate accompanying 'Sonnet IV: To the moon'.

uncontextualized quotation shifts this identification onto the 'I' who is apparently figured by the plate. The next plate, for 'Sonnet XII' (Plate 4), also shows a young woman, this time a more thoughtful, even intellectual figure, who sits 'On Some rude fragment of the rocky shore' with a book, contemplative and seemingly oblivious to the ship foundering faintly to her left. Again, the figure stands in for the poem's 'I', complicating the question of identity: does 'Charlotte Smith' speak, or this unknown young woman? Skipping for the moment the plate to Sonnet XXVI, which shows the 'infant Otway', the plate for 'Sonnet XXXVI' (Plate 5) moves away from embodying the speaker to imaging Fancy and Hope: 'Her pencil sickening fancy throws away / And weary hope reclines upon the tomb'. Weary Hope, in shadow, gazes pensively on Fancy, another beautiful young woman, dressed in classic robes with bare feet and a winged wreath on her head. Whether it is the pencil or Fancy herself who 'sickens', the plate begins to deconstruct the roleplaying of the other plates; here the speaker stands apart from the figure in the plate, except for the fact that both 'Charlotte Smith' and Fancy write, and that Fancy presumably inspires the poem accompanying the plate. The last plate to Volume I illustrates 'Elegy' (Plate 6), a longer poem spoken by a desolate young woman whose lover has been lost at sea. The plate shows the speaker, a dark-haired, dishevelled, and yet still beautiful young woman, who hastens across a churchyard to the sea she hopes will end her misery: '"Approach, ye horrors that delight my soul"/ . . . / The Ocean hears – The embodied waters come – / . . . / And bear the injured to eternal sleep!' (63, 65, 68). In all of these plates, the female figure ornaments the text, and yet also invades it, taking over for the speaker and re-embodying her, substituting youth and beauty for age and experience.

   Three of the four plates to Volume II follow a similar line, but in a more complex way. In each poem, the speaker turns her attention outward: to the Female Exile, the Forest Boy and his family and lover, the Poppy (Plates 7–9). Each plate shows the requisite young and beautiful woman, but patently not conflatable with the speaker except in situation. The Female Exile gazes on her children; 'poor wandering Phoebe' lounges alone by a brook with her pain;[19] the figure in 'Ode to the Poppy' pauses briefly in her writing to gather her thoughts. What I mean by situation is that Smith too presents herself as a mother, as overwhelmed by unconquerable pain, as caught in the very act of writing. But the plates, in these cases, are clearly of someone else – even the last one, where despite her occupation the figure can't represent that speaker directly

4 Plate accompanying 'Sonnet XII: Written on the sea shore'.

5   Plate accompanying 'Sonnet XXXVI'.

6 Plate accompanying 'Elegy'.

7   Plate accompanying 'The female exile'.

8 Plate accompanying 'The forest boy'.

9 Plate accompanying 'Ode to the poppy'.

because in the poem, the speaker never describes herself writing. Instead, the plate seems to offer an idealized portrait of the contemplative poet in an idealized contemplative space: on the steps of a church (there is even a shadowy monklike figure behind her), a setting also not described in the poem. Confusingly, the one plate that could conceivably represent Smith the Poet is the one plate that is least attached to the poem it ornaments. These three plates, then, although apparently more simply ornamental than those in Volume I, actually raise the question of representation even more pressingly: who, exactly, speaks? Who are we looking at?

The answer may lie in the plate to 'Sonnet LXX', and to a lesser extent in that to 'Sonnet XXVI' in Volume I. 'Sonnet LXX' (Plate 2), the 'Lunatic' sonnet, is one of Smith's most familiar for modern readers, resonant with interpretative possibilities. Its plate does the usual job of associating the depicted female figure with the speaker of the poem, but here the conflation seems justified: the woman who shadows the lunatic is clearly older, more careworn than her partners, and resembles the Smith of the frontispiece, wearing a similar hat and clothes. The poem takes a complex stance towards reason and lunacy, simultaneously claiming and rejecting the one, and admiring but denying the other. The plate, however, clearly allies the two figures: their bodies are positioned in exactly the same way, while the Lunatic's cloak encompasses the woman, billowing out over her head and dragging on the ground to her feet. Her shawl, too, billows, as she creeps up behind him. Even as this plate illustrates the poem's subject-matter, it is a powerful statement of identity and alliance. The woman and the Lunatic occupy the same space, which emphatically is *not* populated by young lovelies.

The last plate to be mentioned is that to 'Sonnet XXVI' (Plate 10), and portrays the only non-female figure: the 'infant Otway', also inspired by 'the mournful Muse' on the 'wild banks' of the Arun. The poem describes the Arun as the speaker's childhood haunt, even as it was Otway's. This suggests that despite the incongruities of age and sex, the figure in the plate is more clearly 'Smith' than any of the others beside the woman in the plate just discussed: both Otway and Smith are Poets.

> For with the infant Otway, lingering here,
>   Of early woes she [the Muse] bade her votary dream,
> While thy low murmurs sooth'd his pensive ear,
>   *And still the poet – consecrates the stream.*
>   (5–8, emphasis added)

10 Plate accompanying 'Sonnet XXVI: To the River Arun'.

The 'poet', of course, is Smith, and the figure in the plate is too, more so than any of the figures of idealized female beauty that appear elsewhere. The plates, then, play with ideas of the gendered body and complicate the embodied Self insisted on by the frontispiece and the prefaces. They give readers something nice to look at that furthers Smith's representation of her personal needs – each of the female figures craves succour of some type – but they also unpin the close identification between the poems' speakers, the 'I' of the prefaces, and Charlotte Smith. They further allow for the role-playing that characterizes Smith's approach and suggest her understanding of the implications of textual self-representation.[20]

The notes: will the real Charlotte Smith please stand up?

The prefaces and plates to Smith's poems are about need; they plead with readers to relieve 'Charlotte Smith''s suffering and rescue her from degradation. The notes, on the other hand, offer a voice increasingly authoritative and strong. They function as a space for dissent, where Smith can display knowledge and autonomy. Notes are both of a text and marginal to it; they are simultaneously essential and easy to ignore. In this way they provide an ideal opportunity for subversion. The history of the footnote is a history of the margins; as Anthony Grafton notes in the first contemporary study of this uniquely tangential, retiring, self-abnegating apparatus, they provide the space wherein writers offer proof, support their colleagues, deride their competitors, list their sources.[21] In a scholarly text, they provide the foundation for the writer's claims to originality:[22] 'the text persuades, the notes prove' (Grafton, p. 15). Smith, of course, is not the only poet who saw the potential footnotes offered for explanation, emendation, enlargement.[23] Byron, for instance, grounded many of his 'Eastern Poems' with notes attesting to the veracity of his imagery, or setting out the rationale for his plot devices, or elaborating on the unfamiliar settings he offered his readers. Samuel Rogers in *The Pleasures of Memory* parodies, among other things, poems with notes. Erasmus Darwin, Robert Southey, and Samuel Taylor Coleridge followed similar lines, bolstering their verse with the information contained in their notes – or, in Coleridge's case, his marginal glosses to 'The Rime of the Ancient Mariner', a version of the note that shifted readerly attention to the side margin and demanded a kind of double vision. For these poets, the notes purport to make sense of, or unravel, the mysteries inherent in the verse; a voice emerges that is more authoritative, less overtly imaginative – more factual. The authority contained in the notes enabled the poet: his imagery is substantiated, his poetry justified. For the (male) poet, like Byron, Southey, Darwin, or Coleridge, the notes perform the historian's function, that described by Grafton.

Smith, however, had a trickier terrain to negotiate than her male peers; for her, the display of knowledge and, especially, authority was not an uncomplicated act. The marginal nature of notes proved an opportunity to explore spaces not thought proper for a woman to visit, and there she establishes a marginal persona whose grasp of history, botany, science and culture is unfettered by convention. Taking her cue from her male peers, she uses the notational space to enlarge her creative space; notes open up the restrictive terrain she maps in, say, her prefaces. Smith attaches layers of prose that succeed in simultaneously bolstering her poetic voice and challenging her culturally marginal position as a woman writer, a mother and a wife. She uses her notes to realign authority and poetry, and to house an educated Self aware of the limitations placed on the social body of Woman. Both physically – the notes to the poems appeared at the end of the text – and metaphorically, the notes bolster the poems with a new version of female selfhood, a subterranean challenge to culture that surfaces in *Elegiac Sonnets* and *The Emigrants* and becomes almost literal in *Beachy Head*. The note-space, in fact, functions as a version of the Kristevan chora, allowing Smith to build a persona on/in the margin whose strength necessitates her abjection.[24]

In the two volumes of *Elegiac Sonnets*, Smith uses a variety of note styles; some merely convey information: botanical references or citations and quotation sources, for instance, as signalled by the Preface to the third and fourth editions. Others, however, are both more substantial and more meaningful. In Volume I, for instance, the first few pages of notes (some nineteen notes in all) are solely citational, but in the note to Sonnet XVII, Smith begins to develop a more personal tone, albeit obliquely. The sonnet is subtitled 'From the thirteenth cantata of Metastasio', and Smith sources Line 1 thus: '"Scrivo in te l'amato nome / Di colei, per cui, mi moro." This is not meant as a translation; the original is much longer, and full of images, which could not be introduced in a Sonnet. – And some of them, though very beautiful in the Italian, would not appear to advantage in an English dress'.[25] It becomes clear that this note does not merely source line one; rather, it contextualizes the entire poem, and provides an assertion of authority that subsequent notes will build on. Although Smith does not use the 'I' in this note, she nonetheless tells her reader at least three things: she has read Metastasio, she has done so in the original Italian, and she is using her poetical judgement regarding the translatability of its imagery. She is also, indirectly, announcing to her readers that for her, translation does not mean a mere rendering of Italian into English, but rather a rewriting and a reconceptualizing. The previous four sonnets have been entitled simply 'From Petrarch'; this note invites a reconsideration of what, exactly, has been taken from Petrarch, and what 'from Smith'.

It is not until the note to Sonnet XLII that Smith speaks in her own voice, but she does so in a way that transforms a declaration of ignorance into one of authority and knowledge. As with several previous notes, Smith here displays her understanding of natural science:

> Line 8. The shrieking night-jar sails on heavy wing. The night-jar or night hawk, a dark bird not so big as a rook, which is frequently seen of an evening on the downs. It has a short heavy flight, then rests on the ground, and again, uttering a mournful cry, flits before the traveller, to whom its appearance is supposed by the peasants to portend misfortune. *As I have never seen it dead, I know not to what species it belongs.* (101, emphasis added)

In the context of the sonnets, this note functions on one level metaphorically; it is not difficult to associate the mournful, portentous, seemingly homeless bird with the speaker of the sonnets. However, the note clearly operates on a different symbolic level as well: it evinces that the sonnet's speaker, or rather its writer, has been on the downs 'of an evening' and observed the bird personally. It also shows that although Smith is content to cite her sources for quotations, when it comes to scientific verification she is more cautious, and requires personal observation of a fact before she will convey it to her readers. Thus, having not seen a dead night-jar, she will not commit herself to its species: she will not defer to another's authority. Looking back at the note to Sonnet XVII, this self-reliance is apparent in embryo: there, she refuses to submit to Metastatio's poetic authority or the linguistic authority of any other translator.

Fittingly, the next note, to Sonnet XLIV, moves from the 'missing' dead body of the night-jar to the presence of dead human bodies: the natural disinterment caused by the encroachment of the sea Smith concentrates on in the poem.[26] To the line 'Tears from their grassy tombs the village dead', Smith appends a note that again avoids the 'I' but carries the authority of personal experience nonetheless:

> Middleton is a village on the margin of the sea, in Sussex, containing only two or three houses. There were formerly several acres of ground between

its small church and the sea, which now, by its continual encroachments, approaches within a few feet of this half ruined and humble edifice. The wall, which once surrounded the church-yard, is entirely swept away, many of the graves broken up, and the remains of bodies interred washed into the sea: whence human bones are found among the sand and shingles on the shore. (101–102)

The impersonal tone of the note, its prosaic style, clashes with the morbid details Smith relays. But it is less impersonal than it appears; the poem itself concludes on a highly personalized note ('While I am doom'd – by life's long storm opprest, / To gaze with envy on their gloomy rest') and the note both reiterates Smith's presence at the churchyard, and reifies the poem's tone. The note and the poem work together: the poem expresses need, and the note verifies the authenticity of the sonnet speaker's situation.

The notes to Volume I serve to set the scene; in Volume II Smith more openly deploys an assertive, authoritative, and unhappy Self. In the very lengthy note to Sonnet LXXIX, 'To the Goddess of Botany', Smith begins by reminding her readers that she writes because she is unhappy, referring to 'wearied eyes', and a 'languid spirit' (118). She contextualizes the poem as appropriate to one so afflicted: botany 'seems to be a resource for the sick at heart', and the only 'pursuit' that 'sooths my wounded mind' (118, 119). But from the first sentence she also surrounds herself with figures she presents as peers rather than authorities. A quotation from Milton's *Il Penseroso* leads into her invocation of griefs, while an unsourced quotation from Shakespeare allows her to situate her disaffection with society allusively. She then turns to 'the singular, the unhappy Rousseau' as someone who was also 'dr[iven] from the society of men' to the study of botany, with extensive quotations from the French to establish her picture of his applicability to her situation (119). For, although she proceeds with the conventional proviso that of course she cannot measure up to Rousseau, she moves immediately from a mention of his 'genius' to her remarkably similar 'misfortune to have endured real calamities . . . in contending with persons whose cruelty has left so painful an impression on my mind, that I may well say "Brillantes fleurs, émail des près ombrages frais, bosquets, verdure, venez purifier mon imagination de tours ces hideux objets!"' (119–120). By speaking Rousseau's words with him, she effectively links both her situation, and her genius, with this. Further, she matches this implicit connection with an explicit comparison; calling herself a 'sufferer', she concludes the note with another turn to Shakespeare: 'the sufferer, chained down to the discharge of duties from which the wearied spirit recoils, feels like the wretched Lear, when Shakespeare makes him exclaim "Oh! I am bound upon a wheel of fire, / Which my own tears do scald like melted lead" ' (120). Again, Smith works on multiple levels. She 'feels like' Lear, but with the phrasing 'Shakespeare makes him exclaim' she reminds her readers of Lear's fictionality. She as poet both 'feels like' a character and 'makes' like his creator. In this note, neither Milton, Rousseau, or Shakespeare are presented as anything other than Smith's literary peers, but further she uses their words to claim their status, and, with her turn to *Lear*, to introduce a flavour of theatricality that also, as I discuss in the next chapter, infuses the sonnets. This hint of role-playing challenges the consistency of Smith's thematics of sorrow, and undermines even the apparent sincerity of her notes.

The self-consciousness of the *Sonnets* notes – the sense that Smith exploits them as her opportunity speak 'for real' rather than as the construct 'Charlotte Smith' – allows them to function as addenda to the prefaces. In the note to Sonnet LXXXII, 'To the Shade of Burns', Smith allies herself with 'the original genius . . . of this genuine Poet' by again noting the similarities in their positions, both unhappy and both forced to engage in 'employment to which such a mind as his must have been averse' (122). One such employment is publication by subscription. In the Preface to the Fifth Edition, as I discussed above, Smith is gracious and reticent about her 'list of so many noble, literary, and respectable names'. In this note, she describes herself as 'made the object of *subscription*' (123, Smith's emphasis). The Preface expresses gratitude, the note resentment: here we see the Smith who finds subscription degrading. In the Preface she 'with difficulty . . . repress[es] what I feel on this subject'; in the note she can only ask 'For one, herself made the object of *subscription*, is it proper to add, that whoever *has* thus been delighted[27] with the wild notes of the Scottish bard, must have the melancholy pleasure in relieving by their benevolence the unfortunate family he has left?' (123, Smith's emphasis). Given all we have learned about Smith and her personal situation from her prefaces, the allusion to Burns is purely academic; Smith's note makes sure that the reader persistent enough to pursue her to the notes makes no mistake about his chivalrous function. But she also leaves off the mask of gentility worn in the prefaces: this, we are meant to recognize, is plain speaking.

The further into the notes we read, the bolder Smith becomes. Earlier notes seem to function as camouflage, a reassuring assemblage of citations that blanket the more incendiary assumptions of literary equality that follow. By the time we reach the notes to 'The Dead Beggar' and 'The Forest Boy', Smith no longer compromises. Both of these notes are confrontational and revolutionary, condemning 'those who suffer party prejudice to influence their taste' ('The Dead Beggar') and 'those who make nations destroy each other for *their* diversion' ('The Forest Boy'). The mention of 'the insulted rights of Man' in 'The Dead Beggar' and the description of 'William entrapp'd 'twixt persuasion and force' to join the army in 'The Forest Boy' show Smith's anger at her culture's enthrallment with war and patriotism, but the poems do not contain the same level of contempt as the notes. There, Smith asserts her independence of mind: 'I have been told that I have incurred blame for having used in this short composition, terms that have become obnoxious to certain persons. Such remarks are hardly worth notice . . .' ('The Dead Beggar'). She also maintains her personal experience of the traumas of war: '*I*, who have been so sad a sufferer in this miserable context, may well *endeavour* to associate myself with those who apply what powers they have to deprecate the horrors of war' ('The Forest Boy').[28] In both these notes, Smith rejects concerns that she may alienate a large portion of her audience and shows herself doing so – she may be told she'll incur blame but she'll publish and be damned. This is a far cry from the emollient and supplicatory tone of the prefaces; it demonstrates a turn to the 'real' and a flair for dissent that offers yet another version of 'Charlotte Smith'.

In a way, these notes give us the Writer behind the Poet, whose broad reading and wealth of knowledge allows her to sprinkle her sonnets with allusion and scientific imagery. They supplement the poetic with more personal history, and they flesh out and justify the tone of the poems. But even as the *Sonnets* are an exercise in restraint, so too their notes go only so far. While many are highly personal in tone, and combative in content, especially given their mid-1790s publication, they draw away from such controversy as they conclude, and the final notes calmly explain allusion and little else. The notes follow a dramatic arc that begins slowly and quietly, builds up to a liberal and political climax, and then subsides again. Structurally, the theatrical is again hinted at, suggesting that the notes work with the poetry rather than merely supplementing it. The point seems to be the creation of an alternate Voice, a Self who finds more freedom of expression in the margin than allowable in the poems. Even the peripheral prefaces are too visible for such a project of Self-Determination. In *The Emigrants*, Smith experiments more explosively with the possibilities offered by notes. The Writer uses the notes to form an alternative identity that revolts against the Poet's victimized tone. The notes function as the textual boundary where she reinterprets the dependence she both exposes and embraces in the poem-proper. Smith creates the ultimate Emigrant, the voice in exile from itself, conducting a self-conscious exploration of the marginality to which that poem's persona is exiled. Where in the *Sonnets* notes Smith explores authority, in the notes to *The Emigrants* gender predominates: Smith declares a revolution to shadow and accompany her poetic exploration of the effects of revolution.

Mary Favret has argued that, 'in the context of home, family, and friends, the outsider/woman occupies the central position.'[29] Centrality, however, is precisely what *The Emigrants* rejects, as chapter 4 discusses; she constructs layers of margins that represent the liminality of woman-hood. In her notes, she furthers this marginality: the voice in which they speak asserts dangerously rebellious sentiments. The first substantial note follows Smith's introduction of the cleric-emigrants; she has just referred to the monk's 'pious prison, and his beads' (I: 124). At this point the reader is directed to a note:

> Lest the same attempts at misrepresentation should now be made, as have been made on former occasions, it is necessary to repeat, that nothing is farther from my thoughts, than to reflect invidiously on the Emigrant clergy, whose steadiness of principle excites veneration, as much as their sufferings compassion. Adversity has now taught them the charity and humility they perhaps wanted when they made it a part of their faith, that salvation could be obtained through no other religion than their own.

This voice, prosaic and personalised, expresses impatience at the potential misreading of the poet's intentions she has experienced before; responding to the ambiguity – the multiple interpretations – resident in poetic language, the speaker imports into the notes her awareness of the dangers posed by wayward readers. In addition, she allows herself a straightforward critique of the clerics' religion that anticipates, and eventually authorises, the more veiled, self-consciously poetic stance taken by the poem's speaker. The next note pushes further:

> Let it not be considered as an insult to men in fallen fortune, if these lux-uries (undoubtedly inconsistent with their profession) be here enumerated – France is not the only country, where the splendour and indulgences of the higher, and the poverty and depression of the inferior Clergy, have alike proved injurious to the cause of Religion. (Note to I: 129)

As Curran glosses it, 'the ambiguity of Smith's prose seems meant to imply that such inequality exists as well within the Anglican establishment' (*Poems*, 140). However, at this point in the poem itself, Smith has not yet moved beyond sympathizing with the emigrants. The footnotes seem to function as the space wherein Smith rehearses her more radical, critical assessments of her own culture that, eventually, she expresses in the poem (England's politics, its law), but that are also embedded in patriotic celebrations of England's probity, clemency and valour. Even as the poem's body internalizes its rebellion, so too the notes provide an outlet on the margin for Smith's articulations of her alienation: this becomes explicit when, in crediting the lines ' "amid the sons / Of Reason, Valour, Liberty, and Virtue, / Displays distinguish'd merit, is a Noble / Of Nature's own creation!" ' to Thomson, she adds that 'these lines . . . are among those sentiments which are now called (when used by living writers), no common-place declamation, but sentiments of dangerous tendency' (note to I: 244). The 'dangerous tendency' towards social breakdown threatened by a pro-revolutionary stand, Smith implies, is turned back on the repressive culture that can rewrite 'Patriot Virtue' (I: 346) as its own obverse; as Smith notes, 'this sentiment will probably *renew* against me the indignation of those, who have an interest in asserting that no such virtue any where exists' (note to I: 346, Smith's emphasis).

Smith, then, uses the notes in Book I to make her revolutionary sympathies (marginally) evident. The Self who speaks them is broad-minded and politically liberal. But she is also intellectually adventurous, in a way that seems designed to invoke the personal once again. In a review of the poem in the *European Magazine*, the reviewer notes that the poet is evident 'almost at the bottom of every page, as [is] the portrait of some of the most renowned painters in the corner of their most favourite pictures'.[30] In the note to I: 282 ('But more the Men, whose ill acquir'd wealth'), Smith ascribes the 'birth' of the Revolution to financial mismanagement:

> The Financiers and Fermiers Generaux are here intended. In the present moment of clamour against all those who have spoken or written in favour of the first Revolution of France, the declaimers seem to have forgotten, that under the reign of a mild and easy tempered Monarch, in the most voluptuous Court in the world, the abuses by which men of this description were enriched, had arisen to such height, that their prodigality exhausted the immense resources of France: and, unable to supply the exi-

gencies of Government, the Ministry were compelled to call Le Tiers Etat;
a meeting that gave birth to the Revolution, which has since been so
ruinously conducted.

Smith challenges the more emotive 'storming of the Bastille' image with
a mundane tale of bad money management, interweaving this with jibes
at an overly self-indulgent Court. But for someone who has made no
secret of her own victimization at the hands of 'Financiers', the note
combines political analysis with personal interest.[31] For the sharp-eyed
reader, this note contains hints of personal rebellion as much as an alter-
native history of the French rebellion.

Smith's notes both evince sympathy for Revolutionary principles and
stand as evidence of its maintenance in the face of continuing social dis-
approval; they reveal a voice that reiterates what her readers already know
about her. They attest to an individuality that nonetheless exiles itself to
the margin, a complicated position of assertion and retreat that suggests,
perhaps, the 'structural impossibility' of the 'female citizen or enlight-
ened feminine subject' remarked upon by Vivien Jones (p. 301). Are we
meant to applaud Smith's audacity or decry her timidity? The poem itself
offers a resolution: even as the revolutionary voice of the notes in Book
I authorizes an increasingly critical poetic persona whose strength of
mind is fully utilized in the text of Book II, if we explore the notes to
Book II we see that, while fewer, they maintain an easy authority that
seems an outgrowth of the increasingly strong subject position devel-
oped in Book I. The poem's journey from the chaos of Book I to the res-
olution of Book II is a corollary to the progress of the notes. Besides
sourcing a number of allusions to Shakespeare, and writing feelingly of
the virtues derived from an 'education in the School of Adversity', Smith
focuses her two major notes on further condemning the effects of war,
informing her readers, before the poem-proper does, that war turns men,
not into soldiers, but into marauders, existing on inadequate food
('unripe corn . . . mashed into a sort of paste') and forced into 'disap-
pointment and humiliation' (notes to II: 223 and 245). Reading between
the lines, or rather behind them, one begins to get a fuller picture of the
culture that has created a world in which mothers, for instance, die at
the hands of soldiers.

The chronology of the poem is important: in February 1793 war was
declared between England and France, rendering an anti-war polemic as
politically suspect as a pro-Revolution argument. In Book I, in Novem-
ber 1792, Smith offers to her readers a persona not merely sympathetic

to, but, marginally, supportive of the Revolution. In Book II, in April 1793, Smith condemns 'destructive war' (II: 215). This is itself a politically marginalized opinion; Smith further enacts the unsayability of her critique by using the margins to expose the wretched conditions endured by the French emigrant soldiers and the dehumanizing effect of dishonourable war. Again, the margin authorizes the body of the text, freeing the poetic voice to expose fully the destructive and maddening effects of battle: dead mothers, murdered children, maniac husbands. The notes create a boundary-voice that allows for the increasing pacifism of *The Emigrants*. It is due to Smith's culturally marginalized politics that we can locate the Kristevan abject – here, the boundary between self and (m)other[32] – in the margins; this allows Smith to defamiliarize both pro-revolutionary fervour and standard anti-French posturing, creating instead a Revolutionary sympathy that fully recognizes, exposes, and condemns the ravages and inequities perpetrated by that revolution, and subsequent war. Negotiating the borderline of the unspeakable, Smith fashions a subject-position that, by the poem's end, allows her to direct – not plead, or even bargain with – God to reinstate Peace, in a series of imperatives: 'view', 'cause', 'restrain', 'teach' and 'drive'. The interactions between note-voice and poem-voice result in an authoritative, politicized Smith who explores and enlarges the borders, a self-effected alienation that, paradoxically, strengthens her subject-position. In this way, Smith energizes the abject, revealing an awareness of the constructedness of the margin; and she allows herself to occupy, simultaneously, the centre and the borderline. War becomes the catalyst which activates Smith's exploration, and performance, of her persona.

The path from *The Emigrants* the *Beachy Head* 'leads to no happy home' (Sonnet LXII), but it maps out the development of the notated Self from exile to embeddedness. The history that underlies *The Emigrants* combines with the footnoted voice attendant on the poem to produce a speaking Self capable of challenging the social construction of women's marginalized position. In *Beachy Head* Smith builds on her earlier poem, again siting the unsocialized Self in the notes and inserting self-confidence and authority via the poem's footnotes, which act as a kind of running commentary on her own work. Smith uses her footnotes to underpin the personal exploration she situates at the heart of her poem. She does not merely poeticize the natural; Smith institutes literal layers of selfhood, making use of general poetic and historical allusion in the body of the poem while transferring detailed historical and, by implication, personal, narratives to the copious footnotes that produce the poem's base, much as Beachy Head itself supports Smith's reclining persona. Smith actively questions established authority in her footnotes: Linnaeus, Gilbert White, even Shakespeare, while assuming the self-confidence this grants in subsequent lines of the poem proper. She thus establishes an interrelation between the poetic and the factual – verse and prosaic elaboration – that informs her implied links between the personal and the historical, in a strategy that both gives added importance to the *personal* history she embeds in *Beachy Head* and confirms the legitimacy of her persona's voice.

Smith's extensive footnotes present her readers with a figure commenting on her own poetry as well as anticipating the objections and requests for information of her potential readers. *The Emigrants* uses images of boundaries and edges suggestive of the Kristevan chora; underpinning Smith's poetics in *Beachy Head* one finds notes alive to the application of Kristevan semiotic theory. Toril Moi writes that 'Kristevan semiotics emphasizes the marginal and the heterogeneous as that which can subvert the central structures of traditional linguistics.'[33] In applying Kristevan semiotics to the appearance as well as the structure of *Beachy Head*, I suggest that her division and eventual reconciliation of the poetic and the factual reflect this subversion. In placing herself, her poem, and her notes in layers of margins, however, Smith encodes her own semiotic system: poetry, history, nature and the personal collude across textual space. The poem's notes contain a persona often actively opposed to the 'Poet' who occupies the poem-proper: in *Beachy Head*, much more so than the *Sonnets* or *The Emigrants*, Smith constructs a persona who is, in Shari Benstock's words, 'unrelentingly self-aware and therefore divided against itself'.[34] Benstock refers to the dual personality created in a fictional text when the author adds notes; in Smith's case, importing the prosaic device of footnotes into her poetic text also divides the text against itself. She self-consciously suits her tone and her treatment of subject to its placement in the text, and in doing so she underpins the poem with a factual base that substantiates the more flowery, more colourful, even more fanciful – in short, more poeticized – lines in the poem-proper.

Benstock remarks that notes allow an author to 'spea[k] in two voices at once . . . ballasting or modifying or even bombarding with exceptions his [or her] own discourse without interrupting it' (221, n. 4). The notes to *Beachy Head* are both *of* and *outside of* the text they enhance. In enabling Smith to speak in at least 'two voices at once', they further illuminate the building process that has resulted in poetry. In her earlier notes Smith signalled aspects of the compositional process, but in *Beachy Head* the notes exist almost in competition with the poem. The Selves represented by the two forms of writing thus create a dialectic, with the notes functioning like the Kristevan chora rather than simply elaborating, albeit in a different voice, on the text of the poems. They develop, as it were, backwards, coming finally to embody textually and metaphorically the pre-linguistic state Kristeva describes as 'reced[ing] and underly[ing] figuration and thus specularization' (*Reader* 26), and which Moi glosses as 'the heterogeneous, disruptive dimension of language, that which can never be caught up in the closure of traditional linguistic theory' (*Reader* 159). Both the metaphorical placement of the chora and its linguistic function ally it to the footnotes as displayed in *Beachy Head*; there, they critique, enlarge on, explain, append to the poem-proper, even as the chora precedes, aids in the formation of, supports and opposes signification. This version of chora resonates with the abject; as Moi describes it, the chora, like woman herself, is marginal, to language and to the culture that produces language. So too are the notes to *Beachy Head*, and so too is the poem itself: all function outside of customary discourse, predicating an alternative ideology, so that, for instance, Smith can display an historical knowledge not usually accepted in a woman in a culture that emphasized the feminine virtues of passivity, piety and accomplishments over the 'hard' disciplines. She has intimated her knowledge in her earlier poems, but even the botanical facts contained in the *Sonnets* pale beside the sheer weight of knowledge offered by *Beachy Head*. The earlier poems have acted as warm-up acts to the notational pyrotechnics now offered.

Smith posits a self in her notes who is outside her own culture, who challenges its authorities and its conclusions, and who supports her own poetry with a voice that is confident and knowledgeable and yet always hidden, sub-rosa.[35] As the chora in her poem's semiotic system, Smith's notes are outside of, even previous to, the systems the poem dramatizes. Her identities as poet and as scholar shield each other from censure. The footnotes offer facts and authority that maintain the foundation of the poem, while the body of the poem comports itself in properly poetic ways. As she does in her other poems, she conforms to aesthetic distinctions: her poem contains the personal reflections, her notes the historical voice. The duality created by this kind of thematic distinction plays out Derrida's demonstration that recognizing the nature of notes requires recognizing that a noted text 'is henceforth no longer a finished corpus of writing, some content enclosed in a book or its margins, but a differential network, a fabric of traces referring endlessly to something other than itself, to other differential traces' (in Benstock 220, n. 2). The notes lead us outwards to the writing poet who strategically comments on her own poeticizing, who upholds her own authority by denying that of others, who 'wrench[es] away the inherent supremacy of the text by setting up a countertext' (Benstock 220, n. 2).

As her own background voice, the notes provide a space for her to enlarge on her own poetry. Situating Contemplation as the poem's resident genius, figured by her own reclining persona, Smith begins her survey of Beachy's past, beginning in distant ages with a description of its earliest invaders. Her language is self-consciously poetic; she prepares her readers for her recital of history by invoking Contemplation, then moves slowly backward in time, but she also mythologizes this history in her use of archaic place-names and evocative brevity, depending upon a knowledgeable readership to know about Dogon, Trinacria, Parthenope. However, this allusive poetry has a footnote attached midway, ostensibly about the single word 'Scandinavia' (line 126), and it is anything but brief: in four substantial paragraphs, she gives us all the details we could wish for, referencing the poem from line 121 to line 138. Place-names are defined, historical figures contextualized; this note provides a mini-history, written in factual, informative language (a straightforward narrative tone, action verbs, names and dates), fleshing out the sparse poetic narrative and displaying Smith's knowledgeable grasp of history. The dialogue that is implied, between poetry and note, allows Smith to explore different levels of the place she inhabits: she is poet and historian, dreamer and reasoner. Indeed, as the note shows, she is also determined: despite her assertion that the story of William the Conqueror is 'too well known to be repeated here', she nonetheless proceeds to relate the history. She is reluctant to relinquish narrative control even for 'well-known' history.

However, as yet the voice is muted, restrained: in all the information we are offered, the 'I' is held back, and the tone is impersonal, as when, in other notes, she glosses the vulgar names of plants and animals with their Latin equivalents: knowledge is apparent here, but its origin is less obvious. Smith seems at first merely to rehearse information in her notes, rather than to process it. The notes support this disembodied poetics. We see initially only two 'I's, and each time it is to express uncertainty or to undermine a poetic device. Six lines into the poem, she refers to the 'vast concussion' that separated Britain from the rest of Europe, and footnotes her reaction to this theory: 'Alluding to an idea that this Island was once joined to the continent of Europe, and torn from it by some convulsion of Nature. I confess I never could trace the resemblance between the two countries. Yet the cliffs about Dieppe, resemble the chalk cliffs on the Southern coast. But Normandy has no likeness whatever to the part of England opposite it' (*Poems* 217, note to line 6). Smith questions herself in this note, eroding her poetic reliance on a theory she cannot quite believe in, and immediately instituting the opposing extratextual voice Benstock sees operating in literary footnotes. She is tentative, however, not yet willing to speak authoritatively; the sequential 'yet' and 'but' undermine her own self-questioning. Her next use of 'I' in a note is to confess failure: accompanying her concern to provide the Latinate names for plants and birds is an anxiety that she may not get it quite right, for at this point in the text she is still 'call[ing] on the scientific authorities of her day to verify the accuracy of her observations,' as Judith Pascoe observes.[36] Hence, in this note she confesses 'I can find no species of sea bird of which [Sea Snipe] is the vulgar name' (*Poems* 221, note to line 113). Again, her only opponent is herself, as she is footnoting her own use of 'sea-snipe' in the poem-proper. One can see, however, that underlying this self-doubt is a willingness to question, and although at this point it takes what would be seen as a properly feminine position (that is, self-denigration), it also lays the foundation for what will become an increasingly confident first-person.

Smith follows a poetic trajectory that depends on the gradual construction of a personal voice. But she approaches her goal of full personhood subtly, meanderingly, establishing herself as uncertain, self-doubting, detached, until the point in the poem when she has arrived at her next 'I': line 282, well into the poem and sufficiently well guarded by effusive praises of England's martial past, the glory of its present, the hardiness of its rustics. And having installed herself as the poem's strong central subject, her footnotes take on an increasingly combative tone. Some examples (all emphases for non-Latinate words added):

anémones. *Anemóne nemorosa.* It appears to be settled on *late and excellent authorities*, that this word should not be accented on the second syllable, but on the penultima. I have however ventured the more known accentuation, as more generally used, and suiting better the nature of my verse. (*Poems* 232, note to line 364)

I have never read any of the late theories of the earth, nor was I ever satisfied with the attempts to explain many of the phenomena which call forth conjecture in those *books* I happened to have had access to on this subject. (*Poems* 232, note to line 375)

Ophrys muscifera. Fly orchis. *Linnaeus,* misled by the variations to which
some of this tribe are really subject, has perhaps too rashly esteemed all
those which resemble insects, as forming only one species, which he terms
Ophrys insectifera. (*Poems* 236, note to line 446)

Mr. [Gilbert] White says, that these birds are never taken beyond the river
Adur, and Beding Hill; but this is certainly a mistake. (*Poems* 237, note to
line 461)

Shakespeare describes the Cuckoo buds as being yellow. He probably
meant the numerous Ranunculi, or March marigolds (*Caltha palustris*)
which so gild the meadows in Spring; but poets have never been botanists.
The Cuckoo flower is the *Lychnis floscuculi.* (*Poems* 242, note to line
591)

These notes follow a trajectory of increasing self-confidence, reflect-
ing the personal progress she charts in the poem-proper. There, as
chapter 5 will discuss, isolation eventually empowers Smith, for banish-
ment to the fringes of culture entails an engagement with the liminal,
and the marginal. Once she has established herself as *willingly* on the
margin, as a woman, as a poet, as a figure on a headland, she fearlessly
takes on the authorities she should, by cultural expectation, allow to
dominate her voice. We see her challenging, in turn, 'late and excellent
authorities' (unnamed), 'books', Linnaeus, White and Shakespeare; and
the last appears in what can only be seen as an ironic self-reference. 'Poets
have never been botanists,' she remarks, and in the next sentence coolly
reveals the Latinate name of the Cuckoo flower. Smith, as poet, relocates
her botanical knowledge in the notes she appends to her own poem, a
more 'congenial soil' for the knowledge she clearly has whether as poet
or as botanist. Her comment becomes, not an admission of her own lack
of knowledge, but a dismissal of Shakespeare's inexact and 'poetic' licence
with the facts of nature; underlying her comment is the clear, though
unspoken (the choric?) aside: 'Poets have never been botanists (until
now).'

Beachy Head represents the culmination of Smith's multivocal self-
presentation. Poetry and a variety of histories intermix, even as she care-
fully keeps them separate. Derrida's notion of the marginal allows us to
see that *Beachy Head*, even more than the *Sonnets* and *The Emigrants*,
embodies a hybrid poetry, where facts are grafted onto verse, where
history takes on different guises depending on its placement. The copi-
ousness of the notes, their position as appendage to the body of the

poem, suggests that they signal the marginal nature of the text itself. Smith is not content to speak in only one voice, that of poet; after a twenty-year career and a public reputation as poet, novelist, children's writer, and possibly even playwright, she seems to seek something new: the creation of a composite poem based on and around an experimental self-questioning, self-supporting chorus of voices. The notes embody the knowledge necessary to comprehend all the facets both of Beachy Head and of its composition. Once Smith achieves the 'I' in the poem-proper, she gains the ability to question established authorities and substitute her own conclusions in the footnotes. She thus reifies her poetic persona as a voice to be reckoned with, and she supports this with a choric sub-voice whose knowledge and sense of self replaces decorous femininity with something much less clearly gendered. Moi notes that 'the chora is a pre-Oedipal phenomenon' 'where sexual difference does not exist' (*Reader* 161); if so, then one can see Smith's notes as dispensing with the sexual difference culturally assigned to gender. Her note Self displays all the confidence and authority commonly associated with the educated man of her time.

The opportunities offered by the margins extend beyond mere factual additions, or supplementary material. The space offered by notes encourages the emergence of a flexible, fluent Self, one unfettered by convention, whether artistic or social. Smith takes advantage of the textual location of notes to embed multiple personae within her poem and to shelter her Self behind its text. Although she goes beyond the culturally permissible with her notes, she does so unobtrusively, and in this way she maintains the margin, lingering just within – or is it just out of? – our sight. Her technique in the *Sonnets, The Emigrants* and *Beachy Head* suggests that for Smith, the margins and extra-textual spaces have a definite use-value. They allow the woman to be Writer, Poet, and Image, and they allow the manipulation of the very idea of Identity. The printed page can encourage a theatrical procession of personae, simultaneous voices that mean 'Charlotte Smith' is both 'there' and not 'there'. In her prefaces, plates and notes, Smith sets the scene for the exploration of possibilities offered by the poems, and she tailors her tone of voice (or style of dress and figure) to fit the space it occupies. Need thus displays itself and is underwritten by authority, and all the while there are pretty pictures to look at. In the next two chapters, I will explore the varieties of 'I's on offer in, mainly, the *Sonnets*, focusing on the paradoxes contained by an embodied speaker.

Notes

1 Sarah Zimmerman has also paid attention to Smith's notes, prefaces, and engravings in her book *Romanticism, Lyricism and History* (Buffalo: SUNY Press, 1999), concentrating on Smith's ability to create a sense of intimacy and enlist readerly sympathy. Zimmerman also reads Smith as creating a poetics based on theatricality. Her work chimes with my own; we both see Smith as in control of her text even as she creates personae who have apparently lost control of their destinies. See also my article 'Selling One's Sorrows: Charlotte Smith, Mary Robinson and the Marketing of Poetry', *The Wordsworth Circle* 25 (1994), 68–71.

2 I use this phrasing deliberately, to ally the margins with the feminine and to emphasize the ease with which critical vocabulary can create that which it discusses.

3 Zimmerman, *Romanticism, Lyricism and History*, 39.

4 *The Poems of Charlotte Smith*, ed. Stuart Curran (Oxford: Oxford University Press, 1994), 6 and 132. Subsequent references will be made in the text.

5 Even in the Dedication of the *Sonnets*, where she might be expected to be as meek and unobtrusive as possible, Smith asserts to value of her work: 'While I ask your protection for these essays, I cannot deny having myself some esteem for them' (*Poems* 2).

6 This characterization complicates Smith's observation in the Dedication to *The Emigrants* quoted above: 'It belongs not to a feeble and feminine hand to draw the Bow of Ulysses.' Dated almost exactly a year after the Preface to the Sixth Edition of the *Sonnets* (10 May 1793, where the Preface is dated 14 May 1792), the Dedication is more about female strength and endurance than weakness.

7 Smith's father-in-law Richard seems to have appreciated her shrewdness in legal matters when he made her an executor to his will; his own lack of knowledge and foresight is illustrated not only by the mess he made with the will, but by the very compliment he paid her. As a married woman, she could have nothing to do with the execution of the will.

8 Her awareness of and frustration with this is evident in the emphasized phrase 'scorn and insult'.

9 Zimmerman quotes from a letter in which Smith informs her publisher Thomas Cadell of her intentions to speak openly of her circumstances in her prefaces: 'I think it necessary to say that in the preface [to the sixth edition] I mean to touch on the hardship of my situation – Who after waiting *nine* years while the Estate of Richard Smith the Grandfather was at [?] now, that all his debts are confessedly clear'd – & Effects arising every day, am no better off than before because Mr. Dyer whose children have an 8th share (& that partly conditional, in the property) opposes any division till his youngest child is of age, who is abt. Seventeen – tho he has not the shadow of pretence for it. I am driven almost to despair by these circumstances; and the conduct

of Mr. Smith – who lives upon the interest of my fortune, with a Woman he keeps, leaving me to support as well as I can his seven Children who are in England' (letter to Cadell, April 1792; 59 in Zimmerman, *Romanticism, Lyricism and History*). It is interesting to note which details Smith makes public in the Preface (her wait of nine years) and which she keeps semi-private (names, for instance). It is also significant that in the privacy of this letter Smith not only refers to the inheritance as 'my fortune' (in print it is always her children's fortune), but also lets slip the mask of devoted motherhood she maintains in her writings ('his seven Children'). Even as Smith appeals to Cadell's sense of justice, she also allows herself to be, for a brief moment, an individual rather than the construct 'Mrs Smith'.

10 In an insightful and interesting article, Elizabeth W. Harries notes that Smith's prefaces can be seen as a 'series of shifting rhetorical stances'. In the preface to Volume II, Smith shifts a step too far and hastens to recover her previous position. See ' "Out in Left Field": Charlotte Smith's Prefaces, Bourdieu's Categories, and the Public Sphere', *MLQ* 58 (1997): 457–473: 463.

11 Johnson published Smith's *Conversations, Introducing Poetry* (1804) and her posthumous *Beachy Head* and *A Natural History of Birds* (1807).

12 Indeed, she uses it again in Book II of the poem itself; see chapter 4.

13 Viscount St Cyres, 'The Sorrows of Mrs Charlotte Smith', *The Cornhill Magazine* 15 (1903): 683–696: 691. St Cyres refers to the reaction to a poem in Volume II of the *Sonnets*, 'The dead beggar. An Elegy, addressed to a Lady, who was afflicted at seeing the funeral of a nameless Pauper, buried at the Expence of the Parish, in the Church-Yard at Brighthelmstone, in November 1792', wherein she again uses the word 'vindicates' as well as the phrase 'Rights of Man'. Her extensive footnote, characterized by St Cyres as 'loud assertion', acknowledges the controversy over this phrase but does not back down from it. It is interesting that for St Cyres, even assertion tucked away in a note is loud.

14 My source text for the plates is *Elegiac Sonnets*, cited below.

15 This information is gleaned from an edition in my possession; evidently the dates for the last two plates were cut off when the pages were cut. It is probable, however, that they would bear the same date as the other two plates.

16 This book contains a 'Classified List of Engravers' in which Milton, Neagle and Thornthwaite are conspicuous by their absence (Arthur Hind, *A History of Engraving and Etching* (New York: Dover, 1963; 1923), 378–388). Basil Hunnisett's *Steel-Engraved Book Illustration in England* (London: Scolar Press, 1980), mentions a Thomas Milton as a governor of the Society of Engravers (est. 1802).

17 In her note to 'The Female Exile', illustrated by the Countess's artwork, Smith says 'The drawing from which the print is taken I owe to the taste and talents of a lady, whose pencil has bestowed the highest honor this little book can boast' (127). In this case poem, plate and note illuminate each other: the plate illustrates the poem, the plate's origin combined with the poem's earlier

appearance as part of *The Emigrants* provides the opportunity for a note, the note implies a personal relationship between author and artist.

18 This plate is also discussed by Zimmerman (44–45), who concludes that 'the engraving visualizes . . . the stylized verbal gestures of Smith's poetry' (44).

19 Phoebe is not, of course, the Forest Boy; it is significant in the light of my argument that the plate portrays a minor female character in the poem rather than its protagonist.

20 Loraine Fletcher quotes a long letter from Smith to Cadell and Davies in which she expresses her dissatisfaction with 'Mr Heaths [*sic*] engravings' and offers advice on improving the figure of another figure: 'I wish that, if it can be done without much trouble, a little more of sorrowful, mournful expression may be given to her Countenance which may I beleive [*sic*] be done with a single stroke of the Graver about the mouth or perhaps brows.' The letter goes into great detail about Smith's reactions to the plates and her desired changes, attesting to her overt desire for compositional control and approval. See Fletcher, *Charlotte Smith: A Critical Biography* (Basingstoke: Macmillan, 1998), 262.

21 Anthony Grafton, *The Footnote* (London: Faber and Faber, 1997). Subsequent references will be made in the text. The footnote, and especially the endnote, hides itself, cowering under or behind the might of the main body of print. Indeed, the more bulky the note – if a footnote, the more visible – the less it endears itself to the reader, who often regards the note as intrusive, disruptive, extraneous.

22 As Grafton notes, they also occasionally serve to mislead the reader; see especially pages 17–20.

23 Many Romantic-period poems included notes: most have been stripped of them in present-day printings. *Beachy Head*, for instance, totters over an extremely pared-down version of the notes in Anthony Ashfield's *Romantic Women Poets, 1770–1838* (Manchester: Manchester University Press, 1995). In Jerome McGann's anthology *Romantic Period Verse* (Oxford: Oxford University Press, 1994), the poem itself is reduced to its opening lines: the notes to those lines are entirely absent. However, in Duncan Wu's *Romantic Women Poets: An Anthology* (Oxford: Blackwells, 1997), and Stuart Curran's *The Poems of Charlotte Smith* (Oxford: Oxford University Press, 1993), poem and notes are present in their entirety, the notes as footnotes (the original *Beachy Head* used endnotes, as did *Elegiac Sonnets* and *The Emigrants*).

24 Even as footnotes are susceptible to culturally inflected readings, they are also receptive to a variety of theories, themselves occasionally marginal to the text of the argument. Exploring Smith's use of the note means also exploring their susceptibility to theoretical constructs. I will return to the notes' enactment of the Kristevan chora more thoroughly in my discussion of *Beachy Head*; see below.

25 Charlotte Smith, *Elegiac Sonnets*, Vol. I: London: T. Cadell, Junior and W. Davies, 1797; Vol. II: London: T. Cadell, Junior and W. Davies. 1800: 94–95. Subsequent references to this edition will be made in the text.

26 See chapter 2 for a more detailed discussion of this poem.

27 Smith's slippery syntax performs its usual function: the reader is uncertain whether 'has thus been delighted' refers to reading Burns, or reading him through subscription.

28 Smith's son Charles lost his leg at Dunkirk in 1793. Here, she invokes her identity as Mother but does so highly elliptically.

29 Mary Favret, 'Spectatrice as Spectacle: Helen Maria Williams at Home in the Revolution', in *Literate Women and the French Revolution of 1789*, ed. Catherine R. Montfort (Birmingham, AL: Summa Publications, Inc., 1994), 151–172: 160.

30 *European Magazine* 24 (1793): 42, unsigned review. Quoted in Zimmerman, *Romanticism, Lyricism and History*, 57.

31 In the Curran edition, which uses footnotes, the note is literally at the bottom of the page.

32 The Kristevan abject signals a redrawing of the Freudian uncanny – the unknown – as the unknowable. 'Abjection is above all ambiguity' (in Linda Zerilli, 'Text/Woman as Spectacle: Edmund Burke's "French Revolution"'. *The Eighteenth Century* 33 (1992), 47–72. p. 54); it is allied with the (m)other, the origin. For Smith, the marginal space performs a similar function. See chapter 4 for a full discussion of the abject in *The Emigrants*.

33 *The Kristeva Reader*, ed. Toril Moi (New York: Columbia University Press, 1986), 158. Subsequent references will be made in the text.

34 Shari Benstock, 'At the Margin of Discourse: Footnotes in the Fictional Text', *PMLA* 98 (1983), 204–225: 205. Subsequent references will be made in the text.

35 To import another theoretical analogy, Smith's notes prefigure Deleuze and Guattari's nomadology, allowing her to wander away from, around, and deeper into the topics chosen and more visibly dealt with in the poem-proper. Christopher Miller writes that 'Deleuze and Guattari's footnotes are . . . the footprints in the sand of their nomad intellectual wanderings, enabling readers to follow their steps' ('The Postidentitarian Predicament in the Footnotes of *A Thousand Plateaus*: Nomadology, Anthropology, and Authority', *Diacritics* 23 (1993), 6–35: 9). Smith's notes allow, even command her readers to attend to her display of knowledge, and to wander, themselves, from poem to note to poem, constructing their own nomadic path.

36 Judith Pascoe, 'Female Botanists and the Poetry of Charlotte Smith', *Re-Visioning Romanticism: British Women Writers, 1776–1837*, eds. Carol Shiner Wilson and Joel Haefner (Philadelphia: University of Pennsylvania Press, 1994), 193–209: 197.

2

Elegiac Sonnets I:
the good mother

One of Smith's most common public mantras was her responsibility for her nine surviving children, and she threw much creative energy into her role as mother. Motherhood is important during the late eighteenth century as an energizing image; Victoria's ideological forebear, Queen Charlotte, is the unremarked but persistent matriarch of domestic ideology, and her subjects – among them the mothers who wrote during the Romantic period – embodied the use-value of maternity, both culturally and personally. As a writing mother, Smith deploys the maternal as a metaphor of respectability, building on the expectation that the mother exemplified a specific kind of gendered body; for the mother who wrote, generation encompassed not only parturition and the nurturing and raising of children, but also creativity and attention to oeuvre, the corpus that contained literary identity. By its very title, Smith's *Elegiac Sonnets* alerts the reader to a thematics of loss and of a mourner left behind. Although her sorrows are myriad, there is one species of loss that validates Smith's position as writing woman. This loss is predicated on Smith's role as mother, and in the sonnets expressing Smith's sorrow over her lost daughter Anna Augusta, she uses natural and botanical imagery to strategic effect. Although Anna was an adult when she died in childbirth in 1795, Smith consistently constructs her as a 'beloved child', the nature of the word itself allowing the conflation of age and relation – of description and family position. Smith blurs the boundaries between adulthood and childhood, a stance the sonnets further in their consistent invocation not of a dead *daughter*, but of a dead *child*.

Critics have accepted that Smith wrote for money to support her children. In 1903 Viscount St Cyres observed rather cynically that 'want of money made [Smith] think of obtaining a market for her literary wares', and elaborated in a way that situates Smith thoroughly as the 'proper lady': 'So long as she had lain on 'Prosperity's enfeebling bed / Or rosy pillows' her gentility had shrunk from the vulgar prominence of print. No one held more strongly than she that, for an English lady of the age of George III, as for an Athenian lady of the age of Pericles, the *post of honour was a private station*. Still, there is no arguing with the lack *paterni et Laris et fundi*.[1] In 1987 Judith Stanton makes a similar point (minus the cynicism): 'From 1784 to 1806, Mrs Smith wrote volumes of prose and poetry as a stop-gap measure, expecting [Richard Smith's] will to be settled to benefit her children and to free her from her duty to support them.'[2] Sarah Zimmerman follows this lead when she notes that Smith 'adopted gestures familiar to her readers from literary tradition in order to tell – in a reassuring guise – the story of a late-eighteenth-century woman supporting her children by writing'.[3] While Zimmerman recognizes the literary artifice used by Smith, all three critics reflect the consensus that Smith not only wrote for money, she wrote, visibly, as a mother. Smith designed her poetry so that her readers knew why she wrote; as the previous chapter discussed, her readers were in no doubt as to the nature of her needs. But it is significant how many times references to her children's needs come up; by 1784 her oldest children were of an age to begin to support her, and yet, throughout her writing career, Smith never stops describing them as requiring her aid. Her status as Mother dovetailed neatly with her role as Author: her readers then, as now, received a neat package containing a familiar, and in Zimmerman's word 'reassuring', type of woman. Her sonnets about her dead daughter provoke sympathy, appealing to readers invested in the cultural attractions of maternity; the 'solicitudes for her children which had weighed down her spirits'[4] reflect well on a writer so frequently in the public eye. As Amanda Gilroy notes, maternity 'brings woman "nearer to the perfection of her being"'.[5]

However, Smith does not slavishly follow the dictates of her culture. In her mother-sonnets, she constructs a complex narrative that, on the one hand, reifies her position as the grieving mother, and emphasizes the *nature* of grief itself through reference to flowers and plants. But she also intimates the artifice of her stance in that the flowers and plants are themselves artificial: drawn and painted. Further, she moves beyond simple expressions of grief by calling into question the identity of the speaker who suffers: she writes her mother-sonnets in such a way that the speaker fluctuates in her[6] expressions of devastation between the grief-stricken mother and the lamenting lover. Although Zimmerman asserts that Smith's 'poems exclude the subject of erotic love to protect her self-portrait as a mother who wrote only to support her family' (53), this follows from the rigorous embodying that Smith encourages. Once the poems are, as it were, 'degendered', then very few subjects are excluded. The sonnets are, in fact, binary: they combine dual possibilities, multiple subjectivities. Julia Kristeva has called the mother 'a division of language', and Smith's mother-sonnets exemplify this: they use language to create multiplicity, a kind of simultaneous Mother and Other.[7] In this way, they can be seen to enact the juxtaposition of voices in Kristeva's 'Stabat Mater'. Where Kristeva explores the maternal as an instance of 'primary narcissism', and speculates that the taming of the maternal 'is a requirement for artistic, literary or painterly accomplishment' (163), Smith uses the sonnet to portray a maternity that is both self-obsessed ('narcissistic'?) and in competition with an equally powerful subjectivity. How we read the speaker depends on who we believe 'her' to be, and that follows from our knowledge of the poet.

As chapter 1 showed, Smith does not hesitate to speak openly to her readers about 'who' she is, but she also utilizes appropriately marginal spaces for her most direct revelations. She is thus able to be authoritative while also preserving her dependence on her readers. In the sonnets, she follows a similar path, writing poems that appeal to her readers' assumptions about maternal emotion while also working against those assumptions. Again, she relies on her culture's preoccupations: for the poet who is a mother in a culture that so strongly links the feminine with infancy and child-rearing, the 'child' is both poetic metaphor and natural extension of the self who writes. Smith, in poeticizing her daughter's death and her own unending grief, legitimizes her work: sanctifying her dead child authorizes, in turn, her poetic self. Her dead child thus functions as simultaneously an instance of personal loss and an opportunity to strengthen her poetic persona, as poetry becomes the vehicle by which she expresses her grief. Smith solidifies her position when she utilizes botanical and artistic images in these sonnets; they offer visions of nature and permanence that naturalize Smith's position as bereaved, writing mother and suggest the value of her own art. For Smith in these sonnets, the child both offers a reason to write and signals her fitness to write: the propriety of the subject matter legitimizes her position as a public figure. Once again, Smith reminds her readers that she is an embodied author: in the mother-sonnets, the maternal functions protectively.

Michelle Boulous Walker glosses Lacan to suggest that 'the mother' is 'movement, flux and undecideability ... The maternal acts as a metaphor for tension, ambivalence and ambiguity' (135).[8] However, the maternal Smith does not follow this rubric. Instead, she uses 'the mother' to fix meaning, inserting the maternal metaphor as a counter to the looseness and ambiguity of this cultural picture. In writing herself as mother, Smith offers a textual self-recreation, substituting 'mother' for 'author' and inscribing her writing self *as* mother: 'the maternal is performed through the (public) act of writing' (Walker 210, n. 4). When a woman writer foregrounds her maternal self in her writing, she side-steps the public and offers the private and domestic in its place: print inscribes and hence fixes maternity. The public act of writing and publishing allows Smith to reconstitute her daughter's life and establish her own mother-love, while also creating a public memorial. The mother–daughter bond is thus mediated through a more public, textual space; the relationship establishes itself as much through ink as blood. And yet this kind of maternal imagery presents the text as itself domestic, almost private, an impression strengthened by the sonnet: intimate, homely and individuated. Privacy, not publicity, is emphasized; the maternal and the domestic work together.

The nugatory affect carried by motherhood relates to the near-sanctification of the mother in the Romantic period. The Victorian idolization of the mother finds its roots in the 1780s and 1790s, where to be a (certain kind of) mother was to be forgiven any number of sins. The codification of the domestic sphere wherein 'only mother's law orders life'[9] functions, on the one hand, to disenfranchise women, and especially mothers, from the public space of man-made and man-enforced laws; on the other, it conjures the Hannah-Morish world that glorifies woman's influence and substitutes a 'little elevation in her own garden' for the active power available in public life. And maternal love, the motherly identity, has its secure place in the domestic sphere. There, woman approaches divinity: as William Buchan ponders in 1809,

> The more I reflect . . . on the situation of the mother, the more I am struck with the extent of her powers, and the inestimable value of her services. In the language of love, woman are called angels; but this is a weak and silly compliment; they approach nearer to our ideas of the Deity: they not only create, but sustain their creation and hold its future destiny in their hands. (Gelpi 75)

As Barbara Gelpi notes, the power granted the mother is contingent on her remaining fixed in her motherly sphere, and on her visible contentment with the limitations attendant on being an embodied divinity. And, further, this kind of deified motherhood also depends on its legitimacy:

unmarried mother could easily forfeit such respect. Wifehood, a clear prerequisite to motherhood, sets the domestic scene. When writers enlist mother-imagery, they appeal to the emotional force carried by the 'mother'; in assuming the mantle of the Madonna, they cast out the spectacle of the Magdalen. The natural – that is, biological – link predicated by the mother–daughter bond reifies the attractiveness and power of the image.

Gelpi's analysis of the centrality of the mother-metaphor is complemented by Ruth Perry's reconstruction of its cultural affect. Even as a renewed emphasis on the fittedness of breastfeeding for all classes of mothers focused attention on the breasts, so too the connection to maternity led to a desexualization of the female body. The erotics of the uncovered breast were transformed into a symbol of civic duty; as Perry remarks, 'even Mary Wollstonecraft seemed to believe that a woman's claim to citizenship depended on her willingness to "mother".[10] As the breast was re-imagined as nourishing rather than ravishing, so too 'the maternal succeeded, supplanted, and repressed the sexual definition of women . . . Writers began to wax sentimental about maternity, to accord it high moral stature, and to construct it as noble, strong, and self-sacrificial . . . Natural but learned, instinctive but also evidence of the most exquisitely refined sensibility, motherhood was celebrated in prose and poetry' (Perry 190, 191). In her textual self-presentation as mother, Smith asserts her virtue and her right to be read, as well as a self-respect contingent on her public identity as mother. She transforms what Perry calls 'this new colonization of [women's] bodies' (207) into a declaration of self-determination, one that takes advantage of a cultural approbation of and hunger for public displays of mothering.

During the twenty-three years she lived with her husband, Smith gave birth to twelve children. Nine survived infancy, and after her separation from Benjamin Smith she was their sole means of support, as indeed she had been for at least ten years before the separation. Smith's children were always around: they lived with her, started careers and marriages with her help, and seemed to be constantly needy. Indeed, they benefited by her reputation as a poet, as her son Lionel found in 1799:

> [My sonnets] have been the means of introducing him to all the best society in Quebec & Montreal & have obtain'd for him friends in his profession who have been on great use to him and may be of more . . . Amidst the many mortifications and very severe sufferings to which I am needlessly expos'd, it is some consolation to know that the talents I first exerted to procure bread for the infancy of my Children (Alas! it is now, fourteen years

ago,) have been the means of the success in life of those who are grown up; at least of my Sons – for Mr William Smith was for that reason (after he had read my books) taken up by Sir John Shore in India – Nicholas by the same means found friends in Bombay – Charles got his late appointment almost entirely by Lord Clanniarde & Lady Bessborough my particular friends – And Lionel has been greatly benefitted by them in Canada.[11] (letter to Cadell and Davies, undated)

Again and again Smith's letters refer to her financial hardships in terms of her children, and demonstrate her sense that she alone is responsible for them, both in childhood and once grown: in 1804, three years before her own death and when her youngest child is nineteen, she describes herself as still 'chained to the oar' of writing (letter to Sarah Rose, 15 June 1804) and a year later laments 'the expense of my family are so high that they take away every resource for myself' (letter to Sarah Rose, 30 July 1805). For Smith 'the child' was a material, tangible, demanding being rather than, for instance, 'an ideal image of uninhibited, expressive self-hood which does not carry with it the penalty of isolation or exile'.[12] Her children, living, provide her justification for publicizing her legal plight in her Prefaces to the *Sonnets* and her other works of poetry, and excuse her forays into the legal intricacies surrounding the delayed settlement of her father-in-law's will. Her child, dead, provides the subject matter for sonnets which place Smith as acceptably feminine, a grieving mother whose sorrows flow outwards to form a proper sphere of loss, rather than inwards to focus on the self, the stricken and isolated individual who inhabits most of the sonnets.

The traditional Romanticist figuration of the child as metaphorical – 'the immediate ecstasy of joy without shadow or reflection', for instance, that J. Harvey Darton sees in the childless Blake's *Songs*[13] – derives from texts produced by men, whose investment in fatherhood has little impact on their public writing persona. The Mother-sonnets, however, insist on the presence of very real children. Alicia Ostriker says that 'the advantage of motherhood for a woman artist is that it puts her in immediate and inescapable contact with the sources of life, death, beauty, growth, corruption'; however, as she also notes, a mother 'no longer belong[s] to [herself. Her] time, energy, body, spirit and freedom are drained'.[14] This is the image of Smith derived from her letters: far from regeneration, unity with nature, or opportunity, her children represent *work* to her. And yet, as her textualized reaction to Anna Augusta's death shows, they also represent *worth* to her, confirming her maternal – and hence feminine – status despite her frequent and public lamentings. For Smith, writing about her daughter performs a public duty: she demonstrates, repeatedly, her maternal dedication.

Anna Augusta died in 1795, aged twenty-one, from an illness resulting from childbirth. Smith's preference for this daughter seems to have lain in Augusta's difference from her father; as late as 1806 Smith still referred to her as 'the only one *who had not the remotest resemblance of him*' (letter to Sarah Rose, 26 April 1806). Smith mourns this loss for the rest of her life, framing her grief as a bodily decline: 'the loss of my loveliest and most deserving child, is slowly undermining not only my frame but the few powers of mind I possess'd' (letter to Joseph Cooper Walker, 18 May 1800); 'Every mention of my Augusta, tho almost ten years are gone by since she was torn from me, (under circumstances that pour'd vitriol and aquafortis into a wound otherwise incurable;) Every mention of my Darling Child, tears my heart to pieces' (letter to Sarah Rose, 14 February 1804). Such language suggests that Smith's grief mirrors the birth process itself, and it resonates with a romanticized tone that finds play in the sonnets: Augusta functions as a lover-substitute, ironically most attractive in her *difference* from Benjamin. Gelpi points out that the construction of the maternal in the late eighteenth century meant that fathers were considered simultaneously as on a level with their children and their own children's rival. Certainly, that Augusta has nothing in her to remind Smith of Benjamin reifies Gelpi's observation, while Benjamin's well-documented efforts to secure money from Smith and from his father's estate at the expense of his children casts him as the 'scoundrel father' whose lack of parental feeling creates Smith as 'angelic mother' (Gelpi's terms, 62), images familiar from, for instance, novels of sensibility. Moreover, Smith's continued invocation of Augusta as 'my child' furthers Augusta's position, not as an adult who has died, but as an everlasting child whose loss both intensifies Smith's grief and gives it a proper expression. Smith's sonnets to her dead daughter, then, find their genesis in a wholly tangible, dutiful, even beautiful concentration on what is here rendered as particularly womanly grief.

Smith carefully embodies her mother-love in the mother-sonnets, but she does so gradually. In the first sonnet referring to Anna's death, Smith offers a grief that is so strong it can barely name its source. Sonnet LXV, 'To Dr. Parry of Bath, with some botanic drawings which had been made some years', can only explain itself allusively and tangentially, through a note that identifies Dr. Parry as 'the excellent friend and Physician to whom . . . I was obliged for the kindest attention, and for the recovery from one dangerous illness of that beloved child whom a few months afterwards his skill and most unremitted and disinterested exertions could not save!' (*Poems* 57, note to title). As the previous chapter discussed, Smith slips this information in through the back door; the note occupies the last pages of the volume. It both contextualizes the sonnet, and disguises it; Anna is a 'beloved child' rather than an adult woman, and her death, it is implied, is from a 'dangerous illness' rather than complications following childbirth. Even as the sonnet presents, via the note, Smith as devoted mother, the note erases Anna's potential motherhood, instead constructing her as a vulnerable child. It is significant that Smith allows her readers unwittingly to mistake birth as an illness; Smith underlays this sonnet with a kind of anti-maternity. The reader is directed to the note from the title of the poem, suggesting that Smith wants the sonnet read with its information in mind. The sonnet itself does not mention death, Anna, or motherhood, but relies on the note to supply the necessary information, without which it is simply about friendship in the face of adversity.

> LXV: To Dr. Parry of Bath, with some botanic drawings
> which had been made some years
>
> In happier hours, ere yet so keenly blew
>   Adversity's cold blight, and bitter storms,
>   Luxuriant Summer's evanescent forms,
> And Spring's soft blooms with pencil light I drew:
> But as the lovely family of flowers
> Shrink from the bleakness of the Northern blast,
>   So fail from present care and sorrow past
> The slight botanic pencil's mimc powers –
> Nor will kind Fancy even by Memory's aid,
>   Her visionary garlands now entwine;
> Yet while the wreaths of Hope and Pleasure fade,
>   Still is one flower of deathless blossom mine,
> That dares the lapse of Time, and Tempest rude,
> The unfading Amaranth of Gratitude.

Written with a modified rhyme scheme (abba cddc efefgg) that allows Smith to conflate the English and Italian sonnet, the poem conveys its point through two quatrains and a sestet. Smith relies on a kind of naturalized artifice: botanical drawings, rather than specimens, are used metaphorically to describe her past 'lightness' and her present care. Walker, following Kristeva, notes that 'the poetic is a kind of metaphorical relation with the mother's body' (117). Here, the mother's body is both allusive and elusive; for Smith, drawings stand in for displays of emotion. Thus, the 'pencil light' suggests her past lightheartedness, while the 'slight botanic pencil' inverts the rhyme to suggest the fleeting nature of happiness. The sestet shows that the heaviness of care blights even memory, destroying both Hope and Pleasure and the ability to 'mimic'. Smith builds in layers of representation, moving from the mimicry of drawing flowers to the more physicalized mimicry entailed in memory, and suggesting throughout the nature of art itself, which both mimics and creates. By the end of the poem, a metaphorical Amaranth has replaced the literal drawings of flowers: the logical conclusion in a poem that has been about substitution and re-presentation. The silence at the poem's centre – the subject voiced only in the note – enacts the emptiness of artificial recreation.

But Smith has also used art to, as it were, solidify grief. Even as the drawings mimic what is lost, they also stand in for it; the reference in line 5 to 'the lovely family of flowers' functions at least to hint at what the note makes more plain. Further, the 'deathless blossom' of Amaranth, although purely metaphorical, nevertheless allows for the possibility of cheating death. Returning to the poem's title, we realize that as much as the sonnet dismisses the 'pencil's mimic powers', the drawings themselves show a permanence perhaps more closely allied to the deathless Amaranth than Smith's speaker can acknowledge. The speaker, who can only bring herself to mention her 'child's' death in the margins, overlooks the paradoxical durability of art. The 'family of flowers . . . shrink from the . . . Northern blast', and Anna does not survive her own attempt at maternity, but botanical drawings are deathless. The poem thus combines nature and culture, the real and the imagined, to ensure the permanence both of grief and art.

Historically, 'women's art-making [has been seen] in connection with the home, the family and . . . caring duties'.[15] In Sonnet XCI, 'Reflections on some drawings of plants', Smith conforms to this scenario, refining the art/nature relationship introduced in Sonnet LXV, and imposing a new violence and publicity. 'Reflections' figures Smith's loss as comprehensible, if not appeaseable, through an extended artistic metaphor, and unlike Sonnet LXV does not hide its context in a note. Indeed, this is the only of the mother-sonnets in which the speaker names herself as mother.

XCI: Reflection on some drawings of plants

I can in groups these mimic flowers compose,
    These bells and golden eyes, embathed in dew;

Catch the soft blush that warms the early Rose,
  Or the pale Iris cloud with veins of blue;
Copy the scallop'd leaves, and downy stems,
  And bid the pencil's varied shades arrest
Spring's humid buds, and Summer's musky gems:
  But, save the portrait on my bleeding breast,
I have no semblance of that form adored,
  That form, expressive of a soul divine,
  So early blighted; and while life is mine,
With fond regret, and ceaseless grief deplored –
  That grief, my angel! with too faithful art
Enshrines thy image in thy Mother's heart.

Again, Smith combines sonnet forms: by rhyme scheme, the poem
has three quatrains and a couplet, although the first two quatrains are
Shakespearian and the third Spenserian. By content, however, the sonnet
rejects standardization, a suggestive move that 'reflects' the poem's force.
Smith divides the sonnet neatly in two: she devotes the first seven lines
to an assertion of her artistic expertise combined with an intrusive sug-
gestion of the loss of her visual work and its substitution by words. This
foreshadows the topic she turns to in line 8, Anna's death, and the second
half of the poem makes plain the bereavement that is the focus of the
poem. At the moment she establishes herself as skilled maker of flowers,
Smith leaves behind her flower painting; those very drawings over which
she exerted such steady control evoke the memory of a daughter whose
death she 'with fond regret, and ceaseless grief deplore[s]' (line 12). Here,
the permanent representations of nature only emphasize the evanescence
of human life, while the ease with which she captured nature's hues
in her drawings underscores her sorrows that, 'save the portrait on my
bleeding breast, I have no semblance of that form adored' (lines 8–9).
Again, Anna is transformed through poetry: a 'form adored', an 'angel', a
'soul divine, so early blighted'. Elevated to a kind of deity, Anna's divin-
ity also allows for the transformation of Smith from 'Mother' to 'Mater
Dolorosa', whose 'ceaseless grief' defines and contains her subjectivity.
Kristeva notes that 'milk and tears became the privileged signs of the
Mater Dolorosa' (173), and Smith's maternal persona recapitulates this,
displaying not only her grief but her breast as well.

  For, as we see by the poem's end, she is not entirely without her child's
'semblance'. Indeed, almost sanctifying the art by which the image is
engraved, Smith offers her own body, first the maternal breast that
'bleeds' from its loss, and then her 'Mother's heart', as the canvas on
which the portrait is reproduced. The Christian overtones suggested by

the bleeding heart of the combined images indicates that even as Anna is elevated to the divine, so too is the Mother: Mater Dolorosa and Mater Eterna. Taking to extremes the maternal 'duty' to breastfeed, the speaker displays a commitment that pathologizes this aspect of maternity. Where William Buchan in *Advice to Mothers* directs that the fit and healthy mother cannot neglect breastfeeding 'without material injury to her constitution' (in Gilroy, 22), Sonnet XCI shows that the material injury rests more emphatically in motherhood itself. This image of the lost child is not 'composed', 'caught', or 'copied', as the flowers were, but rather *carved* onto her body, an engraving more permanent than the tints (that may fade) and the paper (that may, significantly, decompose) which make up her flowers. Gelpi has noted that the ideology of the family leads to the mother's body being 'invaded, zoned, and manipulated both literally and figuratively', and that 'attention . . . is focused most particularly on the breasts' (44). But the nurturing maternal breast described by Gelpi finds its alternative in 'Reflections', for here we see blood instead of milk,[16] and self-mutilation instead of self-celebration: a violent mother's grief that ends the poem by ensuring that the dead daughter's image painfully and permanently, 'with too faithful art / [rests] Enshrined . . . in thy Mother's heart' (lines 13–14). The 'ceaseless grief' that renders an image more painfully permanent than 'arrested' nature could be also inscribes the mother: the reader sees not only a drawer of flowers but a woman who both engraves her child's portrait, and is the surface upon which she engraves. Judith Hawley has noted Smith's 'pathological morbidity' and refusal to 'let her [daughter] go', designating Smith a 'mother-martyr'.[17] This is certainly suggested by Sonnet XCI, but Hawley does not go far enough. The very force and violence of the poem create fissures in the maternal speaker's subjectivity. Smith's Mater Dolorosa is inconsolable, epically so; she displays an almost mythic grief. Even as Smith writes a maternity acceptable to her culture, she implies its concomitant unacceptability. Smith's use of nursing imagery in a sonnet describing an adult child is arresting – apparently, the child never outgrows its need for the mother's breast – but her bloody transformation of the 'Maternal breast' suggests an underlying conflict in Smith's devotion to her children's needs.

Carol Smart has noted that the nineteenth-century culture of the family held that 'mothers could not be free-thinkers; mothers follow their maternal instincts'.[18] Indeed, one could say that Smith poeticizes those instincts in her child sonnets – but that would be to re-present her as an emotion-fraught, thought-free female subject. Instead, it is the very strength and violence of her grief that implies free thought: while Smith's other children figure prominently in her letters and are the beneficiaries of her literary work, only Anna appears in the sonnets, a kind of muse, and an indication of her importance to Smith when we remember the importance of poetry in her conception of her writing self. The domestic sphere romanticized as a mother's fitting place, the 'barrage of admonitions' directed at her to submerge herself in the life of her child, the popularity of the picture of the 'blameless wife and mother, morally superior to her scapegrace husband . . . [who] devote[s] total, loving attention to her child, usually a daughter', combine to create a world wherein 'only mother's law orders life' (Gelpi 62, 66). When Smith poeticizes her dead daughter, she poeticizes a part of herself, and alleviates the impropriety of so publicly poeticizing an individual, grieving, female self. As she writes about her daughter, she also composes that daughter, textually recreating a connection broken by death but which lives beyond physical decomposition. Anna inherits the poetical love of her mother, because she *is* the poetry of her mother. The poetry in turn acts partly to support Smith's complicated self-representation as grieving mother and needful woman. Writing, for Smith, re-establishes the mother–daughter bond even as it allows her to provide materially for her other children, and, tautologically, justifies itself. The maternal love that cements filial inheritance thus depends, not on the untrustworthy lawyers negotiating a flawed will – the masculine world – but on the preservation of a publicly private world wherein the daughter rescues the mother. Anna signifies for Smith both loss and need, the one defined by the other.

The image of the proper mother in these two sonnets, then, is both upheld and called into question; the grief-stricken speaker is a model mother, but the very violence of her grief is suspect. And since this mother grieves over the body of the lost child, she is actually more of an ex-mother, hanging onto a composed maternity. But there is another way to approach these sonnets, which involves looking behind or beyond the story they set up. Sonnet XCI only names the speaker as Mother in the last line, while Sonnet LXV avoids the issue, providing the necessary information obliquely, in a note. The remaining mother-sonnets do little more than refer to a lost 'she' who remains unnamed and unidentified. We assume we know who 'she' is because we read the poems as the output of Charlotte Smith, bereaved mother. The extent of the embodying encouraged by Smith's textual apparatus and the very personal nature of her sonnets disguise the actual *impersonality* of Sonnets LXXIV ('The

Winter Night'), LXXVIII ('Snowdrops'), LXXXIX ('To the Sun'), and XC ('To Oblivion'). In each of these poems, the muted reference to a lost 'she' can only be read as the lament of a mother if we follow Smith's directions; if we read the poems on their own terms – if we, in effect, *degender* them – then they transform into poems of lost love, complete with the markers of sensibility noted by Zimmerman as inflecting Smith's poetry. More interestingly, however, in each poem the degendered speaker is regendered as male: the lost 'she' is mourned by the romantic 'he' left behind.[19] The female author creates a male speaker who is most frequently read as a bereft mother: the Kristevan juxtaposition of voices.

Indeed, 'Stabat Mater' describes the 'two fundamental aspects of Western love' as 'courtly love and child love', and quotes John Chrysostom: ' "For where there is death there is also sexual copulation, and where there is no death there is no sexual copulation either" ' (165). The degendered mother-sonnets poeticize, on the one hand, child love, and on the other, courtly love; they locate the moment of intensest love in the outpouring of grief. The speaking Self is simultaneously Mother and Lover.

LXXIV: The winter night

'Sleep, that knits up the ravell'd sleeve of care',
    Forsakes me, while the chill and sullen blast,
    As my sad soul recalls its sorrows past,
Seems like a summons, bidding me prepare
For the last sleep of death – Murmuring I hear
    The hollow wind around the ancient towers,*
While night and silence reign; and cold and drear
    The darkest gloom of Middle Winter lours;
But wherefore fear existence such as mine,
    To change for long and undisturb'd repose?
Ah! When this suffering being I resign,
    And o'er my miseries the tomb shall close,
By her, whose loss in anguish I deplore,
I shall be laid, and feel that loss no more!

LXXVIII: Snowdrops

Wan heralds of the Sun and Summer gale!
    That seem just fallen from infant Zephyrs' wing;
Not now, as once, with heart revived I hail
    Your modest buds, that for the brow of Spring

---

* These lines were written in a residence among ancient public buildings.

Form the first simple garland – Now no more
  Escaping for a moment all my cares,
Shall, with pensive, silent step, explore
The woods yet leafless; where to chilling airs
Your green and pencil'd blossoms, trembling, wave.
  Ah! ye soft, transient children of the ground,
More fair was she on whose untimely grave
  Flow my unceasing tears! Their varied round
The Seasons go; while I through all repine:
For fixt regret, and hopeless grief are mine.

In both sonnets, the speaker is nowhere identified as a mother. Instead, both use the language of romance to suggest lost love. It is a common trope of love poetry for the lover to wish himself laid in the tomb of the beloved, a substitute for the marriage bed; it is here that some of the eroticism that Zimmerman sees as excluded from Smith's poetry emerges. The footnote to Sonnet LXXIV sites the speaker specifically, and colours the scene dramatically, as does the title; it is almost as if readers watch a theatrical scene unfolding, especially given the familiarity of the romantic, almost gothic description. The rhyme scheme mixes Shakespearian and Spenserian quatrains, while the final couplet implicitly returns us to the poem's start, given the close rhyme between deplore/more and care/prepare. The emphasis on death functions to destabilize the quatrains, as line 4 runs into line 5 without pause, linking sleep with death, while the opening quote from *Macbeth* (unsourced by Smith) furthers the sense of theatricality. Sonnet LXXVIII also revolves around death, but substitutes the familiarity of sensibility for that derived from theatre; this speaker could as easily be one of the overwrought heroes of a Smith novel, obsessed with the lost beloved and haunting the 'untimely grave'. This sonnet, unlike the others, seems self-contained, with no notes or quotations, and it follows a strict Shakespearian rhyme scheme, a structure as 'fixt' as the speaker's regret and grief. In each sonnet, the speaker/lover sees death as an ally, the avenue by which union with the lost love can be achieved; in the two sonnets discussed earlier, the speaker/Mother seemed content to live, albeit in pain. Purging the Mother from the poem seems to invite a closer relationship with death.[20]

The last two mother-sonnets function as a pair; Sonnet LXXXIX continues to use the language of romance, while Sonnet XC seems to give up on subjectivity altogether.

LXXXIX*: To the Sun

Whether awaken'd from unquiet rest
   I watch 'the opening eyelids of the Morn',
When thou, O Sun! from Ocean's silver'd breast
   Emerging, bidst another day be born –
Or whether in thy path of cloudless blue,
   Thy noontide fires I mark with dazzled eyes;
Or to the West thy radiant course pursue,
   Veil'd in the gorgeous broidery of the skies,
Celestial lamp! thy influence bright and warm
   That renovates the world with life and light
Shines not for me – for never more the form
   I loved – so fondly loved, shall bless my sight;
And nought the rays illumine, *now* can charm
   My misery, or to day convert my night!

XC: To oblivion

Forgetfulness! I would thy hand could close
   These eyes that turn reluctant from the day;
   So might this painful consciousness decay,
And, with my memory, end my cureless woes.
   Sister of Chaos and eternal Night!
Oblivion! take me to thy quiet reign,
   Since robb'd of all that gave my soul delight,
I only ask exemption from the pain
   Of knowing 'such things were' – and are no more;
Of dwelling on the hours forever fled,
   And heartless, helpless, hopeless to deplore
'Pale misery living, joy and pleasure dead;'[†]
While dragging thus unwish'd a length of days,
'Death seems prepared to strike, yet still delays'.[‡]

As with the previous two sonnets, there is no hint in Sonnet LXXXIX
that the speaker is a mother; the reference to the 'fondly loved' 'form'
could as easily be spoken by a lover. Indeed, Smith's note referencing a
Milton sonnet furthers the idea that the speaker is a lover – 'I woke, she
fled' – and that Smith attaches this note to the sonnet's title rather than,
say, line 1, where it could contextualize the 'unquiet rest', strengthens the
romantic aspects of the sonnet. But we do not even reach the reference

---

  * 'I woke, she fled, and day brought back my night'. Milton
  † 'See misery living, hope and pleasure dead'. Sir Brook Boothby
  ‡ 'Death seems prepared, yet still delays to strike'. Thomas Warton

to a beloved until line 11; after line 1's 'unquiet rest', the rest of the poem's opening lines seem curiously *light* for a mother-sonnet.[21] From the title – 'To the Sun' – on, the poem emphasizes warmth, radiance, and brightness. Structurally, its rhyme scheme of quatrains allows for unimpeded movement; there is little here that suggests trouble until we reach line 11. There, however, it all begins to break down. The quatrains which have seemed to hold the poem together in a nice and tight Shakespearian structure overstays its welcome: the final quatrain extends to a sestet, even as the speaker exchanges light for darkness. The imagery is now revealed as misleading: the speaker has spent most of the poem creating a scenario that the poem itself now discounts. Vision and brightness give way to blindness and wasted light. No matter how brightly the sun shines, the speaker cannot see 'the form I loved'. But the poem carries a further rhyme scheme nuance that works two ways. The warm/form/charm rhyme of the sestet acts as a near-rhyme to morn/born of the first quatrain. Is Smith suggesting that darkness infiltrates the light even of the first quatrain, or is she allowing some of the poem's early light to persist to the sombre conclusion? Such care with rhyme suggests a poet more detached from the emotions of her speaker than readers have wanted to accept.

This artistic detachment finds further play in Sonnet XC, where the speaker allows quotation to express her despair.[22] 'To Oblivion' follows 'To the Sun' as night does day; indeed, even as 'To the Sun' ends with a rejection of the light of the sun, 'To Oblivion' opens with those same 'reluctant' eyes. In this poem, pain and 'cureless woes' are present from the start, but bereft motherhood is it its most invisible. The only clue that the poem grieves over Anna's loss is the (again unsourced) quotation from *Macbeth* that 'allu[des] to Macduff's inability to remain stoic after the murder of his wife and children' (*Poems* 77, note to Sonnet XC). Even the lover motif is muted here; instead, we read the lamentations of a distressed speaker, whose need outgrows any specific cause. The rhyme scheme echoes this general sense of woe, beginning with a Petrarchan quatrain and following this with Shakespearian quatrains and a couplet. As with Sonnet LXXXIX, the couplet harks back to the first quatrain, here through repetition and assonance: day/decay and days/delays. The repetition also suggests a speaker who does not try very hard to find new ways to express grief, a sense enhanced by the turn to quotation in the last three lines. Smith here scrupulously sources not only her reference but also the original form of phrasing, showing how the speaker has merely shuffled the words of others rather than writing her own, and in this way she calls into question the speaker's subjectivity: who is actually speaking here? What is she/he trying to say? The reference to Sir Brook Boothby's *Sorrows. Sacred to the Memory of Penelope* gives only the faintest flavour of romance, similar to the allusiveness of the maternal mentioned above.

It is interesting that Smith follows this sonnet with Sonnet XCI, 'Reflections', which as I noted is the only mother-sonnet to name the speaker *as* Mother. It is as if Smith allows the maternal to be, firstly, over-taken by the romantic, and then overcome altogether by a speaker more interested in quotation than plain speaking. She then pulls her readers back into the world of maternal grief with the visceral, violent and bodily imagery of 'Reflections', and re-emphasizes the identity of the speaker as 'Charlotte Smith', poet and bereaved mother. The turn to the romantic visible once the sonnets are 'degendered' allows to speaker to exist on several planes: grief-stricken mother (female), grief-stricken lover (male), grief-stricken lover (female), despairing 'I' (no sex). The lover-speaker is both male and female because the dead beloved is sometimes 'her', sometimes merely a 'form'; the despairing figure has no sex since the poem lacks any overt gendering, apart from that carried out by Smith herself. The Kristevan double-voicing extends to a model of quadruple voicing, originating with the voice of the mother. The transformations Smith gives to the maternal voice – the imposition of the romantic voice of sensibility – intimates her understanding that her culture considered motherhood to be woman's emotional zenith, and her exploitation of this. There is something almost playful about Smith's last mother-sonnets, as if she is experimenting with how faint a reference can be and still be detected.[23]

Elegiac Sonnets offer two more poems, 'April' and 'Ode to Death', wherein Smith seems to allude to Anna's death as another example in a long line of trials and sorrows. 'April' contrasts the 'return of the Spring, which awakens many to new sentiments of pleasure', with the despair felt by Smith: April 'serves only to remind *me* of past misery. This sensation is common to the wretched – and too many Poets have felt it in all its force'. Smith uses a footnote to point her poem as a personal expression of misery, and to identify herself as Poet, as chapter 1 discussed. The poem itself is reserved; Anna, here again a 'her', is identifiable only by season: as Curran notes, Anna 'died in the spring of 1795' (*Poems* 120, note to line 40). As the speaker says, 'dire Disease on all I loved was preying, / And flowers seem'd rising but to strew her grave!' (lines 39–40). 'Ode to Death' is even more circumspect: 'Can then the wounded wretch who must deplore / What most she loved, to thy cold arms consign'd, / Who hears the voice that sooth'd her soul no more, / Fear *thee*, O Death!' (lines 16–18). Here the 'she' is not the lost Anna but the speaker herself. Where 'April' to a certain extent disguises the event – Anna's death – with its reference to 'Disease' (Anna died in childbirth), 'Ode to Death' goes even further and disguises the speaker. This poem, written in the third person, first describes the 'wretched' figure as male: 'Ah! wherefore fears to die / He'. It then moves to the 'she' in lines 16–20 (16–18 are quoted above), before settling on a gender-neutral 'they': 'Oh! Misery's Cure; who e'er in pale dismay / Has watch'd the angel form they could not save, / And seen their dearest blessing torn away' (lines 21–23).[24] Where the sonnets experiment with structure and voice to explore the ramifications of maternal grief, 'April' and 'Ode to Death' present maternal loss as merely one form of sorrow, and in this way call into question the primacy of motherhood, both in the mother-sonnets and in the pantheon of sorrows. They also show a Smith able to manipulate 'her' grief as a poetic construct; the Mater Dolorosa is just another speaker rather than a fact of Smith's identity.

To read her mother-sonnets as the productions of a speaker detached from the poet means that we need to read Smith against herself, rather than on the terms she offers. Her many references in letters and other non-poetical writing to her efforts as a mother rather than as a writer can be seductive, but the poems themselves offer outlets to the sceptical reader. From rhyme schemes and structures that work to unravel tight-knit images of grief to the curious turn to romantic language evident if the poems are 'degendered' to the disguises wielded in 'April' and 'Ode to Death', *Elegiac Sonnets* play with motherhood as a type of feminine identity, and in doing so show Smith's ability to wear a mask and call it nature. But the *Sonnets* are not Smith's only instance of maternal imagery. In *The Emigrants* she uses the space allowed by the shift in genre from sonnet to blank-verse meditation to explore a different approach to motherhood, one that fuses a personal identity as Mother with portraits of hunted and despairing mothers physically affected by war. *The Emigrants*, published in 1793, interrupts the *Sonnets'* many editions through the 1790s with a version of motherhood that anticipates Freud's description of the uncanny; in this poem the experience of motherhood chimes with exile and alienation, and signals Smith's rejection of culture.

The uncanny works particularly well in analysing Smith's mothers in *The Emigrants* because of its association with the *heimlich/unheimlich*.

Part 'familiar', part 'homely', part 'knowable', the *heimlich* is to an extent the place of the mother; it defines her cultural space. The *unheimlich* undoes the familiarity of the *heimlich*; it is like the other voices speaking in the sonnets. In chapter 4 I will explore in more detail how *The Emigrants* follows the plot of the *unheimlich*; here it is sufficient to note how closely the *heimlich* supports the maternal, and how the defamiliarizing of the *unheimlich* recreates the maternal as itself both alienating and alienated. Smith uses mothers to bind together the two books of the poem; the emigrant mother of Book I foreshadows a collection inhabiting Book II. Her 'softer form reclines' 'where the cliff, hollow'd by the wintry storm, / Affords a seat with matted sea-weed strewn' (I: 202, 200–201). This figure, the first in a sequence of mothers, mourns her lost lavish lifestyle; sheltered not on, but *in* the margin, she watches her children playing and finds in 'Fancy' some respite. This first mother embodies the dissolute aristocracy; she imagines the crowds that 'paid [her] willing homage' since 'Beauty gave charms to empire' (I: 225–226). Smith's observing self cannot identify with this careless mother; like her 'fellow sufferer', her husband, she represents arrogance, conscious haughtiness, and an inability to recognize 'that worth alone is true nobility' (I: 240). Unlike the mothers to follow, this one, 'lost in melancholy thought', lacks maternal care; her error is a concern with self at the expense of deep mother-love. Smith's stance is sympathetic, yet judgemental; from her vantage point, she characterizes this mother as unfamiliar with her maternal duty, as in exile from her appropriate position of care.[25]

Claudia Johnson has observed that 'maternity, as [Mary] Wollstonecraft sees it, in fact entails no necessary or insurmountable division of the public and private spheres'.[26] *The Emigrants*, published in 1793, follows the 1792 *Vindication of the Rights of Woman* by dramatizing how maternity in wartime actually straddles the public/private divide, showing that motherhood itself functions as a metaphor for victimization. Whereas in the *Sonnets* Smith constructed a complicated 'is she/isn't she' embodied persona whose duality effectively questioned its own existence, in *The Emigrants* she devotes portions of the poem to life-writing of the kind that plainly associates the speaker with the author.[27] In the poem's dedication to William Cowper she asks to 'vindicate [her]self from those [faults], that may be imputed to the [poem's] design'. I have noted how her use of 'vindication' resonates with a Wollstonecraftian fervour that spills into the poem, where her self-presentation as a mother struggling to save her children is mirrored by the portraits of mothers affected by martial violence. She 'designs' a pro-Revolution, anti-war poem that concentrates on the civilian victims, especially the mothers whose homes and lives are destroyed. She maintains a careful awareness of chronology, setting Book I in November 1793 (after the September Massacres but before war with Britain is declared), and her Book I mother is, as noted above, criticized for her careless mothering and nostalgia for a dissolute lifestyle. Book II, however, is set in April 1793, and Smith is less concerned with the emigrants and more interested in following through her exploration of victimized maternity. Her choice of April allows her to take on board the founding of the Society of Revolutionary Republican Women in February, as well as the King's beheading in January and the declaration of war between France and Britain. The Society endorsed women as publicly revolutionary figures despite conclusions that, 'in the ideal Republic, women were meant to be 'mothers' not writers ... women were expected to remain in the private sphere ... rather than play a public role, be it political or literary'; as Suzanne Desan elaborates, however, 'in both ideology and practice, women's new-found role as citizens stood in tension with the ideal patriotic role of women as republican mothers and moral guardians of the revolution within the home'.[28] In Book II, Smith responds to this clash of ideologies, encoding in her own self-placement a rejection of strictly domesticized femininity but also exposing the effect of war on the domestic ideal: her mothers are *prevented* from guarding the nation's morals by that very nation's immoral assault on their bodies. Public violence thereby eliminates privacy altogether.

Smith furthers this by focusing first on the imprisoned 'unhappy heir / Of fatal greatness' (II: 127–128) whose 'baby brow' (II: 130) would have been better off 'in an humble sphere' (II: 131). Her protective tone is itself maternal, but she uses the child to gain access to his mother, here divested of Burkean sexual allure and transformed into a 'wretched Mother, petrified with grief, / [Who] views [her son] with stony eyes, and cannot weep!' (II: 152–153). The *heimlich* space of the domesticated mother has become the distinctly *unheimlich* one of the imprisoned mother, but at this point it functions, paradoxically, positively. Like the aristocratic mother of Book I, Marie Antoinette suffers for past folly, but unlike that careless mother, she is focused on her son, petrified not with fear for herself, but grief for what – who – has been lost. The Queen is also a Mother, and Smith 'mourn[s] thy sorrows, hapless queen! / And deem[s] thy expiation made to Heaven / For every fault, to which prosperity / Betray'd thee, when it plac'd thee on a throne / Where boundless power

was thine, and thou wert rais'd / High (as it seemed) above the envious
reach of destiny!' (II: 154–160). Perversely fulfilling republican ideals, the
Queen has been transformed from a public to a private woman, from
frivolous to responsible, from error-laden to a moral guardian, in her
movement from Queen to Mother. That she has also been imprisoned
creates the paradox that Smith exploits; even as she makes clear the
Queen/Mother's fears are 'for those / More dear to thee than life!' (II:
173–174), she also links her personal feelings of loss and despair to the
Queen's through an overt identification of mother with mother. Both are
persecuted by 'sad experience': 'Ah! who knows, / From sad experience,
more than I, to feel / For thy desponding spirit, as it sinks / Beneath pro-
crastinated fears for those / More dear to thee than life!' (II: 169–173).
The Queen's 'eminence of misery' (II: 173–174) proves a metaphorical
analogue to Smith's position, as Book II opens, 'on an Eminence': for
Smith, the eminence is both proof and cause of alienation. That the
home, the protected domestic space, is, for the Queen, exchanged for a
prison only emphasizes the contradictions of a culture that requires a
femininity exemplified by motherhood yet fails to protect mothers. By
recasting a dissolute Queen as a despairing mother, Smith questions easy
assumptions of guilt while further defamiliarizing motherhood itself.

Smith continually returns to mothers and their special victimization
by war: the nightmare landscape created by battle, when 'the flames of
burning villages illum[e] / the waste of water' (II: 226–227), echoes with
'the frantic shrieks / Of mothers for their children' (II: 229–230). Smith
moves from the general to the specific, cutting into her description of
horrors the tale of a 'wretched Woman, pale and breathless'. This latest
mother, 'clasping close / To her hard-heaving heart her sleeping child, /
All she could rescue of the innocent groupe [sic] / That yesterday sur-
rounded her/ (II: 264–267), proves a culminatory figure: driven from her
home by 'lawless' soldiers, she exemplifies the wrongness of war. If the
new republic idealizes mothers, why does it kill them, asks Smith? This
mother is multiply victimized: she lacks a protector in the home since he
has gone to fight, and she is at the mercy of soldiers who do not recog-
nize her motherhood. She even questions her own maternal devotion:
while the earlier lines have implied that she could *save* only one of her
children, she feels 'half repentant now / [Of] her headlong haste[;] she
wishes she had staid / To die with those affrighted Fancy paints / The
lawless soldiers' victims' (II: 269–272). Smith shifts the inference from
justified escape to hysterical flight: the baby who is all the mother 'could
rescue' figures now as the chosen one. In other words, the mother has

run away and left her other children, an act perhaps mitigated by circumstance but still resonating with the violence war wreaks on the maternal. This terrified mother has abandoned her maternal duties even as she has 'saved' one child. With this figure, Smith makes it clear that war destroys what it purports to uphold. The mother dies, pursued by soldiers, but, 'in Death itself, / True to maternal tenderness, she tries / To save the unconscious infant from the storm / In which she perishes / . . . / But alas! The Mother & Infant perish both!' (II: 280–284, 290–291). Even as Marie Antoinette's motherhood will not save her from the guillotine, neither is this woman protected from (doing) violence. The homeliness, the refuge of maternity, in Smith's handling, reveals its own emptiness: motherhood itself is vitiated by war.[29]

Considering that *The Emigrants* concerns itself in part with the errors of the French, it might be expected that Smith would turn to England for relief, but even as her representations of English politics are equivocal, so too her experience of its culture proves alienating. Invoking Memory, Smith finds she can locate personal happiness only in her childhood: the advent of adulthood and almost immediate motherhood mean only 'never-ending toil, / . . . terror and . . . tears!' (II: 350–351). Having dwelt for so long of the terrors of war, it is significant that when Smith turns to herself as mother she uses such diction. Like the mother who died in the wilderness (but with, one hopes, more success), Smith 'attempt[s] . . . / To save my children from the o'erwhelming wrongs / That have for ten long years been heap'd on me! – / The fearful spectres of chicane and fraud / Have, Proteus-like, still chang'd their hideous forms / (As the law lent its plausible disguise), / Pursuing my faint steps . . .' (II: 353–358). Smith, having presented us with a series of mothers victimized by war, now links her own situation with theirs: where they are persecuted by violence, she is by chicanery and fraud. There is a sense that the entire poem has been building to this point, that Smith declares herself an emigrant from a violent and terrible social evil, as she declares that not even motherhood can withstand its force. Underlying Smith's imagery is an accusation: even as the Revolution has betrayed its allegiance to Liberty, so too English law has betrayed its commitment to equality – or rather, Smith's experience has proved the hypocrisy of that commitment. Her 'mother's efforts' find as little support as a French mother's, despite a cultural insistence on its necessity, but part of the thrust of *The Emigrants* has been to 'vindicate [Smith's] humble fame' (II: 383); her repetition of this word from the Dedication strengthens its allusiveness to Wollstonecraft's and is as evocative as Smith's earlier, personalized use of 'terrors'. To be a 'mother', in wartime and in *The Emigrants*, is to be the 'other'; the home is invaded and destroyed by violence, while social forces collude to push women to its margins. Smith's self-placement on the eminence allows her to see this and to embody this. Her delineation of mothers exiled from the protective family space by the very society that insists on the primacy of motherhood underscores her critique of 'the variety of woes that Man / For Man [or Woman] creates' (II: 413–414). The repressed, which here functions as the social violation of the maternal, returns to take up a central space in *The Emigrants*.

Smith's deployment of the maternal in this poem cooperates with what she does in the *Sonnets* in that both suggest her utter devotion to her children and the idea of motherhood. But as my discussion of the mother-sonnets concluded, it is possible to detect a strand of self-subversive commentary; in *The Emigrants*, it surfaces partly in the insistence with which Smith associates her speaking Voice with condemned and dying mothers. While on the one hand it is arguable that in doing so Smith is underscoring the risks inherent in a socialized maternity – as I explore above – it is also the case that Smith draws comparisons that are extreme, and that she does so deliberately (with the repetition of the imagery of pursuit, for instance). Returning to lines 353–358, it is significant that Smith attempts 'to save my children from . . . wrongs that have . . . been heap'd on me'. Does this mean that she is trying to protect her children from the wrongs she has experienced? Or to salvage the family name from such wrongs? Or is there a kind of slip occurring here, as if the speaker cannot help but focus on motherhood and herself as mother at the linguistic expense of her children? And does this function as another example of maternal error, such as that shown by the emigrant mother, the dead mother, and Marie Antoinette? Even as the sonnets began to privilege romantic love over mother-love once 'degendered', *The Emigrants* offers a group of mothers, speaker included, whose individual errors suggest something larger once read *in toto*. There seems to be another voice in this poem, one much less invested in the sanctity of motherhood than the speaker, and this voice becomes audible once we begin to read Smith against herself. If we refuse to accept the terms the poem offers, then the exile and alienation it links to motherhood begin to invade the ideal of maternity it seems to uphold.

The very strength of the speaking voice in the sonnets and *The Emigrants* means that readers feel easy identifying 'her' with Smith. As with Wordsworth, Coleridge, and the other more familiar Romantic

poets, Smith succeeds in creating a personalized subjectivity, and here
she factors in that aspect of selfhood that makes, for instance, 'Frost at
Midnight' an equally powerful statement of personal identity. When she
talks about 'my children' or her 'Mother's heart' there seems to be no
reason to question the image; as Zimmerman says, 'the sonnets them-
selves aim to present the poet with the vividness of a portrait' (44). This
aim is accurate and powerful, hitting most readers straight in the senti-
mental zone. As the poems illustrate, the mother is one of the social
figures most in need of assistance, and most deserving of it. Harsh indeed
would be the reader who would refuse to lend at least sympathy. There
are few more emotive feminine types (the next chapter explores perhaps
the mother's closest rival, the woman in need), and in using maternal
imagery Smith could hardly fail to appeal to her audience. But Smith's
appreciation of the marketability of motherhood is shadowed by a
deconstruction of the maternal voice, a breaking down of its constitu-
tive elements of selflessness, devotion and self-sacrifice. It is this fissure
that suggests Smith's artifice and her self-conscious application of a gen-
dered stereotype.

Notes

1 Viscount St Cyres, 'The Sorrows of Mrs Charlotte Smith', *The Cornhill Mag-
   azine* 15 (1903), 683–696: 685. St Cyres unwittingly points out the limited
   options of the 'proper lady' when he ventriloquizes Smith as believing print
   to be 'vulgar', and shows her willingness to follow this career once money
   was needed. Somehow, the vulgarity has been eliminated; one wonders if the
   necessity to publish served more as an opportunity for Smith than a calamity.
2 See Judith Stanton, 'Charlotte Smith's Literary Business: Income, Patronage
   and Indigence', in *The Age of Johnson* 1 (1987), 375–401: 375.
3 See Sarah Zimmerman, *Romanticism, Lyricism, and History* (Albany: State
   University of New York Press, 1999), 53. Subsequent references will be made
   in the text.
4 In Scott, review of 'Charlotte Smith'. *Miscellaneous Prose Works*, 4 vols.
   (Edinburgh: Cadell, 1834), 123.
5 Gilroy quotes from Martha Mears's *The Pupil of Nature; or, Candid Advice to
   the Fair Sex* (1797), in '"Candid Advice to the Fair Sex": Or, the Politics of
   Maternity in Late Eighteenth-Century Britain', *Body Matters: Feminism,
   Textuality, Corporeality*, eds. Avril Horner and Angela Keane (Manchester:
   Manchester University Press, 2000), 17–29: 19.
6 For the sake of convenience I use the feminine pronoun; however, as this
   chapter argues, it is not always clear what the sex of the speaker is, due to
   Smith's play with gender roles.

7 Julia Kristeva, 'Stabat Mater', *The Kristeva Reader*, ed. Toril Moi (New York: Columbia University Press, 1986), 160–187: 178. Subsequent references will be made in the text.

8 See Michelle Boulous Walker, *Philosophy and the Maternal Body: Reading Silence* (London: Routledge, 1998). Subsequent references will be made in the text.

9 Barbara Gelpi, *Shelley's Goddess: Maternity, Language, and Subjectivity* (Oxford: Oxford University Press, 1992), 66. Subsequent references will be made in the text.

10 See Ruth Perry, 'Colonizing the Breast: Sexuality and Maternity in Eighteenth-Century England', *Eighteenth-Century Life* 16 (1992), 185–213: 187.

11 Letter to Cadell and Davies, undated. This and all subsequent letters are quoted from Rufus Paul Turner, 'Charlotte Smith (1749–1806): New Light on her Life and Literary Career', PhD diss., University of Southern California, 1966. Judith Stanton's long-awaited edition of Smith's letters was not yet available at the time of writing, but see *The Collected Letters of Charlotte Smith*, ed. Stanton (Bloomington: Indiana University Press, 2003).

12 See Jonathan Cook, 'Romantic Literature and Childhood', *Romanticism and Ideology: Studies in English Writing, 1765–1830*, ed. David Aers (London: Routledge and Kegan Paul, 1981), 44–63: 45.

13 See J. Harvey Darton, 'Blake and Verse for Children', *William Blake: Songs of Innocence and Experience, A Casebook*, ed. Margaret Bottrall (Basingstoke: Macmillan, 1970), 108–115.

14 See Alicia Ostriker, 'A Wild Surmise: Motherhood and Poetry', *Imagining Women: Cultural Representations and Gender*, eds. Frances Bonner, Lizbeth Goodman, Richard Allen, Linda Janes and Catherine King (Cambridge: Polity Press, 1992), 103–107: 106.

15 Catherine King, 'Making Things Mean: Cultural Representation in Objects', in *Imagining Women: Cultural Representations and Gender*, 15–20: 17.

16 Gelpi, Mary Jacobus (*First Things: The Maternal Imaginary in Literature, Art, and Psychoanalysis* (London: Routledge, 1995)) and Felicity Nussbaum ('Heteroclites: The Gender of Character in the Scandalous Memoirs', *The New Eighteenth Century*, eds. Nussbaum and Laura Brown (New York: Methuen, 1987): 144–167) all note the political and social importance breastfeeding assumed during the late eighteenth century: in an age of wet-nursing, breastfeeding one's own child was both a social duty and a social faux pas.

17 Judith Hawley, 'Charlotte Smith's *Elegiac Sonnets*: Losses and Gains', *Women's Poetry in the Enlightenment: The Making of a Canon, 1730–1820*, eds. Isobel Armstrong and Virginia Blain (Basingstoke: Macmillan, 1999), 184–198: 187, 188.

18 See Carol Smart, 'Disruptive Bodies and Unruly Sex: The Regulation of Reproduction and Sexuality in the Nineteenth Century', *Regulating Womanhood: Historical Essays on Marriage, Motherhood, and Sexuality*, ed. Smart (London: Routledge, 1992), 7–32: 22.

19 This reading, of course, imposes a heterosexual romance matrix, partly because the romance terminology the poems utilize is most often in the service of heterosexual love.

20 If we read the poems as spoken by the bereft Mother, then death becomes another way of mothering the lost child.

21 The source of the quotation in line 2, *Lycidas*, carries with it the weight of mourning, but unusually, Smith does not reference it; perhaps she felt that a quotation from Milton was self-explanatory. Certainly by the late 1790s Smith was punctilious about sourcing her quotes after charges of plagiarism from Anna Seward, among others, so it seems telling that she allows this one to stand on its own.

22 Adela Pinch has fruitfully explored Smith's use of quotation in *Strange Fits of Passion: Epistemologies of Emotion, Hume to Austen* (Stanford: Stanford University Press, 1996).

23 Since I have followed Stuart Curran's identification of these sonnets as 'about' Anna, this analysis also points out the effects of critical assumptions I discussed in the Introduction.

24 'Angel form' seems another reference to Anna; Sonnet XCI calls her an 'angel'.

25 The emigrant mother later reappears in *Elegiac Sonnets* in 'The Female Exile', where Smith reworks her languidness as a suitable example of her feminine maternity. The female exile, a 'fair stranger', feels her children's woe for them as 'she beholds them with anguish' (line 25), and instead of indulging in fantasies of her lost luxurious lifestyle, mourns the 'multiplied miseries that wait on mankind!' (line 24). An extreme example of feminine sensibility, she is accorded the full mark of approval when Smith's speaker concludes 'Poor mourner! – I would that my fortune had left me / The means to alleviate the woes I deplore; / But *like thine* my hard fate has of affluence bereft me, / I can warm the cold heart of the wretched no more!' (lines 33–36, first emphasis added). Although, as Smith's note to the poem asserts, the female exile and the female emigrant are the same person, the mothers presented in the two poems are diametrically opposed. See chapter 1 for a discussion of the plate that accompanies this poem.

26 See Claudia Johnson, 'Mary Wollstonecraft: Styles of Radical Maternity', *Inventing Maternity: Politics, Science and Literature, 1650–1865*, eds. Susan C. Greenfield and Carol Barash (Lexington: The University of Kentucky Press, 1999): 159–172: 161.

27 This is the 'lyric realist' as defined by Zimmerman, 'who carefully observes the world around her and who strongly resembles Smith herself' (70). My argument differs from Zimmerman's in that I think Smith artfully encourages this resemblance in the *Sonnets* only to destabilize it through poetic structure. In *The Emigrants* she uses war imagery to transform her frustrations at the hands of lawyers into active and malevolent persecution.

28 See Catherine R. Montfort and J. J. Allison, 'Women's Voices and the French Revolution', *Literate Women and the French Revolution of 1789*, ed. Catherine

R. Montfort (Birmingham, AL: Summa Publications, Inc., 1994), 3–17: 3–4.
See also Desan, 'Women's Experience of the French Revolution: An Histori-
cal Overview', *Literate Women and the French Revolution of 1789*, 20.

29 Smith does not neglect fathers; this vignette is followed by one depicting the
return of the 'feudal Chief' to his home, 'alone and in disguise'. Smith implies
that his castle is the same 'mansion' that the mother has fled, and indeed the
Chief soon discovers his slaughtered family: 'o'er a bleeding corse / Stumbling
he falls; another interrupts / His staggering feet – all, all who us'd to rush /
With joy to meet him – all his family / Lie murder'd in his way!' (II: 304–308).
Where the mother loses her life to war, the father loses his reason: 'And the
day dawns / On a wild raving maniac' (II: 308–309).

3

Elegiac Sonnets II:
the woman in need

For all the affectiveness of the mother, Smith did not rely on this figure alone to establish her attractions for her reading public. The justification for her sorrows contained in the poems' prefatory pages allowed for the establishment of a more general feminized construct, the damsel in distress, recast by Smith as a woman in need.[1] As a successful novelist, Smith was well aware of the fashion for romance in the 1790s.[2] When she presents her persona as actively in need of succour, presumably to be provided by a sympathetic and chivalrous readership, she situates that persona as a kind of romance figure, the distressed woman whose sensibility overwhelms her, and whose fate will be determined by forces outside her control. But Smith does not simply write a romance heroine into her sonnets; indeed, as this chapter will show, she goes beyond such limitations even as she seems to accept their bonds. Smith's deliberate embodiment affects the 'distressed woman' sonnet as much as it does the mother-sonnet, while the sonnet genre itself becomes a tool for a poet interested in exploring the ramifications of gendered subjectivity. Even as she pursues a project of writing the sorrows of Charlotte, Smith overturns the very subjectivity this relies on: her manipulation of selfhood reflected in her abstraction of the 'I' results in poetry that is simultaneously highly personal and emptied of personality altogether. And while her establishment of the distressed woman allows for another view of Smith's exploration of conventional gender roles, it is when she strays from this marked path that gender itself is called into question.

The distressed woman sonnets operate in a highly artificial way, taking advantage of both genre and expectations of conventional behaviour. Smith's own insistence on her sincerity has resulted in a picture of her poetry as unmediated, as emanating from the genuine distresses and woes of Smith herself. The previous chapters pointed out some of the problems with this construction; in this chapter I will continue to unpick Smith's careful assumption of personae and show them to be roles, and Smith herself to be exploiting the expectations of her readers. The recent work of Judith Pascoe, Julie Carlson, Catherine Burroughs and other critics has illuminated the theatrical bent of the Romantic period; as Joseph Litvak notes, 'the trope of "theatricality" enables us both to unpack subjectivity as performance and to denaturalize – to read as a *scene* – the whole encompassing space in which that subjectivity gets constituted . . . [T]he self is . . . a contingent cluster of theatrical roles'.[3] If we approach Smith's sonnets as theatrical in this way, then, as Litvak says, her anchored and embodied subjectivity transforms into a series of roles, facilitated by the sonnet genre which allows each poem to encompass in fourteen lines an entire world.[4] Jonathan Hess defines the sonnet's form of subjectivity as 'necessarily finite, one of bounded interiority, an illusion of autonomy' and goes on to say that 'as a form of necessarily finite subjectivity, the sonnet is . . . a naïve form *par excellence*, not a medium of reflection'.[5] The sonnet reinforces by its very nature the impression of wholeness unfettered by 'reflection': that is, it is offered as a momentary effusion (despite its concurrent status as formally one of the most difficult of genres) which encourages readings that stress its finiteness. The suggestion, of course, is that the sonnet cannot contain anything greater than itself; Hess's 'naiveté' ensures against any serious exploration of subjectivity. But what happens if the sonnet's speaker rejects such boundedness, and splits or fragments? What happens if a series of sonnets constructs, not an illusory autonomy, but an intermingling of subjective stances that can only be called theatrical? Smith's role-playing gains coherence from the 'finite' sonnet, a kind of generic protection that disguises her creation of a 'contingent cluster of theatrical roles'. This, combined with the embodiment enforced by the prefaces, means that the sonnets' play with subjectivity takes place undercover, protected by what we think we know about the speaker and her sorrows.

Indeed, most readers remain convinced that the sonnets express a particularly female subjectivity, reading them as 'express[ing] a female point of view . . . Smith takes up the position of a woman of sensibility in her poems . . . [H]er speaker is a creative and talented figure who has suffered betrayal and disillusionment'. The 'sonnet series establishes a woman's right to position herself as a subject . . . The protagonist in Smith's autobiographically based sonnets defines herself as a melancholy woman.' Her 'state of abjection can be seen as symptomatic of the position of the woman /poet'; Smith is 'virtually an archetype of the female condition of the late eighteenth century'.[6] These critical responses have no hesitation in reading the sonnets as inherently gendered because clearly spoken by a woman who writes from her own experience. The sensibility that is displayed is feminine, dealing with a variety of personal losses but returning again and again to lost happiness and a need for succour and assistance: the inscription of an abandoned and distressed woman. And yet this style of response to Smith, as appropriate as it may be to the response she solicits, fails to understand sensibility as both felt and performed. As Markman Ellis has established, the performative aspect of sensibility has been consistently underplayed in favour of its more obvious status as *feeling*, which in turn ascribes to an understanding of the Romantic period as a whole as sincere, genuine and self-reflexive.[7] The need to see sensibility as in some way 'real' connects to a desire to read subjectivity as also 'real': a mirror of the soul that justifies readerly identification with a speaker's emotion. As with the use-value of form attached to the sonnet, an acceptance that emotion displayed is emotion felt (especially if the speaker is female, but not exclusively so) means that readers of the sonnets effectively collude in their own manipulation; they agree to be affected when they agree not to notice affectation.[8] For Smith's original readers as much as for modern critics, this amounts to a willing suspension of disbelief to the point that disbelief itself is disallowed. And so while some of Smith's readers through the centuries have become weary of her *tone*, fewer have felt suspicious of her *style*.

Of course, as I have suggested already, readers are effectively seduced into belief by the trope of embodiment that informs Smith's work, which combines with the emotiveness of the sonnets to mask artifice. What Joseph W. Donohue, Jr calls 'the late eighteenth-century movement toward subjectivity in the arts'[9] suggests that Smith's culture, not just Smith herself, was engaged in a redefinition of what constituted art itself – an investigation of art *qua* artifice that is perhaps more closely associated with poems like 'Ode on a Grecian Urn'. Smith's culture was interested in looking at things and in being entertained, but it also required authenticity: the feeling/posturing dichotomy described by Ellis and borne out by the appeal to vicarious emotion carried by sentimental novels. The immediacy of poetry, enhanced by the intimacy of the sonnet, assured readers that Smith was genuine and that her distress was really felt: it was as embodied, as physical, as the poet herself, the same poet who stresses her own sorrowful ageing in the volume's frontispiece.

The link between spectacle and surveillance described by Litvak (ix) works to maintain Smith's 'reality': even as she displays her emoting subjectivity, her readers require a consistency of emotion by which to know her.[10] The very emphasis on the value of authenticity in the presentation of selfhood, however, implies its artificiality, its theatricality: once something like selfhood becomes an aspect of art, art inevitably becomes an aspect of selfhood. The appealingly embodied author is as much a construct as the distressed woman in need.

Another way to approach this is provided by Thomas Crochunis when he situates 'authorship' as something 'performed on a discursive stage'.[11] The author here is the construct 'Charlotte Smith', who sets a scene of unremitting sorrow starring herself. The convincing nature of the performance effectively disguises its own provenance: a masked masquerade. The distressed woman takes centre stage and engrosses our attention. But recognizing the theatricality of the sonnets does not mean merely recognizing the performative nature of this distress; as with the mother-sonnets, the distressed woman sonnets perform the 'woman' part of the equation as well. Indeed, as much as Smith's speakers affect distress, they affect gender as well; the discursive stage textualizes a gendering wherein femininity itself – the very essence of the distressed woman in need, and the very underpinning of a readerly chivalric response – is no more than a costume. The discursive again comes into play, linked to the 'performative' as theorized by Judith Butler: 'gender is an "act," as it were, that is open to splittings, self-parody, self-criticism, and those hyperbolic exhibitions of "the natural" that, in their very exaggeration, reveal its fundamentally phantasmatic status'.[12] As I will discuss, the 'I' that inhabits the distressed woman sonnets is exactly split, self-parodic, self-criticizing, and only nominally 'natural'; moreover, if 'gender is a series of mimetic, socially constructed, stylized acts, which operate discursively and as such are only naturalized and appear as authentic expressions of biological sex through a process of constant repetition',[13] then the sonnets operate as a kind of textbook on engendering, employing the discursive and the repetitive to authenticate gender itself. Each time the distressed woman – or more accurately the distressed 'I' – is reiterated, gender is inscribed, an adjunct or corollary to the genuine self understood to inhabit the sonnets. And each time this occurs, a complicit readership agrees to see the 'I' as the engendered 'Charlotte Smith'.

Joan Riviere has described femininity as a 'masquerade', and Geraldine Harris has elaborated by saying that '"femininity" is always "drag", the poor copy, even when performed by a woman, because masculinity is the norm and the original' (59; Riviere quoted in Harris 59). This has interesting implications for the kind of performativity that Smith's sonnets engage in. As I noted in the Introduction to this book, the subjectivit(ies) in Smith's poetry are signalled as feminine partly because of the overt – that is, costumed – gender of the frontispiece. The 'I' is derived from and constantly harkens back to this embodied figure. But since so much is conveyed through dress, and through the repetition of the prefaces and the iterated 'I' of the poems, while so little is left to the chance identification of the reader, the authorial presence of Smith is used theatrically to stage this femininity. What lingers behind the set, however? Does Smith manifestly have to establish the femininity of her subjectivity exactly because the referent, the 'norm', is masculine? When she stages femininity, does this work to recover or reiterate gender? Butler discusses the problematic nature of authority when it comes to gender: 'a performative tends to have the *appearance* of issuing from the authority of the subject who utters it, [but this disguises] the way in which this subject only reproduces that authority in so far as they are "quoting" an already established set of conventions' (in Harris 68). So when Smith's speakers put on the costume of femininity, when they engage in what is demonstrably a masquerade, are they actually exposing their own complicity as well as enlisting that of the reader? Is the demonstration of gender visible in the sonnets actually a series of plagiarisms, 'quoting which operates to conceal its own status as quotation' (Harris 68)? By presenting the 'I' as in distress, by appealing to the chivalric impulses of a readership well versed in romantic literature, Smith bolsters the embodied 'I' with additional femininity, but the closer this is examined, the more like a pantomime dame the 'I' comes to seem: exactly a figure in drag, 'passing' as feminine.

The distressed 'I' sonnets function as masquerades because they are, in actuality, by no means consistent when it comes to the gendering of the 'I'. Although nominally the 'I' is nominally 'Smith' and hence feminine, as this chapter will discuss the figure of the feminine is always assumed: adopted, rather than 'natural', staged rather than authentic. This runs counter to the picture of Romantic subjectivity as coherent and self-contained, but as Pascoe proposes in *Romantic Theatricality*, the Romantic self is more indebted to the staged than critics have wanted to see. When Smith writes subjectivities that exist on several simultaneous levels, she supplies a model taken up by the more familiar figures of Romanticism for whom the 'I' is as much a construct as it is for Smith (even if this often goes unrecognized). The difference is that Smith's sexed body presupposes a gender more culturally insisted on as significant to the writing process. Her play with gendered subjectivities in the sonnets shows her own investment in the performative: her speakers' multiplicities attest to her theatrical skill. In turning to the sonnets, my discussion will unpick Smith's complex of identities, and demonstrate the ways in which Smith loosens gender from identity, only for her readers to refix it. This loosening takes place on several levels, some more deliberate than others. In beginning with the distressed 'I', it will be necessary to return briefly to the simpler figure of the distressed woman, before moving on to investigate how the 'woman' transmutes, shedding her gender while retaining subjectivity. I will then look more closely at the theatrics of gender in the sonnets, their function as masquerades.

Dorothy Mermin has remarked that for the Victorian woman poet, the figures of the damsel and the knight functioned as emblematic of her necessity 'to be two things at once, or in two places, whenever she tries to locate herself with the poetic world'.[14] The mutually exclusive roles of 'poet and his fairy inspiration' fragmented the female writer, who 'looked for a place where a woman could situate herself without self-contradiction and in which she could not just daydream, but speak' (66, 65). The romantic imagery assumed by Victorian woman poets is that familiar to Romantic poets as well. The enforced femininity of the damsel – that is, her automatic association with any forlorn woman – and her definitive need to await rescue means that almost any poem where the speaker exhibits distress and the author is a woman activates the trope, and the *Sonnets* are no exception. An early reader, Sir William Jones, wrote a friend in 1787 to thank him 'heartily, my dear Sir, for the tender strains of the unfortunate Charlotte, which have given us pleasure and pain; the sonnets which relate to herself are incomparably the best'.[15] Although in 1787 Smith had not yet published the very personalized Preface to the Sixth Edition that laid bare the troubles under which she suffered, Jones has no hesitation in naming her as a distressed woman, 'the unfortunate Charlotte', his familiar use of her first name increasing the impression that he read her 'strains' on a personal and yet spectative level.[16] Her romantic position as 'damsel' secure, it is only through her own mechanics of the performative that Smith can also be the 'knight': she literalizes the doubleness discursively.

It is striking how few of the sonnets actually manifest a distressed female speaker, and yet how many of them seem as if they do. For instance, 'Sonnet LXVII: On passing over a dreary tract of country, and near the ruins of a deserted chapel, during a tempest', immediately challenges gender stereotypes with its very title; although putatively the experience of a woman in need, this woman is not awaiting rescue, but out in the storm, or 'tempest', at night, as the poem itself makes clear when it describes the owl 'forgo[ing] his evening flight' and the fox 'elud[ing] the tempest of the night' (6, 8). As in 'Sonnet LXII: Written on passing by moonlight through a village'[17] this speaker engages our sympathy as a woman in need by refusing to act like one, 'passing' as a different creature altogether, a 'being' (3). The owl and fox, both referred to as 'he', avoid the tempest that the speaker actively seeks; the 'gloom' 'hides me from a World I wish to shun' (10). Since the speaker opposes 'her' position to that of the masculinized owl and fox, we could conclude that Smith genders the speaker feminine and reverses accustomed gender roles, since the male owl and fox have homes and stay there, while the feminine speaker wanders, as in 'Sonnet LXII', 'cheerless and unblest'. The final couplet, 'Nor is the deepest shade, the keenest air, / Black as my fate, or cold as my despair', emphasizes the speaker's isolation and emotional emptiness, and encourages readerly sympathy. But the sonnet presents a more complicated gender genealogy than at first apparent. Although Smith does not note it, the sonnet is drawn from her novel *Montalbert* where it was spoken by a male character, Sommers Walsingham. Her lack of attribution suggests, as it does in the other cases where the sonnets first appeared in one of her novels, that Smith is reclaiming the poem, recasting the speaker and setting aside its earlier associations. But it also means that lingering behind the scenes is the original male speaker, which contributes to the 'passing' of the title. This sense of the theatrical is heightened in lines 11–12, as the speaker invokes 'That *scene* where Ruin saps the mouldering tomb, / [Which] Suits with the sadness of a wretch undone' (emphasis added). In the end, while this sonnet certainly dramatizes need, the sexual identity of the speaker remains a mystery: we have a female author presenting an apparently feminine speaker voicing lines that once belonged to a male speaker in a situation more traditionally masculine but markedly rejected by the male owl and fox.

Crochunis also formulates this kind of authorial multiplicity as performance, saying that 'the meta-authorial figure, the woman author as agent of her own literary production in multiple media, was a subject apart from her own textual objects. She was an author of a multi-faceted authorship . . .'[18] Crochunis probably does not intend the multifacetedness to apply even within the body of a sonnet, but as Smith's poems show, the identity of the 'I' can never be assumed. The success of *Elegiac Sonnets* depends on a readership willing to believe in the 'I' as the tragically distressed author: 'critics hardly ever reviewed her [Smith's] poems without commenting directly on her personal life. They chivalrously leapt to the defence of the respectable gentlewoman-in-distress . . . offering their condolences to her as a woman struggling to support many children and to maintain her upper-middle-class status' (Kennedy 49). To this extent, then, Smith's performances were a success; readers read her 'as a woman' and offered assistance in the form of sympathy and encouragement to others to buy her books. They were unbothered by, or did not notice, her theatrical dedication to staging feminine distress, accepting the presentation of 'heart-rending sorrows' as read.[19] And yet as 'Sonnet LXVII' suggests, the association between author and speaker(s) is more implied than obvious. The 'meta-authorial', in the *Sonnets*, is matched by a poetics of trickery even as the style of the poems does much to inaugurate a Romantic tradition of sincerity and authenticity.[20]

When Smith writes the 'I' as sexually mutable, as she does in 'Sonnet LXVII', while also maintaining the putative identity of the author as 'Charlotte Smith', she is in danger of creating what Butler refers to as the 'unreadable'. For Butler, as Harris explains, this means the 'improper cit[ation of] sexed positions' especially if 'sex is one of the norms that qualifies a body for life within the domain of cultural intelligibility' (Harris 71). Smith's readers, seduced by her successful depiction of distress, 'neglec[t her] technical and imaginative achievements as a poet' (Kennedy 49); that is, they are unable, or refuse, to read her multifaceted authorities because they do not match the culturally accepted template. Instead, the sonnets return repeatedly to Smith's own sorrow because that is what her society can see; Smith repeatedly presents sorrow as her own while simultaneously showing the impossibility of 'owning' sorrow, the implausibility of unified subjectivity. 'Sonnet LXVII', for all its irregularities, follows a strict Shakespearian rhyme scheme that works to contain and stabilize its eccentricities of content: for Smith's contemporaries, a more culturally readable 'citation'. In evoking distress, her other sonnets, while equally playful in terms of identity, also use form constructively, to mask or disguise – or sometime enhance – the lack of fixed subjectivity.[21]

Smith uses the familiar Shakespearian rhyme scheme in several sonnets where the trope of need is balanced by violent or unconventional imagery. Sonnets I, IV, XXXV, LXVIII and LXXX all present a speaker who fulfils our expectations of a woman in need, overwhelmed by distress. 'Sonnet I' introduces the picture of a sorrowing speaker, establishing the 'I' as feminine both by implication (we know who the author is) and by allusion; Smith sources her couplet in Pope's *Eloisa to Abelard* while also subtly changing its phrasing, so that 'He best can paint [woes] who shall feel them most' becomes '*If those paint sorrow best – who feel it most!*' (14, Smith's emphasis). By echoing the words of Eloisa, the speaker suggests a feminine identity; by changing the quotation slightly, Smith actually *suppresses* gender, which embeds in the first sonnet a hint of her strategy: it is all about suggestion and a/illusion. The sonnet's references to 'rugged path[s]', 'doo[m]', 'the thorn [that] fester[s] in the heart', 'pang[s]' and 'sigh[s]' (2, 8, 11) effectively convey distress, while the penultimate line, 'Ah! then, how dear the Muse's favours cost', combines an image of the speaker as victimized poet with the less savoury image of the speaker as a kind of ravisher of the Muse – an intriguing turn to the masculine just before the allusion to the feminine Eloisa. The last two lines carry the paradoxical implication that while the speaker feels the deepest sorrow ('feel it most'), this also allows for the most effective poetry ('paint sorrow best'), so that the best condition for poetry is intense sorrow. The implied destruction of the speaker, 'her' doom, is also 'her' salvation; the perfect Shakespearian structure of the sonnet attests to the speaker's skill (even as it suggests artifice, and hence the artificial). 'Sonnet I' thus superficially presents a sorrowing, distressed woman whose poetry both soothes and exacerbates her pain, while at a deeper level beginning to explore identity, subjectivity, and how both are assumed.

'Sonnet IV: To the moon' plays on the feminine associations of the moon to suggest the gender of its speaker, this time one who 'delights to stray' (2) the same 'rugged path' of 'Sonnet I' as long as it is lighted by the moon's 'pale beam'. The moon is the 'Queen of the silver bow', 'mild and placid' (1, 5), and the octave of the poem, while 'pensive', is also relatively peaceful. This changes in the sestet, when the speaker transforms the moon into a kind of pagan haven for 'wretched' souls: 'The sufferers of the earth perhaps may go, / Released by death – to thy benignant sphere; / . . . / Oh! that I soon may reach thy world serene, / Poor wearied pilgrim – in this toiling scene!' (9–10, 13–14). The unexpected turn to the moon as a new version of Heaven is mirrored in the poem's structure: a Shakespearian rhyme scheme married to a Petrarchan octave/sestet. Again, Smith in an understated way calls attention to the constructed nature of the poem, to its status as art, while her non-Christian imagery challenges the conventions of her readership – the

Heaven of God the Father is set aside in favour of that of the Moon-Mother.[22] Functioning alongside the artistry of the poem's structure is the reference in the last line to 'this toiling scene', a theatrical image that calls into question the authenticity of the poem. The subtitle, 'To the moon', suggests a soliloquy, and the accompanying plate, as chapter 1 discussed, features not 'Charlotte Smith' but a stand-in young beauty. The poem's careful pacing and octave/sestet division contribute to a dramatic feel, to the point that the distressed feminine speaker comes to resemble a player in a scene. The feminine connotations of the poem's imagery both situate the speaker as a woman and intimate that this is merely a pose. As with 'Sonnet I', the very aspects of the poem that seem to establish identity: imagery, tone, the decided 'I', also work behind the scenes to unfix it.

The relatively low-key imagery of distress in Sonnets I and IV sets the tone of need and distress that later sonnets more explosively take up. While still intimating the feminine identity of the 'I', Sonnets XXXV ('To fortitude'), LXVIII ('Written at Exmouth, midsummer, 1795'), and LXXX ('To the invisible moon') offer newly violent challenges to the stabilizing influence of the regular rhyme scheme. Sonnet XXXV invokes Fortitude with a series of powerful images of the 'beating storm', the 'bitter winds that howl / Round thy cold breast', 'the deep thunder', and the 'bursting waves' and contrasts them with the 'vain . . . cares that press / On my weak bosom' (2–4, 5–6). But the contrast seems forced; having read by this time thirty-four sonnets of woe it is hard to credit the speaker's frailty, and indeed the speaker, whose 'weak bosom' connotes femininity, identifies with the feminine Fortitude ('Nymph of the rock', 1) to the point of renouncing her humanity in favour of Fortitude's 'cold breast' (3). Once again the poem is divided into an octave and a sestet, which allows the speaker first to set up her distress as opposed to Fortitude's hardiness, and then to assume Fortitude's strength in order to court death. While the poem ends with an emotive wish for death, sure to affect readers well-versed in feminine sensibility, its very emphaticness begs the question of sincerity. Each sentence – there are only two – ends with an exclamation mark, and the first sentence sports an additional two embedded exclamation marks. The unconvincing description of the vanity of the speaker's cares furthers a sense of performance: Fortitude is soliloquised just as the moon was. The poem's heightened insistence on the sorrows of its speaker is matched in Sonnet LXVIII, where the speaker again displays her distress by 'keep[ing] / The vigil of the wretched!' (5–6). The images of sensibility – 'my burning breast', 'these ever-streaming eyes', 'my bursting heart' – pile up, culminating in 'hearts o'erwhelm'd with grief, [and] eyes suffused with tears' (13–14). Here, the rhyme scheme holds in check an emotional excess that signals the speaker's intense need but also figures as a critique on that need. Smith's familiarity with the language of sensibility, and her more restrained use of it in other sonnets, indicates an underlying playfulness; the violence of the emotions here displayed, like the emphatic punctuation of Sonnet XXXV, calls sincerity into question, and hence undermines the notion of a coherent, feminine subjectivity. By the time we reach Sonnet LXXX, the theatrical self-placement of the speaker (on 'some steep rock to look / On the obscure and fluctuating main', 7–8) combined with the dramatic images of 'the martial star with [its] lurid glare', 'the troubled deep', 'the red comet' and 'the fire-ting'd waves' (9, 10, 11, 12) dissipates any sense of authenticity in favour of a staged feminine sorrow, especially with the last line's mentions of 'beings less accurst than I'.[23] The feminine moon of Sonnet IV is now 'invisible', 'dark and conceal'd' (1), and the speaker identifies more closely with the 'martial star'; a process of unwriting the feminine 'I' has taken place, and even thought the speaker's self-placements and sentiments have not substantially changed, 'her' points of reference have.

The regularity in these sonnets maintained by the rhyme scheme, however, is a more recognizable 'norm', in Butler's and Harris's terms, than the 'improper citation' comprised in the speaker's variable gender adherence. Likewise, the distressed 'I' sonnets that experiment with rhyme scheme exchange traumatic imagery for softer references to pleasure and tranquillity in the midst of sorrow. 'Sonnet XXXIV: To a friend' allows the speaker to find some solace in her vocation as poet and a friend's approval. Unlike Sonnet I, here poetic skill serves as a balm, although the rhyme scheme of *abba abba cdcddc* inserts a note of uncertainty, as the seeming regularity of the Spenserian rhyme is undercut at the last moment. The speaker's 'hop[e] to die' (8) in 'Sonnet XLI: To tranquillity' is redeemed by 'her' characterization of tranquillity as only found in death, while death itself assumes a low-key register antithetical to the tone of the regular distressed 'I' sonnets. And yet, this sonnet's rhyme scheme of *abba cbcb defdef* infuses the poem with uncertainty and flux. Is it death, tranquillity, or speaker that defies definition, despite the poem's best efforts? The interaction between the sonnet's content and its rhyme scheme furthers the idea that Smith approaches the sonnets as exercises in artifice, balancing irregular imagery with a stable rhyme scheme and vice-versa. Indeed, in Sonnet XLIV she takes this further by creating new a rhyme scheme that is regular and yet unconventional. 'Sonnet XLIV: Written in the church-yard at Middleton in Sussex' contains powerful images of a graveyard at the mercy of the tide (itself guided by the moon), which 'tears from their grassy tombs the village dead' (7). And yet the speaker envies the bones, despite their rough treatment, because '*They* hear the warring elements no more: / While I am doom'd – by life's long storm opprest, / To gaze with envy on their gloomy rest' (12–14). The speaker's need is turned inward; there is little sense here of display, although the Gothic scene is inherently visual and dramatic. The rhyme scheme is also enclosed: *abba cddc ecce ff*, returning on itself like the waves. The two, imagery and structure, work together by design, just as the sonnets' distressed I is designed: the artistry of the sonnets point to their inherent artificiality.

But poetic design is more easily discerned than designs on identity, and Smith's readers noticed her experiments with structure while ignoring their deeper implications, although their discomfort with her irregularity may perhaps indicate other forms of unease.[24] Smith's parade of distressed speakers, then, contain their own subversions, and once we acknowledge their artifice then it becomes possible to recognize that in none of these poems is the 'I' plainly feminine. That is, despite what we think we know about 'who' the speaker is, the sonnets hold themselves aloof from such identity assignments. In all the sonnets discussed so far, the gender of the speaker is no more than implied, hinted at, or suggested through allusion; it is not a *fact* that 'the sonnets show oppressed and depressed womanhood' (Kennedy 51), but an *assumption*. If we return to the sonnets and degender them, then some interesting aberrations of identity and subjectivity become apparent; indeed, identity and subjectivity are themselves transformed into aberrations.

As much as the distressed 'I' sonnets *imply* the femininity of their speakers, then, that femininity is not anchored in the text. There are, for instance, a number of sonnets where the 'I' cannot be feasibly given any fixed gender identity. For instance, 'Sonnet XII: Written on the sea shore. – October, 1784' constructs an 'I' who takes a 'solitary seat' 'on some rude fragment of the rocky shore' (3, 1). Identifying with a 'shipwreck'd . . . poor mariner' (9, 10), the speaker makes no other move towards sexing itself. Harris, following Butler, calls this 'a process achieved through the identification with one or the other of the sexed positions within language' (69), which may give added significance to the speaker's reference to the mariner, but this must be balanced by the poem's accompanying plate, which shows a female writing figure (not Smith). The two effectively cancel each other out. In 'Sonnet XXXI: Written in Farm Wood, South Downs, in May 1784', the speaker gives the first twelve lines to a rather conventional description of a 'thoughtless', 'unconscious', 'careless' hind (9, 11, 12) whose ease contrasts with the miserable speaker's inability to forget sorrows. The 'I' observes and records, but gives no clue as to a personal identity other than a loose reference to the 'dear days' of the past (13). 'Sonnet XXXII: To melancholy. Written on the banks of the Arun, October 1785' implies the physical presence of a speaker who 'listen[s]' and has 'poet's eyes'; the poem's closing image of 'the pensive visionary mind' avoids all mention of sex, leaving a vision of a Poet who somehow escapes gender definition despite the presence of a body (3, 6, 14). 'Sonnet XXXVI', like 'Sonnet XII', offers a male figure whose situation mirrors that of the speaker: a 'lone Wanderer' who pauses on his weary way to 'pluck the wild rose, or woodbine's gadding flowers' so that 'the sense of sorrow he awhile may lose' (4, 6). The speaker, too, has 'sought thy flowers, fair Poesy!' (7), but under the threat of 'new clouds of evil yet to come', 'Her pencil sickening Fancy throws away' (10, 11). The speaker uses a poem to prophecy the end of poetry and the uselessness of transient enjoyments; as with 'Sonnet XII', the accompanying plate, showing the female Fancy, counteracts the momentary identification with the male Wanderer the speaker initially sets up. The theme is more pronounced in 'Sonnet LIV: The sleeping woodman. Written in April 1790', where, as in 'Sonnet XXXI', the speaker first conjures up an image of an 'unthinking hind' whose repose the speaker envies (11), then declares the impossibility of gaining even 'such transient respite from the ills I bear' (10).[25] Although this poem contains the same marginal allusion to Eloisa that features in 'Sonnet I', here Smith contracts her reference simply to 'Pope', leaving the source unidentified, which effectively disguises any residual femininity in the quotation. As a final example, 'Sonnet LXXII: To the morning star. Written near the sea' offers a counterpoint to the sonnets to the moon; where the moon is the 'mute arbitress of tides' ('Sonnet XLIV', 1), the morning star is a 'lucid arbiter 'twixt day and night' (1). Although this poem again features male figures (a seaman and a lover), both stand in contrast to the speaker, who cannot feel what they feel (hope) although able to see what they see (the star). The speaker merely 'marks' the morning star, but disallows readers to mark the identity of the 'I' with any certainty.

What this sketch reveals is how many of Smith's sonnets resist gendering if read outside the context of Smith's personal history and critical assumptions. Indeed, those sonnets that I have identified as even

putatively feminine are not hard to ungender. But the process requires a
kind of unwriting of Smith's heavy insistence that the 'I' is 'Charlotte
Smith', and it also means deconstructing the process of self-reflexivity we
are used to in Romantic-period writing. When 'readers . . . engag[e] the
text, [they] repeat the production of the text as it generates its own self-
understanding',[26] but that self-understanding depends at least in part
upon the expectations and experience of readers. Smith embodies her
'I' so that both are met; she creates an elaborate artifice that calls
both into question. The distressed 'I' functions both as an exemplar
of femininity and a rejection of the ramifications of embodiment – the
limitations imposed by gendering. By acting out feminine sensibility in
sonnets that show the 'I' to be incoherent and fragmentary, the distressed
'I' transforms from a woman in need to an embodiment of Need, a fluid
construct independent of the body. Distress itself becomes a dramatic
tool.

The masquerade of sex, then, disguises the adventurous subjectivity
that Smith constructs in the sonnets. The gendering we assume in the
sonnets, assisted by Smith herself, means that in certain ways each sonnet
is initially 'feminine': that is, the 'I' is assumed to be female, a version of
'Charlotte Smith'. But as my discussion of the sonnets above also show,
many of these speakers occupy positions we would more closely associ-
ate with a masculine figure: when the speaker roams alone at night, or
stands on an eminence, or portrays the female Muse as a kind of lover.
Similarly, some sonnets overtly emphasize a masculine referent while
maintaining an undercover feminine speaker. These sonnets produce a
kind of cross-gendering by which Smith exploits the cultural imperative
to assume an identity through gender; in these sonnets the speaker is
always at least doubly, and sometimes triply, gendered: that is, an initially
assumed femininity (the Poet) gives way to an imposed masculinity, or
a previously existing masculinity is colonized by authorial femininity
only for a masculine identity to be reintroduced. And then there is the
most intriguing group of all: those where, despite the embodied Self,
despite the personalized 'I', despite all efforts to maintain the femininity
of the sonnets overall, the speaker is nonetheless marked as male. In dis-
cussing the sonnets Smith transplants from her novels, and her transla-
tions, we will see how the construction of subjectivity and gender creates
a house of many mansions.

Smith peppers many of her novels with sonnets spoken or written by
both male and female characters, which she then includes in her *Elegiac
Sonnets* either without attribution or without revealing the poem's origi-

nal speaker. The most obvious result is that a poem first written from a man's point of view is usurped by a feminine speaker. For instance, Sonnets LXI and LXII, which first appeared in *The Old Manor House* (1793), and LXVI and LXVII, from *Montalbert* (1795), are spoken by the male protagonists Orlando Somerive and Sommers Walsingham respectively. However, Smith reveals only the novels in her notes, not the speakers, which effectively translates the sonnets from masculine to apparently feminine. 'Sonnet LXI: Supposed to have been written in America', presents a speaker weak in both body and mind, occupying the feminized position of distress that characterizes the sonnets. The style of femininity here dramatized is the helplessness of the romance heroine, 'wounded', 'enfeebled', and in need (8, 14). Although Smith does not reveal the original speaker, his shadowy presence contributes to the crowded subjectivity of this sonnet: the feminine 'Charlotte Smith' who speaks with the voice of Orlando Somerive whose words are handed back to 'Charlotte Smith'. Readers of Smith's novels would presumably recognize the original speaker; Smith teases them with her incomplete reference. 'Sonnet LXII: Written on passing by moon-light through a village, while the ground was covered with snow', similarly reveals novel but not speaker. As I argued in the Introduction, this sonnet, with its subversive suggestions of feminine wandering and straying and its happy use of the word 'passing' in the title, on the one hand exemplifies the possibilities of a gender-aware reading of the sonnets. But it also points out the pitfalls, since again the speaker is both feminine and masculine, both subversive and conventional – both 'authentic' (when Orlando) and theatrical (once he is removed). The sonnets from *Montalbert* function in the same way: 'LXVI: Written in [*sic*] a tempestuous night, on the coast of Sussex' contains the highly theatrical tone discussed above; images of violence and turbulence are this case only partly contained by a regular rhyme scheme. The Shakespearian rhyme of the other regular sonnets is here disrupted by the last two lines, where the couplet is replaced by a reversed rhyme transforming the last six lines into a sestet: *efeffe*. 'Sonnet LXVII', discussed earlier in this chapter, also uses the word 'passing' in its title, which in the context of these cross-gendered sonnets come to seem less a coincidence than a clue. In all four of these sonnets, Smith explores the effect of doubling gender, but her tone of grief and need does not change.

   The cross-gendering of these sonnets is facilitated by the hints Smith gives, but in many of her other transplanted sonnets she does not reveal their novelistic origin.[27] This means that their original gendering is a closed secret, and points to the mystique of gender itself, for if Smith can write a sonnet that in one genre (novel) exemplifies masculine sensibility and in another (poetry) writes the feminine, then the fixity of gender itself comes into question. In Sonnets XXVIII and XXXIX, Smith reassigns her speakers' identities, and again uses rhyme scheme to suggest the resulting confused subjectivity. Both are from *Emmeline* and originally spoken by the excitable Godolphin, Emmeline's lover, but this information is erased from the world of the *Sonnets*. 'Sonnet XXXVIII' offers an 'I' whose need is represented by the absent Emmeline. Although the speaker eulogizes Emmeline, this is not enough in itself to establish 'his' identity, since as I have discussed the mere fact of a romantic or sexualised tone does not necessarily identify the speaker. Indeed, the tone of this sonnet, while emphatic, is less lover-like than some of the mother-sonnets discussed in the previous chapter; Emmeline could as easily be an absent friend like Mrs G. (Sonnet X) or Mrs O'Neill (Sonnet XXXVII). Instead, the sonnet more resembles the ungendered poems discussed earlier in this chapter: there is very little here to evoke either masculinity or femininity. What Smith does give us is a curiously elliptical rhyme scheme: *abab baba ccdcdd*. The two quatrains reverse each other, while the sestet is both reversed and reordered. Such a confused yet intricate rhyme scheme speaks to Smith's care in crafting this sonnet, which suggests that the poem's lack of a clearly gendered subjectivity is again down to design rather than chance. In 'Sonnet XXXIX: To night', the speaker's femininity is implied by 'her' position 'repose[d] on [night's] dark breast' (9). The pleasure the speaker feels in 'sober-suited Night' (1), unlike the yearning of the previous sonnet, carries distinctly romantic overtones, here working to gender the speaker given Night's aura of masculinity. But the clarities of the sonnet are qualified by a wandering and confused rhyme scheme: *abab cbbc cddc ee*, and, reading further, we see that this pleasure 'is calm, tho' wretched; hopeless, yet resign'd' (12). The distressed 'I''s appeal to Heaven to hear the sorrows 'lost on earth' (14) carries a subtle chastisement and situates the poem as one of the more recognizable 'woman in need' sonnets, and yet the poem's provenance, hidden as it is, militates against this association. In these transplanted sonnets, it is clear that something is being staged, but what the spectacle might be is less obvious.

Cross-gendering effectively calls into question the fixed notion of subjectivity subscribed to by those of Smith's readers who see the sonnets are emblematic of 'woman's condition'. It also shows Smith's creative play with established assumptions of gender and identity: if a sonnet of sensibility can be equally ascribed to a masculine and feminine speaker – if the speaker's gender can be both simultaneously or neither at all – then the display of sexualized behaviour can itself be exposed as *display*, a theatrical staging for effect of a certain kind of role. While the sonnets explore other forms of dramatic self-assertion,[28] at this point I turn to the most significant group of poems in terms of theatrical play with subjectivity: the translations from Goethe, Petrarch and Metastasio. If one leaves in place the establishment of the 'I' as spoken by 'Charlotte Smith', the personal and familiar speaker reacted to by her contemporary readers and current criticism, then a group of poems that cannot possibly be spoken by 'Smith' are especially significant. Smith's play with identity in the sonnets, as I have discussed it, takes place in many ways on subterranean levels; the challenges to a coherent 'I', the woman in need, are, as I noted above, superficially 'unreadable' given the strength of the embodiment of the 'I'. But in the translations, the female 'I' is upstaged by a male voice, that of Werther and Petrarch's and Metastasio's male speakers. The 'I' *becomes* male, even though the sensibility displayed does not change.

Claudia Johnson has noted that 'during the 1790s, sentimentalized masculinity is . . . prevalent' and that 'Werther is . . . the culture's paragon of feeling'; his 'exquisite, delicious, and finely textured sensibility mark him *not* as effeminate . . . but as an estimable man of feeling'.[29] Ironically, when Smith ventriloquizes his voice she is establishing even more strongly the sensibility of the sonnets – but she is disestablishing their femininity. Sonnets XXI–XXV are all, as Sonnet XXI phrases it, 'Supposed to be written by Werter' and take the reader from Werther's despair at Lotte's indifference to 'Just before his death'. The ambivalence of 'supposed' (meant? thought? imagined?) is stabilized in the following four sonnets which are unequivocally 'by the same'. It seems that Smith means to anchor the sensibility of her sonnets by speaking with the voice of 'the paragon of feeling', and yet 'his' sentiments are markedly similar to those expressed in the sonnets as a whole. Werther feels despair, seeks solitude, 'wander[s] 'mid the tempests drear' ('Sonnet XXIII: By the same. To the North Star', 5), welcomes death, and feels 'the force of hopeless care' ('Sonnet XXV: By the same. Just before his death', 5). In Sonnet XXI, he compares himself to 'the poor maniac' who 'haunt[s] the scene where all my treasure lies; / . . . / Tow'rds the deep gulf that opens on my sight / I hurry forward, Passion's helpless slave! / And scorning Reason's mild and sober light, / Pursue the path that leads me to the grave!' (5, 9–12), a scenario Smith returns to in 'Sonnet LXX: On being cautioned

against walking on an headland'. In that poem, as I discuss in the Intro-
duction, the speaker both identifies with the lunatic and distances herself
from him, but the overall effect of sonnet and plate is to link the two. In
this sonnet, the speaker Werter, who cannot be 'Charlotte Smith', sees
himself as a kind of maniac: the two are one. When she rewrites this
scene, Smith creates enough detachment from the lunatic to intimate
'her' difference from Werter, but she also builds in enough similarities to
suggest the ineffectualness of her detachment.[30] Werter, however, encour-
ages the association, just as he does in the next poem when he situates
the nightingale (solitude's 'own sweet songstress', 12) as his emblem.
Solitude's 'sequester'd vale', 'wild-woods, and untrodden glades' (1, 5) are
familiar from most of the other sonnets, particularly 'Sonnet LIV' with
its 'pathless bowers'. Werter's adoption of the nightingale, who 'weeps my
wayward fate' instead of her own, further links his voice with the dis-
tressed I of other sonnets (for instance, 'Sonnet III: To a nightingale' and
'Sonnet VII: On the departure of the nightingale'), and suggests a version
of the cross-gendering discussed above.

Where the putatively feminine distressed 'I' invokes the moon, Werter
turns to the North Star, flickering in and out of sight in 'the tempests
drear' that 'Smith' too frequents. The North Star seems to figure as a mas-
culine analogue to the feminine moon, and finds another version in
'Sonnet LXXII: To the morning star'. The desire for death expressed in
the final two Werther sonnets rehearses a familiar trope of the sonnets,
while the presentation of a sinless suicide[31] rewrites Christianity along
the lines of 'Sonnet IV: To the moon', where the moon became a haven
for unhappy souls. All five Werther sonnets situate Werther as the same
distressed 'I' that we find in the other sonnets, which works to blend them
and further destabilize fixed gender identities. But Smith also builds into
the fourth Werther sonnet an ironical turn to self-reflexivity when she
anglicizes the German Lotte as 'Charlotte', which in light of the sonnets'
interweaving of the personal and the theatrical threatens an implosion
of identity:

> And sometimes, when the sun with parting rays
>   Gilds the long grass that hides my silent bed,
> The tears shall tremble in my CHARLOTTE'S eyes;
>   Dear, precious drops! – they shall embalm the dead!
> Yes – CHARLOTTE o'er the mournful spot shall weep,
> Where her poor WERTER – and his sorrows sleep!
>   (9–14)

Werter, who in these sonnets stands in for, or represents the same subjectivity as, the distressed 'I' who readers see as 'Charlotte Smith', imagines for himself an ideal audience, Charlotte herself. This theatrical solipsism points to the artificiality of the sonnets as a whole: how can subjectivity be coherent if the self can be self and other, if one version of the self surveys another, if indeed the most appropriate mourner for the loss of self is another fragment of the self? When Smith allows Werter to imagine 'Charlotte', she takes her sonnets beyond the representative to the meta-representative: another version of the 'meta-authorial' described by Crochunis (224).

In the Petrarch sonnets, Smith assumes the identity of Petrarch himself, pursuing Laura with a lover's passion. The Petrarch sonnets, XIII–XVI, are free translations based on specific Petrarchan sonnets identified by their first lines and sonnet number in the notes, and they function more obviously than do the Werther sonnets as ventriloquisms. Nonetheless, they rely on the same formulations of sensibility and sorrow as do the *Elegiac Sonnets* as a whole, and contribute more to the sense of a developing company of identities precisely because of their more open status as translations. In 'Sonnet XIII: From Petrarch', Smith assumes Petrarch's poetic identity seamlessly, writing a sonnet to Laura asserting that 'his' 'faithful heart still burns for thee!' (14). While Smith seems to make a bodily exchange – the distressed feminine 'I' becomes the ardent masculine 'I' – she also again uses poetic structure to suggest an underlying critique. Not only does this 'Petrarchan' sonnet have a strict Shakespearian rhyme scheme, but it also is written in iambic tetrameter; Smith both disrupts her readers' expectations of who speaks in the sonnets, and also confounds the very form of the sonnet. If the originator of a traditional sonnet form fails to write his sonnet correctly – that is, if he fails to embody his own corpus – then his identity is called into question. Similarly, if we read the sonnet as spoken by an *imitator* of Petrarch, someone who speaks his lines but gets them wrong, then the image of a bad actor is conjured up: the speaker is, so to speak, underrehearsed. In fact, not one of the Petrarchan sonnets follows correct Petrarchan form. 'Sonnet XIV: From Petrarch' begins well: *abba cddc*, but then carries on with another Shakespearian quatrain, *effe*, and ends with a rhyming couplet. 'Sonnet XV: From Petrarch' is straightforwardly Shakespearian, and 'Sonnet XVI: From Petrarch' combines the two forms, laid out as two Shakespearian quatrains followed by a Petrarchan sestet with a Shakespearian rhyme scheme.

Smith underscores the theatricality of the Petrarchan sonnets in 'Sonnet XV' when she allows the 'angel form' of Laura to address the speaker directly:

> Unhappy Petrarch, dry your tears;
> Ah! why, sad lover! thus before your time,
>   In grief and sadness should your life decay,
> And like a blighted flower, your manly prime
>   In vain and hopeless sorrow fade away?
> Ah! yield not thus to culpable despair,
> But raise thine eyes to heaven – and think I wait thee there.
>
>   (8–14)

Laura's words are as applicable to any version of the distressed 'I' in the sonnets, and her naming of Petrarch shows how transferable are the sentiments of grief and sorrow the sonnets explore. Indeed, in 'Sonnet XVI', as Petrarch mourns over the lost Laura, his words seem drawn from any of the sonnets in which the maternal Smith grieves her lost daughter:

> While busy Memory still delights to dwell
>   On all the charms these bitter tears deplore,
> And with a trembling hand describes too well
>   The angel form I shall behold no more!
> To heaven she's fled! and nought to me remains
> But the pale ashes which her urn contains.
>
>   (9–14)

Even as 'Charlotte Smith' temporarily inhabits the body of Petrarch, Petrarch speaks with the familiar tones and images of 'Charlotte Smith': the distressed 'I' is both consistent and fragmented, and gendered subjectivity is rendered fluid and changeable. 'Sonnet XVII: From the thirteenth cantata of Metastasio' reinscribes this, as the speaker assumes the identity of the male lover of Miranda only to write the familiar Shakespearian rhyme and describe a 'beauteous tree' (2) of love that will shelter the dove and the nightingale, both birds emblematic of the sonnets' distressed 'I'.

Lucy Newlyn writes that 'the integrity of the subject [is] placed disturbingly (but also excitingly) under question every time we write or read'.[32] Smith exemplifies this statement, using writing itself to question the integrity of the subject, along with the viability of a fixed and stable gender identity. For the distressed 'I', both subjectivity and gender identity are equally problematic, and both are placed under the strain of continual flux. I will end this chapter by juxtaposing two sonnets; they dramatize a mutually exclusive gendered identity, and each proposes a subjectivity impossible to reconcile with the other.

Sonnet LXXV

Where the wild woods and pathless forests frown,
  The darkling Pilgrim seeks his unknown way,
Till on the grass he throws him weary down,
  To wait in broken sleep the dawn of day:
Thro' boughs just waving in the silent air,
  With pale capricious light the Summer Moon
Chequers his humid couch; while Fancy there,
  That loves to wanton in the Night's deep noon,
Calls from the mossy roots and fountain edge
  Fair visionary Nymphs that haunt the shade,
Or Naiads rising from the whispering sedge;
  And, 'mid the beauteous group, his dear loved maid
Seems beckoning him with smiles to join the train:
Then, starting from his dream, he feels his woes again!

Sonnet XCII: Written at Bignor Park in Sussex, in August, 1799

Low murmurs creep along the woody vale,
  The tremulous Aspens shudder in the breeze,
Slow o'er the downs the leaden vapours sail,
  While I, beneath these old paternal trees,
Mark the dark shadows of the threaten'd storm,
  As gathering clouds o'erveil the morning sun;
They pass! – But oh! ye visions bright and warm
  With which even here my sanguine youth begun,
Ye are obscured for ever! – And too late
  The poor Slave shakes the unworthy bonds away
Which crush'd her! – Lo! the radiant star of day
Lights up this lovely scene anew – My fate
  Nor hope nor joy illumines – Nor for me
  Return those rosy hours which here I used to see!

                                              (emphasis Smith's)

Both sonnets place their sorrowful figure in the woods, under trees, haunted by dreams of what has been lost. The Pilgrim, resolutely masculine, is not in this poem replaced at the last minute by an 'I'; the speaker in 'Sonnet XCII' is one of the only clearly female first-person speakers in the whole of the *Elegiac Sonnets*. 'Sonnet LXXV' essentially erases the subjective self in favour of a dramatic stand-in, while 'Sonnet XCII' finally allows the 'real' Charlotte Smith to take centre stage, at the last possible moment given that this is the last sonnet in the series.[33] Reading these two sonnets together, and taking into account the contents of *Elegiac Sonnets* as a corpus, it is clear that far from offering a sustained picture of personal sorrow, the *Sonnets* are a compendium of identities and voices, linked by an 'I' who changes costume with ease,[34] and stage-managed and directed by Smith. They are as theatrical, with voices as multiple, as the work of the more overtly shape-shifting Mary Robinson, but they disguise their theatricality with a consistent return to the same woes. Nonetheless, by ascribing the same kind of sensibility to a variety of speakers, Smith demonstrates the looseness of the ties of gender and subjectivity; when her readers, then and now, see the sonnets as drama-tizing the state of miserable femininity, they demonstrate their desire to tighten them. In a letter of February 1795 to her publishers Cadell and Davies, Smith wrote 'I hope . . . I shall no longer write for actual bread or *appear in the mortifying character of a distrest Author*' (quoted in Hawley 190, emphasis added). As the *Sonnets* attest, however, the 'distrest Author' was to prove her most popular and enduring role.

Notes

1 Judith Pascoe names her as the 'tragic heroine . . . sorrow personified', and goes on to note that her 'poetic persona grew into a dramatic version of her equally dramatic private self'. See *Romantic Theatricality: Gender, Poetry, and Spectatorship* (Ithaca: Cornell University Press, 1997), esp. chapter I, 'Sarah Siddons and the Performative Female': 12–31, 16, 17. I am indebted to Pascoe's formulation of Romantic theatricality in this chapter.

2 She was also aware of the controversies surrounding this genre. For a selec-tion of the writings on the topic of the romance, see Appendix B in my edition of *The Old Manor House* (Peterborough: Broadview Press, 2002). As Smith's combination of genres in this novel shows, she was interested in exploring the possibilities of the novel as well.

3 Although Litvak concentrates on the nineteenth-century novel, his observa-tions are apropos to the Romantic period: see *Caught in the Act: Theatrical-ity in the Nineteenth-Century English Novel* (Berkeley: University of California Press, 1992), xii. See also Pascoe, *Romantic Theatricality: Gender, Poetry and Spectatorship*; Julie Carlson, *In the Theatre of Romanticism: Coleridge, Nation-alism, Women* (Cambridge: Cambridge University Press, 1994); Catherine Burroughs, *Closet Stages: Joanna Baillie and the Theater Theory of British Romantic Women Writers* (Philadelphia: University of Pennsylvania Press, 1997). The field of Romantic drama and theatricality is a burgeoning one; see *Women in British Romantic Theatre: Drama, Performance, and Society,*

1790–1840, ed. Burroughs (Cambridge: Cambridge University Press, 2000) for an excellent bibliography.

4 See Pascoe, *Romantic Theatricality*, 27–28, for another account of the sonnet's appropriateness for the theatrical woman writer.

5 Hess, 'Wordsworth's Aesthetic State: The Poetics of Liberty', *Studies in Romanticism* 33 (1994): 3–29, 17, 19. Hess argues that Wordsworth rescues the sonnet from obscurity and positions it as politically self-reflexive. The total absence of any mention of Smith suggests that Hess is unaware of her *Elegiac Sonnets* and their interventions in the politics of the personal.

6 See Stella Brooks, 'The Sonnets of Charlotte Smith', *Critical Survey* 4 (1992), 9–21: 17, 19; Deborah Kennedy, 'Thorns and Roses: the *Sonnets* of Charlotte Smith', *Women's Writing* 2 (1995), 43–53: 43, 44; Judith Hawley, 'Charlotte Smith's *Elegiac Sonnets*: Losses and Gains', *Women's Poetry in the Enlightenment; The Making of a Canon, 1730–1820*, eds. Isobel Armstrong and Virginia Blain (Basingstoke: Macmillan, 1999), 184–198: 188; and Stuart Curran, 'Romantic Poetry: The "I" Altered', in *Romanticism and Feminism*, ed. Anne K. Mellor (Bloomington: Indiana University Press, 1988), 185–207: 200. In fairness to Hawley, she notes Smith's 'ventriloquiz[ing]' of Goethe and Petrarch, among others, and that the poems are not 'merely autobiographical' (189), but as all these quotes show, the critical consensus is that Smith's sonnets reveal something specific about the female condition and female authorship. Subsequent references to these essays will be made in the text.

7 As Ellis says, 'recent critical studies of sensibility have consistently privileged [powerful feeling] at the expense of [artificial posturing], making the philosophical again the master of the popular and fashionable' (*The Politics of Sensibility: Race, Gender and Commerce in the Sentimental Novel* (Cambridge: Cambridge University Press, 1996), 36–37). The 'philosophical' – that is, the intellectual, rational, and 'real' – is the only thing that can rescue sensibility from accusations of flimsiness. But as Ellis maintains, this attitude itself refuses to see anything of value in conscious artifice, whereas part of the appeal of sensibility is exactly its status as posture.

8 Sensibility is both personalized and depersonalized by Smith: her sorrows are both 'hers' and, as I will discuss, Werther's or Petrarch's or Metastasio's.

9 Joseph W. Donohue, *Dramatic Character in the English Romantic Age* (Princeton: Princeton University Press, 1970), 3.

10 Smith seems to recognize this when she includes two sonnets in her collection that speak directly to her status as distressed woman. In 'Sonnet XXIX: To Miss C— on being desired to attempt writing a comedy' she describes herself as 'unfit' to 'tempt the comic scene / Of gay Thalia', while 'Sonnet LXXIII: To a querulous acquaintance' suggests that only those with something worth complaining about should do so. Both poems insist on their speaker's personal knowledge of grief.

11 Thomas Crochunis, 'Authorial Performances: Romantic Women Playwrights', *Women in British Romantic Theatre: Drama, Performance, and Society,*

1790–1840, 223–254: 248, n. 5. Crochunis refers specifically to Elizabeth Inchbald and Joanna Baillie. Subsequent references will be made in the text.

12 Judith Butler, *Gender Trouble: Feminism and the Subversion of Identity* (New York: Routledge, 1990), 146–147.

13 Geraldine Harris, *Staging Femininities: Performance and Performativity* (Manchester: Manchester University Press, 1999), 57. Subsequent references will be made in the text.

14 Dorothy Mermin, 'The Damsel, the Knight, and the Victorian Woman Poet', *Critical Inquiry* 13 (1986), 64–80: 67. Subsequent references will be made in the text.

15 Letter to J. Shore, 16 August 1787, in *The Works of Sir William Jones*, 13 vols. (1806; Delhi: Agam Prakashan, 1976–80), 2:119. Quoted in Pascoe, *Romantic Theatricality*, 17.

16 As Mermin also notes, for the Victorians (and, I would add, earlier readers as well), '*poems* are women'. Certainly for Jones, Smith's sonnets reveal 'Charlotte' to him.

17 See Introduction, pp. 13–14.

18 Crochunis notes that the female author's 'performances repeatedly demonstrated her alienation from cultural institutions' (224). But it is a condition of Smith's gender play that she as much exploits or relies on cultural institutions as is alienated by them. It is my contention that her 'alienation' is more apparent in her longer poems; see chapters 4 and 5.

19 *Monthly Review* (1797): 458, quoted in Kennedy, 'Thorns and Roses', 49.

20 This tradition is most commonly explicated through readings of Wordsworth. See chapter 5 and the Coda for a discussion of some aspects of the Smith/Wordsworth connection.

21 The following discussion groups the sonnets according to my readings of their explicit and/or implicit gendering; the critical culture of gender informs my decisions. It is, of course, entirely possible to create other groupings based on, say, images of memory and childhood, or, as in chapter 2, maternal imagery. As in chapter 2, however, part of my aim in this chapter is to establish the by no means straightforward gender politics of the sonnets, one of the things that make possible manifold groupings.

22 This anticipates the archetypal moment in *Jane Eyre* when the moon, Jane's unearthly mother, advises her 'daughter' to leave Rochester (chapter 27).

23 The speaker's placement and despairing speech call to mind the more famous figure of Manfred, whose soliloquy on the Jungfrau is as heightened and theatrical as Smith's sonnet-speaker's.

24 Anna Seward famously chided Smith for her 'perpetual duns' on her readers' pity, and was distinctly unhappy with her unconventional rhyme schemes. Indeed, her own series of one hundred 'regular' sonnets was expressly in opposition to Smith. See *The Poetical Works of Anna Seward, with Extracts from her Literary Correspondence*, ed. Walter Scott, Esq. (Edinburgh, 1810).

25 With its opening image of a 'lone shelter of . . . pathless bowers' sought by
   the speaker's 'soul depress'd' (4, 3), this poem may well have suggested the
   'pathless rocks' and 'dear nook / Unvisited' of Wordsworth's 'Nutting' (14,
   16–17), while the 'untrodden region of my mind' (51) that will house the
   temple of Psyche in Keats's 'Ode to Psyche' also resonates.

26 Marc Redfield, 'Romanticism, *Bildung*, and the Literary Absolute', *Lessons of
   Romanticism: A Critical Companion*, eds. Thomas Pfau and Robert F.
   Gleckner (Durham: Duke University Press, 1998), 41–54: 43.

27 There are more than I have the space to discuss in this chapter: Sonnets L–LIII
   are originally spoken by Celestina in *Celestina*; Sonnet LXIV is originally
   spoken by Mrs Denzil in *The Banished Man*, Sonnets LXXXV–LXXXVII are
   from *The Young Philosopher*, Sonnet LXXVI is by Edward-Armyn Marchmont
   in *Marchmont*, and Sonnet LXXXI is from *Rambles Further*. Smith notes the
   origin for the sonnets from *The Banished Man*, *The Young Philosopher*, and
   Rambles Further, but not *Marchmont* or *Celestina*. It is interesting that the
   group of sonnets most closely associable with her own sonnet persona, those
   from *Celestina*, are kept resolutely hidden from the reader, while the sonnet
   from *Marchmont* is recontextualized to the reader through a mention of
   Smith's son, thus anchoring it the more firmly to Smith *as* Smith.

28 For instance, Sonnets III, XLIX, L–LIII, and LXIV can be viewed as overtly
   dramatizing the feminine in that the speaker is more obviously female than
   in many of the other sonnets, while Sonnets VII, VIII, XXVI, LIX, LXIV, and
   LXXV seem to abandon subjectivity altogether by rejecting first-person
   narration in favour of a kind of omniscience.

29 Claudia Johnson, *Equivocal Beings: Politics, Gender, and Sentimentality in
   the 1790s. Wollstonecraft, Radcliffe, Burney, Austen* (Chicago: University of
   Chicago Press, 1995), 12.

30 Of course, since Smith writes both poems in the first person, the two
   speakers are, essentially, the same.

31 Werther chooses his place of rest as 'the corner of the church-yard' (note
   to line 1 of 'Sonnet XXIV') while also calling himself 'the unhappy suicide'
   ('Sonnet XXIV', 8) who has gone 'uncall'd – to mercy and to heaven!' ('Sonnet
   XXV', 8). If he commits suicide, of course, Werther would not be permitted
   a churchyard burial; suicide is a mortal sin. Smith counters this by writing
   both sonnets with a strict Shakespearian rhyme scheme.

32 Lucy Newlyn, *Reading, Writing, and Romanticism: The Anxiety of Reception*
   (Oxford: Oxford University Press, 2000), ix.

33 Both Volumes I and II also contain other poems; 'Sonnet XCII' is the last
   sonnet in Volume II, and effectively sums up the imagery and tone of all the
   sonnets.

34 Or at times linked only by the *assumption* of an 'I', given that not all the
   sonnets feature a first-person narrator.

4

On the edge: politics and the strictures of subjectivity in *The Emigrants*

In the previous chapters, I have discussed Smith's manoeuvres as an embodied speaker, and attempted to untangle her complex approach by showing how the sonnets, in particular, are susceptible to a process of engendering encouraged both by Smith's style and our own desire to assign gender to bodies. Julia Epstein and Kristina Straub have noted that 'the gendered body' is a 'site of ambiguity [as well as] identity ... [T]he body would seem to promise resolution both as physical evidence of gender identity and the site of claims from the corporal body to the body politic'.[1] In the *Sonnets*, Smith parades a series of bodies through images and text, giving her readers an abundance of 'physical evidence' of gender but also avoiding any final resolution. In *The Emigrants*, published in 1793 at the height of her *Sonnets* fame, she concentrates on a single unifying persona, herself – or at least the 'Charlotte Smith' by this time well-enough known to her readers that the *European Magazine*, as quoted in chapter 1, could 'discover' her 'almost at the bottom of every page, as we may the portrait of some of the most renowned painters in the corner of their most favourite pictures'.[2] *The Emigrants* is in part a poem about the misfortunes of the French émigrés, in part a poem denouncing the harm 'Man inflict[s] on Man' (II: 319), but it is also a poem about a speaker who attempts, through her engagement with the political situation in France the England, to move from passive spectator to active director. As the *European Magazine* goes on to note, the 'whole Poem may be considered as a soliloquy pronounced by the authoress' (42). Again, the reviewer's choice of terminology is instructive: the reviewer sees the poem as artificial, infused with the drama of the Self that marks Smith's poetic oeuvre. And parts of the poem are highly theatrical, especially the sensational scenes of hounded mothers and maniacal fathers in Book II.

But as the reviewer notes, in this poem 'Charlotte Smith' intrudes onto another's platform, rather than seamlessly inhabiting the variety of selves on show as 'she' does in the *Sonnets*. Although Smith's putative subjects occupy a large portion of the poem, nonetheless the speaker is omnipresent, not least due to her reiterated presence 'on the Cliffs' and 'on an Eminence' in the 'Scenes' to Books I and II. Drawing on the visual mastery afforded by this prospect self-placement, the speaker is always already *there*, even when she seemingly highlights the plight, and presence, of the emigrants. This poem is an uneasy hybrid: it is both political commentary and personal revelation, both objective and subjective. Where the form and contents of the *Sonnets* essentially worked together to establish subjectivit(ies), here the two seem to compete; the objective, disinterested prospect viewer who describes the emigrants does not mesh with the alienated speaker for whom exile from a hostile culture is both sought and enforced. Whereas *Beachy Head* will see Smith experimenting with the possibilities of multiple subjectivity, in this poem she seems to want to merge the political and the personal. While this allows for an approach to the poem that reads 'exile' as its theme, situating the speaker as making use of the political troubles of the emigrants to highlight her own cultural alienation, such a reading also means smoothing over the poem's jagged edges and following Smith's suggestion that her experience of exile creates a special bond between herself and the emigrants. In effect, this kind of response signifies a collaboration between poet and reader, where the reader submits to Smith's direction, turns his/her attention to the 'soliloquizing' speaker, and agrees that the 'play's the thing'.

The artificiality that pervades this poem arises from the incompatibilities of its competing projects. Remembering that the poem's Preface contains one of Smith's two nods towards a conventional self-presentation ('I am perfectly sensible, that it belongs not to a feeble and feminine hand to draw the Bow of Ulysses'[33]), which it then undercuts by references to her 'Poetical talents' and desire to 'vindicate herself' (*Poems* 133), we can see that from its first pages the text attempts a combination of approaches. In this chapter, I will pursue a reading sympathetic to Smith's self-presentation as exiled, arguing that she stage-manages an image of subjectivity able to converse with equal authority on the political and the personal. I will do this because Smith's stance is itself politically significant; her Revolutionary sympathies extend beyond an enthusiasm for Liberty to a pervading sense of the necessity for equality in an enlightened society – with the clear corollary that her society's

dedication to inequality define it as unenlightened. The voice she estab-
lishes moves from objective to subjective unpredictably, but the poem
desires structural consistency even as its speaker desires peace and social
justice: its mirrorings and repetitions attest to this. However, even though
the poem, and my reading, emphasize a uniform thematics of exile,
Smith's poetic efforts, and my critical ones, cannot fully compensate for
the antagonisms inherent in Smith's attempt to marry the personal and
the political.

Who speaks *The Emigrants* and how can we tell?

By offering her readers a distinctive identity, Smith steps away from the
multiplicity of the *Sonnets* towards a more unified body. However, this
does not mean a more simplified approach, since even as the speaker is
'discoverable' as 'Charlotte Smith' she is also content to redirect our
attention, in Book I of the poem at least, to the emigrants of the title.
This move from 'the corporal body to the body politic', as Epstein and
Straub phrase it, depends on the intermediary bodies of the emigrants
to shield Smith's move from passive to active; as this chapter will discuss,
The Emigrants is a political poem on many levels, but Smith is also aware
of the constrictions she faced as a woman writing about politics and as
a writer showing a political bias in 1793. Stephen Behrendt has noted
that '[f]or a woman to engage in explicitly anti-war writing was as
dangerous economically and socially as it was politically ... her known
public stance could result in the denial of even minimal assistance, which
she might otherwise receive, from a community prone to reading into
her misfortune divine retribution for her "disloyalty".'[4] Smith, as a
novelist, had already shown pro-Revolutionary sympathies in her 1792
novel *Desmond*, and reviews had critiqued her harshly for so doing.[5]
Smith, as a poet, uses the émigrés in *The Emigrants* to create an aura of
sympathy which effectively disguises her increasingly engaged political
tone: her move to the 'body politic'. Zimmerman argues that Smith 'pub-
licly distances herself from radical politics in defending the exiles of the
ancien régime',[6] but in fact this is exactly what Smith does not do; while
the tone of her poem is sympathetic, the speaker openly and consistently
criticizes the emigrants' actions when still in France. Instead of distanc-
ing herself from politics, Smith uses the situation of the emigrants to
construct a case detailing her own sense of exile, a radical gender poli-
tics that depends on Smith's deployment of an embodied speaker and
her understanding of the particulars of engendering.

Smith, then, follows through on a commitment to political commentary, and she also shows her awareness of the need for caution in so doing. The emigrants serve both to focus her critique and deflect attention from it. Her sympathetic attention allows her to perform a properly feminine role of care and nurturance,[7] earning her praise from reviewers who were able to overlook the poem's undertones:

> ... she draws several interesting and affecting pictures of their misfortunes, and applauds that generous sympathy, which ministers relief to a brother in distress, *without listening to the chilling remonstrance of national or political prejudice* ...

> ... poetry, like charity, will dwell only on such circumstances as are best fitted to excite its proper feelings ... *Mrs Smith has judiciously confined her attention to those particulars in the case of the emigrants, which have excited sympathy in the minds of the humane of all parties;* and she describes their condition with that propriety and tenderness, which those who are acquainted with her former productions will be prepared to expect ...

> ... There is but too much reason to fear, that *this creature of her imagination* has been many times realized in the course of the last two years, and that similar scenes are transacting at the very hour in which we are amusing ourselves with the contemplation of *these fictitious sorrows!*[8]

As these excerpts show, Smith was considered either to be transcending politics in her ability to arouse sympathy, or in the case of the last reviewer, accidentally able to portray probable real events (with a concomitant underlying moral unease) but with little real understanding of them. For these reviewers, Smith occupies the feminine position of the depoliticized woman writer, a reaction encouraged by a speaker who 'often' 'half abjure[s] Society' and longs for a 'lone Cottage, deep embower'd / In the green woods' (I: 42–43). But this is only 'half' the story; the speaker also observes, critiques, and condemns, and dispassionately rejects Society for its crimes, a more traditionally masculine stance that brings to mind the tone of the critiques levelled by, for instance, Shelley.

What the reviews confirm, however, is the success of a strategy that relies on the power of 'half'. Smith, writing in 1792/93, not only brings into her poem a historicity derived from events in France, but also wants to dodge any charge of sedition; the Libel Act of 1792 meant that *The Emigrants*, for instance, was more open to risk than *Desmond*. The very open-endedness of the Act – its implication that, in the matter of seditious writings, the intent of the author mattered a great deal less than the interpretation of the work by its readers – had well-recognized effects on the writers of the period. For Smith, self-packaged as a mother and sole provider for her family, openly furious with lawyers and chicanery since the publication of the Sixth Edition of the *Sonnets*, toasted as a 'lady defende[r] of the Revolution' along with Helen Maria Williams and Anna Letitia Barbauld by a group of British democrats in Paris celebrating the advances of the French army in November 1792[9] – an approach that stressed feminine compliance while also allowing for a more masculine defiance was in order. By 'half abjuring' she leaves open the other half, and creates a sense of the marginal – of things half-said, of stances half-embraced, of anger half-expressed, and of loyalties half-withdrawn. In doing things by halves, Smith invites a reconsideration of a variety of borders, filtered through the experience of exile that is the putative subject of the poem.

The imagery of halves chimes with a theoretical approach that privileges the marginal and the liminal – in this case, a fusion of the Freudian and the Kristevan. The development of proto-psychological tools and theories in the nineteenth century uniformly followed the given that men and women occupied emotional territory as separate as their social spheres. Whether because of her tendency to hysteria, to melancholy, to lust, to chastity, to heat, to coolness, to earth(li)ness, to the angelic, woman provided the disorder against which men defined their own order. The psychological untrustworthiness of women grew out of and was contingent on their irrationality; this, coupled with a woman's *potential* to achieve reason – usually suspended – constructed her as the not-quite-but-almost-human figure whose weaknesses justified her restrictions.[10] Smith, for instance, signals her knowledge of her pre-prepared social position when she states publicly, in print, her awareness that, 'for a Woman, "the Post of Honor is a Private Station"' ('Preface' to the Sixth Edition of the *Sonnets*), glossing over the paradox her public/private self-placement creates. Freud's contribution to this tradition of defining woman through her body, and relationally[11] – as mother, as daughter, as sister, etc. – is a theory that depends on the physical difference of women to the standard of humanity – men. Freudian terms like the uncanny, the repressed, and the *unheimlich* perpetuate difference, but go further than that: the female and the feminine is not necessarily foreign, but rather forgotten. As he says, the uncanny only appears that way: 'this *unheimlich* place [the female genitals], however, is the entrance to the former *Heim* of all human beings . . . In this case too, then, the *unheimlich* is what was once *heimisch*, familiar; the prefix *"un"* is the token of repression.'[12] The uncanny – the unknown, the odd – is associated with a lack, the unfamiliar nature of women's bodies: this is, paradoxically, an expression of recognition of a common home. The return of the repressed can be seen as the return to the familiar, the acceptance and understanding of difference. And yet, because the standard is still the male understanding, the female mind remains, notoriously, defamiliarized to itself; it has no home. Freud's solution is that women accept their repressed desire to fit the pattern, which involves, of course, an acceptance of their own essential *unheimlich* nature. They are only whole if, confusingly, they accept they are incomplete: in permanent exile from subjectivity, in permanent thrall to the expectations of others.

The *heimlich*, akin to the Home, is the place by which one defines oneself as female (on a literal and cultural level). Kristeva, in her exploration of the individual's need to erect barriers between self and (m)other, implicitly redraws the uncanny as the abject; she realigns the unknown as the unknowable, the undefined. Where Freud's *heimlich* is the entry to the *unheimlich*, Kristeva's abject is a 'boundary':

> abjection is above all ambiguity. Because while releasing a hold, it does not radically cut off the subject from what threatens it – on the contrary, abjection acknowledges it to be in perpetual danger . . . Abjection preserves what existed in . . . the immemorial violence with which a body becomes separated from another body in order to be. (in Zerilli, 54)

The abject is that by which the One defines him/herself against the Other – for Kristeva, the (m)other, the origin. For both Kristeva and Freud, the originary point is, more accurately, an edge or boundary, the point at which things can go either way: a metaphorics of halves. Smith's self-marginalized world offers a dense weaving of exile, identity, the *unheimlich/heimlich*, and the abject. Smith deploys the uncanny: *The Emigrants* reveals the *unheimlich* nature of the *heimlich* by showing the disfamiliarity between the preparation for life and the living of it, exploring the very definition of alienation, the legal as well as cultural ramifications of which her own long-running lawsuit made her familiar with.[13] She creates a knowing, chosen marginalization that bears its own uncanny relationship to a kind of self-conscious abject, an exile from an *unheimlich* culture to the boundary of the heimlich, a flight which in itself figures a new *heimlich*. Her competing social identities reconstitute gender boundaries as themselves uncanny. In discussing Burke's *Reflec-*

tions, for instance, Linda Zerilli defines 'abjection' as 'attest[ing] to the instability of borders, of the demarcating line that separates the feminine beautiful from the masculine sublime' (p. 56). Smith's reflections on the Revolution in France also focus on separation, and from this starting point on gender, as she considers and condemns the deadly and deadening effects of war; but it is in her exploration of boundaries and her embracing of the margin that she locates peace.

Combining Freud's and Kristeva's notions of the boundary illuminates Smith's approach. Whereas in the *Sonnets* she manipulates identity by introducing multiple speakers, all apparently 'herself', in *The Emigrants* she shows the malleability of even an apparently unified subjectivity once the margin is attained. From her position on the edge, she constructs a Self both aware of and dismissive of social niceties. As Joan Landes has observed, '[h]ow difficult it is to uncouple women from domestic life. How much more difficult, once uncoupled, to imagine a world in which women's proper place is in the public sphere'.[14] Smith has signed her Dedication to Cowper (discussed in chapter 1) 'Brighthelmstone, May 10, 1793', a domestic location not borne out by the poem itself, which opens 'on the cliffs to the Eastward of the Town'. She is already on a margin; she is already laying claim to a space which, by rights, she has no business with. And although the Dedication is dated May 1793, Book I of *The Emigrants* opens in 'a Morning in November, 1792'. Smith builds into her poem a sense of the significance of place and time, and her self-conscious use, in the subheadings, of terms like 'Scene' and 'Time' also begin to hint at the theatricality of the poem; it is less a meditation than a series of tableaux, with the main character an actor well aware that the post of honour is not consistent with a private station, but equally well aware of a woman's need for a domestic identity, especially in the public eye. *The Emigrants*, as a poem that calls, not just for a 'REVOLUTION in Female Manners' (as Wollstonecraft phrased it), but a revolution in English (read: human) culture, creates a poetics of the marginal wherein the Home is reimagined as exactly the public space described by Landes – but where the public space itself is reimagined as derived from the personal. The émigrés function not merely as representatives of victims of the French Revolution, but as metaphors for Smith's own sense of marginality, personal and cultural. The violent uncoupling suffered by the émigrés mirrors Smith's own exile from a society that simultaneously requires her domestic identity, and renders its sphere uninhabitable.

Landes describes a 'specific, highly gendered bourgeois male discourse that depended on women's domesticity and the silencing of "public" women', and goes on to note that while a 'public man is one who acts in and for the universal good . . . a public woman is a prostitute, a commoner, a common woman' (2, 3). Although she is concentrating on French society, the public/private dichotomy structures British society of the time as well, spiced with more than a little complacency of the 'we in enlightened England' variety. Smith herself appeals to this nationalistic self-pride when she describes the 'just compassion' of 'English hearts', a feeling as natural as the obedience of 'our element, the deep' to 'the mild dominion of the Moon' (I: 360–363). The feminine associations of the moon are not unknown to Smith (remember her frequent turns to the 'mute arbitress of the tides' in the *Sonnets* (Sonnet XLIV, 1)); here, the virtues of being English find their definitive origin in a trope of femininity. Smith rewrites English culture to a feminine template, rejecting the masculine 'marring' of what was once 'fair' (I: 33).[15] Her strategy, however, is not one of simple reversal: Smith displays a disarming awareness of the complexities of class, gender and nationality, and her development of the metaphorics of exile reveals a simultaneous exploration of the theme of alienation, both linked to and derived from the marginal: the Freudian *Unheimlich*, the Kristevan abject. For Smith, exile is both ejection and rejection, and alienation is both felt and performed. Her continual deployment of her name and personal circumstances on the title-pages and in the Prefaces, Dedications, parentheses, and footnotes, as well as (more poetically) in the body of her poetic works not only announce her ownership of her own experiences and texts and insist on a coherent self-portrait; they also show Smith to be manipulating the gendered nature of the 'public' remarked by Landes. For as soon as Smith steps into the publishing sphere, named, she is a public woman, always at risk that the selling of her body of work may be interpreted as the selling of her body.[16] Her awareness of the connotations of her own publicity creates the paradox that Smith's self-declared marginality becomes central to her work; she exemplifies Suzanne Desan's description that 'women's position [is] on the border between the public and private spheres'.[17] The paradox is exploited by Smith when she poeticizes her own movements as 'straying' from marked paths (a common image in the *Elegiac Sonnets*), or on cliffs and eminences (as in *The Emigrants*) or on 'stupendous summits' (as in *Beachy Head*, 1807). Smith thus secures our attention: the readerly eye is caught by an 'I' whose separation from domestic life has resulted in personal, intellectual and poetic rupture.

As I noted earlier, in this poem Smith makes more of the 'I' as a unified facsimile of 'Charlotte Smith' than she does in the *Sonnets*. And yet even as she does so the embodied persona threatens to fade away, replaced by a disembodied, omniscient observer. In fact, her version of subjectivity is exactly about halves, about liminality. In certain ways she is the 'I-less reflection' described by Walter Benjamin: irreducible to a single version of the Self by virtue of the gradual loss of the body in the poem.[18] But this formulation is seen as superior by Benjamin precisely because it derives from the unified masculine self, which it is necessary to display before it can be dispensed with. Kristeva counters by saying 'Within this strange feminine see-saw that makes "me" swing from the unnameable community of women over to the war of individual singularities, it is unsettling to say "I"'.[19] For Kristeva, the idea of self-naming, of claiming the 'I', is always already complicated by the assumptions which colour Benjamin's version. Does Smith, then, approach subjectivity as a sign of masculine privilege, the attainment of which enrols her in a specialized community of Poets, in which case assuming the 'I' is a moment of simultaneous risk and triumph? Does she see the 'I' as a marker of her social and cultural invisibility, and retreat to the margin as the only space from which feminine subjectivity can be approximated? Does she allow the dissipation of the body in the service of the omniscient 'I' because she has no choice: the female body is simply not consonant with the observant Ego? Certainly, as the *Sonnets* show, Smith is aware that the 'I' carries a significance far beyond mere grammar, even as her self-placement 'on the Cliffs' show her understanding that *where* the poet is can be as significant as what she says. But even as readings of Smith's use of subjectivity that conclude she is either claiming the masculine or embracing (or in thrall to) the feminine are tempting, it is, I think, possible to argue that Smith does none of these things, but that instead the margin becomes the place where such binaries can be dispensed with. The embodied speaker can coexist with the disembodied observer; the poet can be half here, half there.

The Emigrants thus teases its readers on a variety of levels. Smith starts at the level of politics: she reconciles a pro-Revolutionary sentiment with a deep and extensive sympathy for the émigré priests and aristocrats the revolution has spent most of 1791–92 persecuting. Curran notes one aspect of her identification in his opening note to the poem:

As the Revolution unfolded in France, a great many who had enjoyed power and privilege under the *ancien régime* sought refuge in England ... [T]o

the numbers of unprotected women who had been sent abroad with their
children for safety were added others whose husbands had emigrated with
them but had then returned to France to fight and die . . . The extent to
which the rules made by men at once keep women dependent and leave
them no recourse when left alone links these distressed emigrants and the
poet who observes them. (*Poems* 131)[20]

And it is quite true that Smith concentrates her most moving imagery
on the plight of the mothers whose role has been denaturalized by
revolutionary violence, from Marie Antoinette down.[21] But the poem's
scene-setting evokes both contemporary history and literary tradition.
As noted, Book I opens in November 1792, just two months after the
abolition of the monarchy and imprisonment of the Royal Family, the
proclamation of the French Republic, and the September Massacres
that dismayed and disillusioned so many liberal thinkers. Further, in
November 1792 there was widespread alarm that Britain was on the verge
of its own revolution. Tom Paine's *Rights of Man Part 2* was followed by
his suggestion that 'social welfare . . . could only be financed . . . at the
expense of sinecure placement and pensioners' (Goodwin 263); Smith
echoes his radical tone when she lambasts the 'Pensioners / Of base
corruption, who, in quick ascent / To opulence unmerited, become /
Giddy with pride, and as ye rise, forgetting / The dust ye lately left, with
scorn look down / On those beneath ye' (I: 316–321). Paine's conviction
for seditious libel in December 1792 did not stop Smith from represent-
ing her countrymen as 'venal, worthless hirelings of a Court!' (I: 329),
although of course Book I is meant to take place before this has
happened. November also saw the formation of the Association for the
Preservation of Liberty and Property against Republicans and Levellers,
and a direct campaign by the Home Office to aggressively hunt out sedi-
tious libel (Goodwin 264). The publication of an Alien Bill in December
'to control the movements of French immigrants' (Goodwin 266)
directly affected Smith's emigrants, and perhaps her own sense of alien-
ation from an increasingly repressive culture. November, then, is more
than simply a transitional month from autumn to winter; in the histor-
ical context that Smith does not want her readers to forget, it is pivotal
as marking the period during which events in France took an increasing
toll on Britain.

Book II moves forward to April 1793, after the conviction of Paine in
December for seditious libel, the execution of the King in January, and
France's declaration of war on Britain in February (also, interestingly, the
founding on the Society of Revolutionary Republican Women). Early

1793 also saw an increasing number of prosecutions for seditious libel only weakly countered by the associated Friends of the Liberty of the Press. The inexorable clampdown on freedom of speech and the wavering of politicians on the issue of reform culminated in the defeat of Charles Grey's motion for parliamentary reform on 7 May 1793 (three days before Smith's dated Dedication). Whether coincidental or not, Smith's Book II 'Time', 'an Afternoon in April, 1793' is as politically significant as Book I's 'a Morning in November, 1792'. But it also carried literary resonances, especially given her opening emphasis on the 'half reluctan[t]' spring with its 'capricious winds' (II: 26, 24). Rather than 'showres soofte', this April 'comes, / With fragrant airs' (II: 17–18); rather than joining a pilgrimage to the shrine of a saint, the speaker situates herself even more distantly from her fellows. The 'Cliffs to the Eastward of the Town' have been exchanged for 'an Eminence on one of those Downs, which afford to the South a View of the Sea; to the North of the Weald of Sussex'. Smith allows herself a panoramic view and combines the margin with the commanding height only possible 'on an Eminence'. Her political stance is thus backed up by literary authority garnered both through her allusion to Chaucer and her claiming of the masterful prospect view.

Both Books, then, open with the speaker already in possession of political savvy and literary and historical authority, but she deploys both more subtly within the body of the poem via contrasting constructions of subjectivity. She is sheltered and initially passive in Book I – the *scene* is 'on the Cliffs', a spectacular position, but the 'I' enters only in line 42, 'half-adjur[ing] Society / And sigh[ing] for some lone Cottage, deep embower'd / In the green woods' (I: 42–44). However, the authoritative Eminence of Book II foreshadows a more powerful subject; the 'I' enters in line 5. Whereas in Book I Smith's speaker wishes to 'hide' herself from her sorrows, here she emphasizes her presence on the eminence, walking 'along the wave-worn cliff . . . lost in despondence' (II: 4, 6). Here, too, the margin functions to bring home the sense of an abjected speaker: not only is she on a cliff, but the cliff itself is 'wave-worn', undermined by the sea so that the image suggested is one of the speaker literally walking on the most marginal of boundaries, jutting out over open air. In this book Smith immediately moves to the personal details that ally her with the emigrants; Book I merely alludes to 'sorrows' and 'labour' and the 'involuntary exile' she experienced when she fled to France with her husband to avoid debt collectors. Book II, however, wastes no time in mentioning the speaker's 'wayward destiny' (II: 7), comparing the emigrants' lot to hers ('They, like me, / From fairer hopes and happier prospects driven', II: 14–15) rather than the other way round, referring to her own lost happiness (II: 36–42), and above all in linking her position as a grieving mother with Marie Antoinette's. Book II shows the development of the 'I' from hesitant and contemplative to angry and participatory: 'Ah! who knows, / From sad experience, more than I, to feel / For thy desponding spirit' (II: 169–171), she apostrophizes Marie Antoinette.

Even in Book I, moreover, Smith begins to establish a respectable, yet highly politicized and visible 'I'. This comes about partly through her facility with grammar – before we reach the first-person of line 42, we have travelled from the omniscient and disembodied third-person, to the docile and cooperative first-person plural ('[God] surely means / To *us*, his reasoning Creatures, whom he bids / Acknowledge and revere his awful hand, / Nothing but good' (lines 29–32, emphasis added)). Smith's desire to 'hide' herself in the 'lone Cottage' further functions to disarm the powerful cliffside position she has manifestly claimed, while her description of her powerful feelings – 'my swol'n heart . . . bursting with its sorrows' (62) – confirm her feminine sensibilities. In a typical Smithian move, the very lines that indicate a desire for seclusion also maintain the energy of individuality: 'there do I wish to hide me' (I: 48), she says, infusing her gesture towards domesticization with both agency and division. By simultaneously locating herself both on the cliffs and in the green woods, Smith claims both a masculine and a feminine subject-position in the first 93 lines of *The Emigrants*. She is, even at this early stage, half one and half the other, and it is this doubleness that figures throughout the poem, allowing Smith a consistently layered approach. She refuses to privilege one approach over the other – her speaker is both on the cliffs and in the woods, both above it all and an emigrant herself – and this correlates with her ability to be embodied and disembodied, an actor and a spectator.

In writing of Helen Maria Williams, Mary Favret remarks that, for Williams, 'the experience of revolution is only realized as the experience of spectators, foreigners, and strangers'.[22] Smith's emigrants are also 'foreigners and strangers', but rather than distancing them from her speaking self, Smith sees their strangeness as uniting them with herself: 'I too have known / involuntary exile', she says, and so can 'mourn [their] sorrows' (I: 55–56).[23] Again in Favret's words, 'her heart and soul understand the French people precisely because she is a woman and [to them] a foreigner' (159). In Smith's case, the 'people' function as representative types, 'banish'd for ever and for conscience sake / From their distracted country, whence the name / Of Freedom misapplied, and much abus'd / By lawless Anarchy, has driven them far to wander' (I: 97–101).²⁴ Book I's 'Time' functions as a contextualizing date that allows her readers to understand that 'lawless Anarchy' does not necessarily characterize the revolution itself, but rather its turn to Terror; the 'name of Freedom' suffers under this harsher regime, but as Smith will make clear, not the original desire for freedom and equality that, she understands, drove the revolution heretofore. On the beach, then, the boundary between land and sea, wander a group by role hostile to the new Republic. Smith's sympathy is not unalloyed; even as she introduces the 'group' she deplores their 'prejudice', their 'Bigotry (the Tut'ress of the blind)' and 'errors' – that is, their Catholicism – that teaches them narrow ways: the monk who seeks to please God by 'renounc[ing] God's works', the cardinal 'dwelling on all he had lost', the abbot 'lighter of heart than these, but heavier far / Than he was wont' (I: 119, 128, 147–148). These men 'hang / Upon the barrier of the rock' (I: 109), their position replicating their marginality, and Smith watches them and remembers her own 'involuntary exile': 'while yet / England had charms for me, [I] have felt how sad / It is to look across the dim cold sea, / That melancholy rolls its refluent tides / Between us and the dear regretted land / We call our own' (I: 156–161).

Of all the clerics, the one who garners Smith's most sympathetic lines is the parish priest: 'even such a Man / Becomes an exile; staying not to try / By temperate zeal to check his madd'ning flock, / Who, at the novel sound of Liberty / (Ah! Most intoxicating sounds to slaves!), / Start into licence' (I: 190–195). The priest's 'temperate zeal' is matched by his flock's enslavement to the tyranny of class; it is in lines like these that Smith reveals her pro-Revolutionary stance. Despite her sympathy, then, the speaker is far from defending the emigrants; she extends her compassion to them as exiles but does not ask her readers to take their side in the conflict. All these emigrant figures are in error – religious, class-based – and in this way their exile mirrors their moral position. Smith's own position is double: she both identifies with, and condemns, the émigrés, in the same way that she both supports the Revolution's principles, and deplores its current 'distraction' from those principles. To this point, her engagement with the émigrés is openly textual, observational – she watches them, sympathizes, empathizes and critiques, but she does not interact with them. The furthest she goes is to create a link with the female emigrant based on their shared maternity, but even here she creates a deeper identification with, first, Marie Antoinette, and then with the fleeing mother in Book II (as discussed in chapter 2). Her approach is even-handed and dispassionate, rather than eager and identificatory: more traditionally masculine than feminine in tone, more feminine than masculine in topics emphasized (for example, motherhood).

Throughout Book I Smith leavens her sympathy for the emigrants with veiled critiques of her own society. Her humanitarian representation of the émigrés supports, on the one hand, English compassion (the émigrés find to their surprise that 'we [English] for them / Feel as our brethren' [I: 359–360]), but on the other allows for pointed and open critique of English 'venalities'. Moving from depicting the émigrés' homelessness to the 'wide-extended misery' that contradicts Britain's self-image as a 'land of highly vaunted Freedom' (I: 307, 245), Smith uncovers the inequities that infect her own nation:

> Ye pamper'd Parasites! whom Britons pay
> For forging fetters for them; rather here
> Study a lesson that concerns ye much;
> And, trembling, learn, that if oppress'd too long,
> The raging multitude, to madness stung,
> Will turn on their oppressors; and, no more
> By sounding titles and parading forms
> Bound like tame victims, will redress themselves!
> Then swept away by the resistless torrent,
> Not only all your pomp may disappear,
> But, in the tempest lost, fair Order sink
> Her decent head, and lawless Anarchy
> O'erturn celestial Freedom's radiant throne; –
> As now in Gallia; where confusion, born
> Of party rage and selfish love of rule,
> Sully the noblest cause that ever warm'd
> The heart of Patriot Virtue!
>
> (I: 329–346)

These lines are plainly revolutionary: not only are the basic tenets of the French Revolution upheld, but England's 'highly vaunted Freedom' is revealed as an empty show, and an English revolution is actually threatened as an appropriate, if not inevitable, action. As if she collects herself, Smith pauses after 'throne': the long dash builds in a deep breath and a deliberate turn away to 'Gallia'. The subsequent return to 'compassionate Britain' is expedient; it allows Smith to end Book I with a decorous praise of British virtue, a paean to British liberty, and a plea to avoid 'wide wasting War' (I: 381) – three months before war was openly declared.

Having approached, identified with and then defamiliarized the unhoused emigrants, Smith uses their situation to 'other' Britain itself, presenting it as a version of pre-Revolutionary France. Even as the French rose up against tyranny, and cast out the corrupt, so too, she warns, those 'who feed on England's vitals' deserve French justice. The progress from proud aristocratic emigrants to an England teeming with venality shows that Smith's émigrés, in Book I, serve to illuminate the weaknesses of English culture as much as the violence of the French Revolution. Her persona judges on a personal and a political level – the inattentive mother serves as a representative of inattentive England, and this serves to import a distinctly politicised tone not only to Smith's ruminations of war, but also her understanding of that microcosm of the social order, the family. Indeed, the speaker is unable to find in any of the cultural institutions she reviews a model for a just society; while the mothers she represents are victimized, the fathers are ultimately ineffectual. The female emigrant's husband is debased by his class prejudices; the dauphin's father is even less helpful than his mother, who at least still lives to comfort him in the poem. The final father pictured, a French aristocratic soldier, leaves his family to the depradations of war and returns to find them all slaughtered: 'And the day dawns / On a wild raving Maniac, whom a fate / So sudden and calamitous has robb'd / Of reason; and who round his vacant walls / Screams unregarded, and reproaches Heaven!' (II: 308–312). It is not the most effective response, and because Smith does not offer an English father who can make up for French deficiencies, it seems that patriarchal authority itself is being questioned.

The rapid and unsignposted movements from individuals to classes to institutions to governments builds into Book I a desire to associate the personal with the political and, further, to reveal the hollowness of each sphere. Even as Book I ends with a (not entirely convincing) celebration of English compassion towards the emigrants, it also straightforwardly denounces war for its personal cost: 'bloodless laurels' 'far better justify the pride, that swells / In British bosoms, than the deafening roar / Of Victory from a thousand brazen throats, / That tell with what success wide-wasting War / Has by our brave Compatriots thinned the world' (I: 369, 378–382). Smith roundly condemns war just as Britain is entering into one; she expresses (guarded) support for the Revolution just when its turn to Terror was losing it many ardent supporters; she maintains an identification with émigrés who yet provoke her criticism. The 'Cliffs to the Eastward' of Brighton loom over an abjected landscape, the confusion of which arises from the poem's attempt to present a pro-Revolution, anti-war, personally politicized, objectively subjective point of view. Like the chaos arising from the Terror, the mixture of stances and attitudes pervading Book I threaten to overshadow its strengths: an underlying sense of structure that needs the addition of Book II to clarify itself. Smith builds into Book I an alienating unconcern with its potential incoherence; while her presentation of events and vignettes is straightforward enough, it is the rationale behind it that destabilizes and defamiliarizes the reader. I would suggest that this is not inadvertent, but rather a kind of poetics of unknowability: even as Smith invites complex readings, she still treads the margin.

Book I's ending emphasis on British virtues and its denunciation of war accomplishes the double task of allowing Smith to level a critique even as she seems to occupy a passive, compassionate position. Her benedictory tone lauds Britain for what it has not yet done: that is, avoid war. She enlists God as her trump card: 'May thy foes, / By Reason's gen'rous potency subdued, / Learn, that the God thou worshippest, delights / In acts of pure humanity! – May thine / Be still such bloodless laurels!' (I: 365–369). Her subtle privileging of the Protestant God over the Catholic God suggests a form of flattery, as if the speaker attempts to make her point in a particularly conventional feminine way. The French may make war, she implies, but the wiser British prefer the 'bloodless laurels' of peace. The critique resides in the alternative; if the British also go to war, they are no better than the French. This sotto voce effect has characterized Book I, allowing Smith to maintain a subjectivity which only occasionally takes centre stage.

It is as if, occupied with the conflicting techniques of sympathy and judgement, desire and repression that characterize Book I, and mirrored in her liminal self-placement 'on the Cliffs', Smith uses Book I to populate her polemic and intimate the direction Book II will take, where many of her characters reappear. Smith bolsters her more assertive physical self-placement 'on an Eminence' with the Chaucerian echoes discussed above, and with a Latin epigraph from Virgil, deploring the eruption of war.[25] Untranslated, the epigraph signals that the speaker in Book II feels at home in the masculine world of the Classics, and that further this speaker will go further than her Book I counterpart. It is, of course, now April, and Britain and France are now at war. It is now both more mean-

ingful and more dangerous to take a publicly anti-war stance. To empha-
size her new sense of agency, Book II begins, as noted above, in the first
person:

> Long wintry months are past; the Moon that now
> Lights her pale crescent even at noon, has made
> Four times her revolution; since with step,
> Mournful and slow, along the wave-worn cliff,
> Pensive I took my solitary way,
> Lost in despondence, while contemplating
> Not my own wayward destiny alone,
> (Hard as it is, and difficult to bear!)
> But in beholding the unhappy lot
> Of the lorn Exiles; who, amid the storms
> Of wild disastrous anarchy, are thrown,
> Like shipwreck'd sufferers, on England's coast,
> To see, perhaps, no more their native land,
> Where Desolation riots: they, like me,
> From fairer hopes and happier prospects driven,
> Shrink from the future, and regret the past.
>   (II: 1–16)[26]

The reader senses a new firmness in Smith's explicit identification with
the émigrés; no longer merely an observer, she is now a kind of partici-
pant in exile. Her use of the word 'revolution' to describe the moon's
progress resonates politically, and recalls the moon's 'mild dominion'
described at the end of Book I. With 'revolution', the moon's dominion
seems no longer 'mild', but rather more potent. In Book II, the
personal/political link will be both cemented and more fully explored:
the defamiliarizing process of Book I results in a new ability to express
the repressed, to unhouse the *heimlich*. And so Smith moves from a
statement of her personal sorrows, through four lines decrying the
beheading of the king, to a more sustained reverie on war's violent effect
on the landscape (for Smith, this April is indeed a cruel month – Spring
hesitates to enliven a countryside 'stain'd with blood' (II: 71)). Smith
devotes some 75 lines to describing the historical uselessness of war in
her movement from beheaded father (King) to imprisoned mother
(Queen), via the 'unhappy heir / Of fatal greatness', whose 'baby brow' is
too young to comprehend 'the savage howl of Murder' heard daily in his
'sullen prison' (II: 127–128, 130, 150, 149).

In her allusions to the King's death, Smith treads a dangerous line, for
she comes perilously close to, as John Barrell has recently phrased it,

'imagining the King's death'.[27] Of course, the king in question is not the British monarch, and his execution in January meant that on one level Smith merely reiterates a historical event. But by representing the dead king, even as elliptically as she does it, Smith forces her readers to imagine *a* king's death, if not *the* king's death, and this is an explicitly political move. It directs her readers' attention, and again we see that the speaker of Book II is a more active 'I' than that of Book I. Where the speaker of Book I describes events, the speaker of Book II points and colours them: so, for instance, the imprisoned dauphin becomes a 'baby' victimized by 'regal mischief', and Marie Antoinette becomes, as discussed in chapter 2, a 'wretched Mother' (II: 130, 131, 152). The speaker's rhetorical skills complement her political aims; but she also maintains her place on the margin. We remember that even as she brings up the dead King, she goes no further than to allude to 'fatal greatness' (II: 128). Her readers must fill in the gaps.

Smith picks and chooses her historical moments because she is doing more than reproducing the world the emigrants have escaped. Her earlier references to her personal history are matched in Book II when she identifies with Marie Antoinette on the basis of their shared mother-hood, when she turns from her vignettes of martial horror to her memories of a childhood spent in Nature, and most vividly when she speaks of the 'o'erwhelming wrongs, / That have for ten long years been heap'd on me' and the 'fearful spectres of chicane and fraud' (II: 353–354, 355). It is jarring that when Smith, after her anti-war polemic of earlier lines, turns now to Peace, it is her personal peace she speaks of: 'Ah! yes, my friends, / Peace will at last be mine; for in the Grave / Is Peace' (II: 371–373). From here to (nearly) the poem's end, the speaker's subject is 'Charlotte Smith'; the personal has overtaken the political. This is what prompts her reviewers to remark irritably 'Herself, and not the French emigrant, fills the foreground; begins and ends the piece; and the pity we should naturally feel for those overwhelming and uncommon distresses she describes, is lessened by their being brought into parallel with the inconveniences of a narrow income, or a protracted lawsuit'.[28] But her turn to the personal in Book II reminds the reader of her identification with the emigrants in Book I: even as she too has been an exile, so now she too has experienced victimhood and conflict. The banality of a 'narrow income' and a 'protracted lawsuit' are not the point; what Smith explores is the condition of being female, and she can only do so if she can assume a masculine, observant and active persona. It is being female that leads her to the margin, and it is being female that encourages a strategy of halves. It is being male that allows her to enter the political arena, risk sedition, and imagine the deaths of fathers. And it is her sexed body that means her reviewers read her as querulous rather than dangerous.[29]

By dragging the personal into the limelight, Smith creates a scene wherein the personal gains the same sort of political relevance as the events in France. She uses her horror of war to suggest a horror of culture itself. Far from using the imagery of exile to 'redefine . . . culture or subjectivity from [a] (middle-class) wom[an's] point of view'[30] – in that way participating in culture – Smith underscores the impossibility of such a move. For her, culture itself remains an Other, intent on ejecting *differance*. She rejects the notion of 'a compliant form of femininity' either as 'the demarcating lines of gender identity' or 'as a necessary form of political artifice' (Zerilli 55). Her politics of the personal, conveyed through a poetics of halves and margins, brings home the cost of viewing the world as do the 'Wise Politicians': 'woes such as these does Man inflict on Man; / And by the closet murderers, whom we style / Wise Politicians, are the schemes prepar'd / Which, to keep Europe's wavering balance even, / Depopulate her kingdoms, and consign / To tears and anguish half a bleeding world!' (II: 319–324).[31] In this poem, Smith skirts the rules usually thought open to even revolutionary women: in Vivien Jones's words, 'sexual object or asexual "respectability"' (305).[32] Jones argues that Wollstonecraft, Helen Maria Williams, 'and other women writers of their generation' sought in the representation of Revolution a release from the strictures of gender; 'they struggle to construct a new subject position, a feminine agency, but the repressive binary categories on which nationalist identity, gender, and, it would seem, emergent Romanticism are constructed are essentially unbroken' (305). Smith's perch on the margin allows her at once to combine and opt out of these binary categories, even as her rhetoric encourages a pro-Revolution, antiwar stance.

Smith's persona, then – poet, mother, liberal, pacifist, revolutionary – is self-consciously constructed; readers become spectators in a drama played out on the very edge of the nation. Zimmerman calls this 'the theatrical dynamic of "overhearing" private thoughts' (63), but Smith makes no attempt at privacy; although on a cliff, or an eminence, or to the east of town, she is always on view, her thoughts directly exposed to her readers. However, as she will do in *Beachy Head*, Smith extrapolates from a physical margin – the edge of a cliff, the coast – a symbolic alienation from her culture. *The Emigrants* offers a specific moment that crystallizes Smith's self-exile, a moment in history that proclaims a self-evident centrality. The revolution, the overthrow of a monarchy, the violence of the Terror, the declaration of war with an historic enemy – the events of 1792–93 constituted 'history' even as they occurred, and Smith's understanding of this embues *The Emigrants*.[33] But Smith's engagement with history masks a deeper disaffection; even as her opposition to war with France encompasses but goes beyond the 'humanitarian reasons' described by Matthew Bray,[34] so her creation of historic 'spots of time' function as much to separate Smith from history as to facilitate her participation. Bray, for instance, argues that in *Beachy Head* Smith rejects the 'ideological Anglo-Saxon yoke' of history 'that allows English people to support an untenable division with France': *Beachy Head*'s version of history is one that realigns misplaced Anglo-French hostility, substituting a Humean history and denying the Anglo-Saxonesque perception of the Norman invasion as the introduction of a foreign tyrant (158). Bray calls this Smith's 'seditious historiography' (157). Smith lays out the groundwork for *Beachy Head*'s sedition, however, in her challenges to authority contained in *The Emigrants*: maintaining the morality of peace in the face of a cultural emphasis on the patriotic value of war constitutes one aspect of this challenge. Setting her speaker up as ultimately capable of speaking directly to God is another, as she does in the poem's last lines.

Smith is a poet ill at ease with dominant voices of her own culture; the footnoted challenges described in chapter 1 authorize a more centrally textual anger. Because she has placed herself outside her culture, developed a speaker able to voice both the masculine and the feminine, and above all introduced the political resonances of her personal circumstances, Smith is able to conclude the poem as the active director of the scenes before her, and the active denunciator of 'the variety of woes that Man / For Man creates' (II: 413–414). Smith plants in *The Emigrants* an anti-war stance that does not preclude the need for radical change in England. Her condemnations of 'Party Rage' and 'base Venality' refer not only to a blind following of Robespierre and his policies but also to an equally blind veneration of leaders closer to home: allusions to 'private vice / [That] makes even the wildest profligate recoil' (II: 120–121) are as applicable to, for instance, the Prince of Wales as they are to Jean-Paul Marat.[35] But the trajectory of Book II is not geared towards an ever-more-explosive exposé of British cultural shortcomings, nor even, despite the almost rhapsodic closing invocation of Divine interference, a dismissal of this world in favour of God's; rather, the significance lies

in Smith's turn to the personal. *The Emigrants* witnesses Smith's growing
alienation from her society; her presentation of the émigrés fosters her
identification with them; and her rejection of history is catalysed by her
immersion in another version of it: her own personal history, her private
sorrows that have, paradoxically, become a public property. Smith's cir-
cumstances provide a micro-instance of the unhappiness and dissatis-
faction that resulted, in France, in revolution, and by forging a direct
bond between herself and the emigrants, she completes her image.
Even as Smith-as-woman follows 'the rugged path, / That leads at length
to Peace!' (II: 370–371), so Smith-as-Poet proclaims that, with God's
intervention,

> . . . the fierce feuds,
> That long have torn their desolated land,
> May (even as storms, that agitate the air,
> Drive noxious vapours from the blighted earth)
> Serve, all tremendous as they are, to fix
> The reign of Reason, Liberty, and Peace!
>   (II: 439–444)

Personal peace foreshadows historic peace: the woman's resolution
inexorably allows for that of 'fierce feuds'. The turn to personal history
thus creates the conditions for a return to a natural and cleansed culture.
War has been rejected, but not, it is important to note, Revolution.

By making the personal central, Smith pushes the margin centre-stage.
Her speaker, a unified 'I' but, so to speak, pan-gendered, acts as the stage-
manager for a drama that explores the meaning of emigration, of being
a stranger in a strange land. By the end of the poem, she has achieved an
agency that allows her to transform her presentation of a personal reli-
gion into an ability to direct even God:

> And if, where regulated sanctity
> Pours her long orisons to Heaven, my voice
> Was seldom heard, [say] that yet *my prayer* was made
> To him who hears even silence; not in domes
> Of human architecture, fill'd with crowds,
> But on these hills . . .
> . . . – I made my prayer
> In unison with the murmuring waves . . .
>   (II: 387–390, 401–402, Smith's emphasis)[36]

The communion thus asserted leads directly to Smith's turn to the 'Power
Omnipotent', and a series of imperatives that resonate with strength:

O Power Omnipotent! with mercy *view*
This suffering globe, and *cause* thy creatures cease,
With savage fangs, to tear her bleeding breast:
Restrain that rage for power, that bids a Man,
Himself a worm, desire unbounded rule
O'er beings like himself: *Teach* the hard hearts
Of rulers, that the poorest hind, who dies
For their unrighteous quarrels, in thy sight
Is equal to the imperious Lord, that leads
His disciplin'd destroyers to the field.
                    (II: 421–430, emphasis added)

Whether she speaks with the voice of the ecstatic preacher or the powerful prophet, Smith here has effectively left behind the world of 'Man' and established a new, almost omniscient voice for a speaker who began, as we remember, longing to hide herself away in a deep-embowered cottage.

Smith achieves this conclusion by observing, and maintaining an attachment to, the culture of revolution. For Smith, her marginalization as a married woman and mother – culturally revered yet voiceless – offers an opportunity to embrace the liminal and explore its territory. What she finds is an area of flexible boundaries, characterized by what has been culturally forgotten – repressed – and sidelined – made abject. Playing with these 'entities', she repopulates the margin, making visible the repressed and utilising the abject, until the edge becomes central and unavoidable, the familiar becomes strange, and the strange becomes homely. By re-presenting the invisible, by voicing the unspeakable, Smith transforms *The Emigrants* into a polemical document, not merely anti-war or pro-Revolution, but rather anti-cultural and pro-active. From her position on the headland, Smith overlooks the émigrés, their adopted refuge, the country they have fled, and she notes the *unheimlich* nature of all three. But the deepest revolution is the one Smith herself embodies: in this poem, she takes up a complex involvement with conventions of gender and culture. As she concentrates on war and exile, she also manoeuvres her persona, performing gendered stances and roles as suggested by her construction of scenarios, vignettes of Revolutionary import, and use of theatrical language. *The Emigrants* is a poem about war and about being at war; it is a rejection of war; and it is a declaration of war on a culture that continually seeks to marginalize and cast off – abjectify – segments of itself. The repressed returns seeking vengeance, and Smith herself assumes the *unheimlich* stance of a woman on the verge: 'and all the various pain / I now endure shall be forgotten there' (II: 374–375).

Loose ends

As this chapter has suggested, *The Emigrants* invites a reading that privileges Smith and her trials over those of the emigrants, but it also requires that the reader not lose sight of them altogether. By situating her speaker as a stand-in for the exiled French, Smith at once promotes a politics of identification and one of critique. Which do we regard as final? The emigrants, representatives of a flawed society, are far from guiltless; indeed, Smith's critical voice is unambiguous even if often parenthentical. And yet if the emigrants function as springboards to Smith's own sense of exile and alienation, how do we reconcile their compromised nature with Smith's pure victimhood? At what point do the emigrants become simply imagery, emptied of their own personal identities and hence ready to receive the imprint of Smith's? Likewise, if Smith wants her speaker to occupy the detached position of the observer for political commentary, and the engaged position of the participant for personal expression, how do we regard the double imposition of the prospect view – on the cliffs and on an eminence? While it can be argued, as I have done, that Smith's strategy converts the prospect from a solely masculinized position to one inflected by the feminine, it further suggests the inherent contradictions of the poem. It is as if Smith attempts to carry on in *The Emigrants* what the *Sonnets* so successfully maintained: an infusion of the Self into the Other, and a combination of the personal 'I' with the depersonalized, or disembodied, 'I'. But where the fourteen lines of the sonnet required brevity and compression, the two Books and 826 lines of *The Emigrants* allow the unleashing of the subjective. Smith steers her readers one way, but the poem's details pull against her attempts to unify her speaker's competing subjectivities. In 1793, then, it seems that Smith's deployment of the personal problematizes her turn to the political, and vice-versa. The next chapter demonstrates that by 1806, she overcomes these difficulties with incompatible subjectivities and, in her masterpiece *Beachy Head*, ties up her loose ends.

Notes

1 See J. Epstein and K. Straub, Introduction to *Body Guards: The Cultural Politics of Gender Ambiguity* (New York: Routledge, 1991), 9.

2 *European Magazine* 24 (1793): 42, unsigned review. It is interesting that the
   reviewer locates the painter's 'portrait' in the space traditionally reserved for
   the signature; here, identity resides in the written name rather than a picto-
   rial image, which encapsulates Smith's approach perfectly.

3 *The Poems of Charlotte Smith*, ed. Stuart Curran (Oxford: Oxford University
   Press, 1993), 132. Subsequent references will be made in the text.

4 Behrendt, '"A Few Harmless Numbers": British Women Poets and the
   Climate of War, 1793–1815', *Romantic Wars: Studies in Culture and Conflict,
   1793–1822*, ed. Philip Shaw (Aldershot: Ashgate, 2000), 13–36: 14.

5 In the Preface to *Desmond*, Smith engages directly with the need for women
   to participate in politics: 'But women it is said have no business with politics
   – Why not? – Have they no interest in the scenes that are acting around them,
   in which they have fathers, brothers, husbands, sons, or friends engaged? –
   Even in the commonest course of female education, they are expected to
   acquire some knowledge of history; and yet, if they are to have no opinion
   of what *is* passing, it avails little that they should be informed of what *has
   passed*, in a world where they are subject to such mental degradation; where
   they are answered as affecting masculine knowledge if they happen to have
   any understanding; or despised as insignificant triflers if they have none.' The
   Wollstonecraftian tone is unmistakable.

6 Sarah Zimmerman, *Romanticism, Lyricism, and History* (SUNY Press, 1999),
   57. Subsequent references will be made in the text.

7 Interestingly, Smith in real life opened her lodgings to the needy and home-
   less emigrants, thus fulfilling her womanly duty of caring for the less fortu-
   nate. But it is not the intention of this book to argue that Smith the woman
   rejected her social role; rather, as I hope is by now clear, I am interested in
   how Smith demonstrates her awareness of the parameters of this 'role', and
   also how we as readers fill in the gaps for her.

8 I quote from the *Analytical Review* 22 (1793): 91, the *Monthly Review* 12
   (1793): 375, and the *European Magazine* 24 (1793): 45, all emphases added.

9 See Albert Goodwin, *The Friends of Liberty: The English Democratic Move-
   ment in the Age of the French Revolution* (London: Hutchinson, 1979): 249.

10 'Sonnet LXX: On being cautioned against walking on an headland', with its
   emphasis on reason claimed and simultaneously rejected, provides a concise
   answer to this assumption.

11 Smith, of course, relies on these associations in her strategy of embodiment.

12 From 'The Uncanny', quoted in Linda Zerilli, 'Text/Woman as Spectacle:
   Edmund Burke's "French Revolution"', *The Eighteenth Century* 33 (1992),
   47–72: 52. Subsequent references to Zerilli will be made in the text.

13 As Curran notes, 'a sense of the legal system as an arbitrary machine of power
   operating without any essential relation to equity runs deep in Smith's
   writing' (*Poems* xxi).

14 Joan Landes, *Women and the Public Sphere in the Age of the French Revolu-
   tion* (Ithaca: Cornell University Press, 1988): 1. Although Landes concentrates

on women in revolutionary France, her conclusions are applicable to late eighteenth-century Britain as well.

15 Smith fully exploits the meanings suggested by 'fair': both 'beautiful' and 'balanced'; only a few lines later, she parenthetically dwells on the 'vain boast / Of equal Law' as 'mockery' (I: 37–38). 'Man' mars the fairness of natural law, which is defined by equality, when he creates his own laws.

16 For a further discussion of Smith's marketing strategy, see Labbe, 'Selling One's Sorrows: Charlotte Smith, Mary Robinson, and the Marketing of Poetry', *The Wordsworth Circle* 25 (1994), 68–71.

17 Suzanne Desan, 'Women's Experience of the French Revolution: An Historical Overview', *Literate Women and the French Revolution of 1789*, ed. Catherine R. Montfort (Birmingham, AL: Summa Publications, Inc., 1994), 19–30: 20.

18 As delineated by Marc Redfield in 'Romanticism, *Bildung*, and the Literary Absolute', *Lessons of Romanticism*, eds. Thomas Pfau and Robert F. Gleckner (Durham: Duke University Press), 41–54: 48.

19 Julia Kristeva, 'Stabat Mater', *The Kristeva Reader*, ed. Toril Moi (New York: Columbia University Press), 160–186: 182.

20 Although Curran implies that Smith's emigrants are only women, in fact just one of the five is: she describes three clerics, an aristocrat, and his wife.

21 See chapter 2 for a discussion of mother-imagery in the poem.

22 Mary Favret, 'Spectatrice as Spectacle: Helen Maria Williams at Home in the Revolution', *Literate Women and the French Revolution of 1789*, 151–172: 157. Subsequent references will be made in the text.

23 In 1784, Smith's husband Benjamin fled England to France to escape further imprisonment for debt. Smith, as the dutiful wife, accompanied him there, and regarded her six months' stay in France as 'exile'.

24 As with 'fair', Smith uses a word that carries multiple meanings: 'distracted' means both 'mad' and 'preoccupied'.

25 Smith displays her knowledge of the (masculinized) classics when she includes a Latin epigraph.

26 One should also note the 'Tintern Abbey' resonances of the first lines of Book II: 'Long wintry months are past; the Moon that now / Lights her pale crescent even at noon, has made / Four times her revolution; since with step, / Mournful and slow, along the wave-worn cliff, / Pensive I took my solitary way' says Smith. 'Five years have passed; five summers, with the length / Of five long winters! and again I hear / These waters, rolling from their mountain-springs / With a sweet inland murmur', says Wordsworth. Given that *The Emigrants* is published five years before 'Tintern Abbey', what should be noted is Wordsworth's use of Smith's trope of memory. For a further discussion of Smith/Wordsworth interweavings, see chapter 5. See also Bishop C. Hunt, Jr, 'Wordsworth and Charlotte Smith', *The Wordsworth Circle* 1 (1971), 85–103: 94. Hunt's article carefully notes a number of Smith/

Wordsworth parallels, although always from the point of view of Wordsworth's unquestioned superiority.

27 See John Barrell, *Imagining the King's Death: Figurative Treason, Fantasies of Regicide* (Oxford: Oxford University Press, 2000).

28 *The Critical Review* 9 (October 1793): 299–302, 299; quoted in Hunt, 'Wordsworth and Charlotte Smith', 96.

29 Or, in the case of the reviews quoted earlier, womanly rather than politically engaged.

30 Patricia Chu, '"The Invisible World the Emigrants Built": Cultural Self-Inscription and the Antiromantic Plots of *The Woman Warrior*', *Diaspora* 2 (1992), 95–115: 100.

31 Given that men fight wars, and women wait at home, one wonders which 'half' of the 'bleeding world' Smith means.

32 Vivien Jones, 'Femininity, Nationalism and Romanticism: The Politics of Gender in the Revolution Controversy', *History of European Ideas* 16 (1993), 299–305: 305. Subsequent references will be made in the text.

33 Wordsworth's 'Tintern Abbey', of course, familiarly elides revolutionary history to concentrate, instead, on the history of the poet's development; yet, as Marjorie Levinson has shown, history is inevitably present. In the context of this essay, it might be said that history constitutes Wordsworth's repressed.

34 Matthew Bray, 'Removing the Anglo-Saxon Yoke: The Francocentric Vision of Charlotte Smith's Later Works', *The Wordsworth Circle* 24 (1993), 155–158: 155. Subsequent references will be made in the text.

35 Curran's note to these lines remarks that 'this attack appears directed at Jean-Paul Marat, the most violent of the Jacobin propagandists, who was assassinated by Charlotte Corday later in 1793' (*Poems* 153).

36 It is interesting to note that Smith's lunatic in Sonnet LXX also 'murmur[s] responses to the dashing surf' (8).

5

Locating the poet in
Beachy Head

Through this book I have attempted a dual project: both to understand Smith's deployment of multiple poetic personae, and to understand what happens when we read her poetry through the lens of gender criticism. So far we have seen that as open as Smith's poetry is to the application of gender theories, it also fights a too-easy mapping of gender onto sex. That is, while it seems evident that Smith manipulates identities based on gender in her poetry, she also writes poetry that in effect denies the power of gender altogether. Thus, the *Sonnets* both forward an ideology of the gendered speaker and refuse it, and *The Emigrants* combines feminine and masculine tones of voice. Even the apparatus surrounding the *Sonnets* both conforms to and challenges stereotypes of gender. Turning to the posthumously published *Beachy Head*, it is possible to read this poem as the culmination of Smith's poetic project, and it functions on several levels to confirm this in its constructions of an authoritative poetic voice that is, eventually, undermined by the Poet herself, the Smith who may or may not have shadowed the 'Charlotte Smith' who has made herself so well known to her readers since the 1780s. *Beachy Head* creates a strong narrative voice who is in the end as unreliable as any post-modern narrator, undercut by several literary techniques that simultaneously serve to strengthen the speaker's authority – that is, the speaker's position as author and the power that derives from that. *Beachy Head* contains a complex poetics of multiplicity and simultaneity, symbolized by the myriad parts of Beachy Head itself.

Beachy Head is a contemplative blank-verse poem, and in it Smith locates herself and her reader atop Beachy Head, investing the poem with the authority culturally allied to the prospect view and making use of her vantage point to explore nature in all its 'multitudinous, uncanny particularity', in Stuart Curran's words.[1] *Beachy Head* participates in the

Romantic revival of the prospect poem; it arises from the same impulse that produced 'Tintern Abbey' and that will produce, for instance, 'Mont Blanc'. In it, Smith creates a tableau fixing her own place – as poet, as woman – in a cultural, social, natural and poetical landscape, utilizing tropes of height, vision and dispossession. It is important to note *where* Smith situates herself and her poem: the prospect view, allied as it was with political and cultural power and dominance, and allied also with masculinity and breadth of vision, is not common property. Smith's daring opening move is to claim the prospect, but to do so in typically Smithian fashion; that is, she gestures towards power but cloaks her moves in decorous propriety. Again, as in so much of her work, she gradually unfolds to the reader's eyes a more assertive, authoritative persona. In this poem Smith preserves a persona reliant on a multiplied sense of self; characterized by a keen awareness of the suitability of voice, tone, self-construction, self-placement and even self-promotion; ultimately, cognisant of the necessity of strategy and skilful self-manoeuvring in a culture itself dependent on increasingly rigid gender roles.

Throughout her writing career Smith represents herself as writing out of necessity, 'chained to her desk' in Cowper's words, 'liv[ing] only to write & writ[ing] only to live'.[2] Her poetry, however, always occupied a different category to her prose writings; it was 'artistic' (Turner 160) and as such contains, as it were, more 'art': a more devoted and thoroughly worked out attention to the artifices and guises offered by language. This is partly how Smith has exploited her readers' expectations of personae and identity, as we have seen. In *Beachy Head* Smith relies on her readers to remember who she has been poetically; the poem consolidates Smith's personae into a speaker who, more than in any of her other poems, is both there and not there. This extends, of course, to reality, since by 1807, when *Beachy Head* is published, Smith has retired to the permanent home of the grave; her death in 1806 means that the poem, as its Preface says, is 'not completed according to its original design' (*Poems* 215), but instead exists as a self-designated fragment. As with most Romantic fragments, it carries within it the potential for something more, but more so than other Romantic fragments, it also figures as something already lost. As the last words of a poet for whom 'home' has always been a vexed category, *Beachy Head* signifies the final resting place of a peripatetic speaker, whose wanderings have figured disenfranchisement on many levels: Smith's poetic self is always outdoors, always unhoused, always seeking shelter.[3] Chained to her desk the author may have been, but her speakers have been among the more mobile of Romantic personae. In

Beachy Head, described as 'a work that begins atop a massive feature of the landscape and ends immured within it' (Curran, *Poems* xxvii), the speaker traverses a landscape littered with the remnants of history – geological, social, cultural – and populated with vagrants, of which the speaker is only the most unexpected. *Beachy Head* supports and contains its poet; the poet in turn infiltrates its structure. By the poem's conclusion, the speaker is not so much a representative of Smith as an aspect of the landscape itself.

The poem is usually read as a statement of Smith's knowledge; Judith Pascoe and Donelle Ruwe have both argued that Smith's extraordinary display of botanical knowledge both in the poem and the poem's notes amounts to a manifesto of female intellectual capability.[4] And certainly the poem functions in this way: Smith follows the structure described in chapter 1 to allow her poem to convey information descriptively (by using, for instance, the common names of flowers) while reserving a more informative, factual, authoritative voice for the notes (where she backs up common names with their Linnean classifications). This multivocality is another version of the multiple Selves Smith has continually deployed in her poetry, but it has the added benefit of encouraging a kind of learnedness; the speaker in this poem does not merely feel, but thinks as well. Indeed, as I showed in chapter 1, the speaker in the notes thinks to the extent that 'she' dismisses the accumulated authorities of leading figures in both science and art, which only makes 'her' declension into silence by the poem's end all the more significant.[5] Stuart Curran calls this Smith's 'powerful . . . impulse to resolve the self into nature' (xxvii), a resolution made possible by a display of the poet's complete knowledge about nature. Whereas Wordsworth, for instance, shows his mastery over nature by smoothing out details and creating a harmonious whole (that is, 'hardly hedgerows, little lines / Of sportive wood run wild'[6]), Smith approaches the whole as a sum of its parts, each of which deserves her full attention. Her display of botanical knowledge, then, is one way of paying attention to the parts.

But even as the poem functions to demonstrate the poet's scientific accomplishments, it also works to further the long project of Self-presentation Smith's career represents. The speaker in this poem fulfils the reader's expectation that 'she' is 'Smith',[7] revisiting the part of the country that acted as the setting for *The Emigrants* but also specifying the locale more closely: the 'stupendous summit' of the 'rock sublime' (1): both the familiar headland of Beachy Head and a defamiliarized, grand landmass in the Burkean tradition. In the same way the speaker

visits familiar scenes of sorrow ('*I once was happy*' (282)), combining a
version of the detail that characterized *The Emigrants* with a generalized
appeal to 'Memory', which here functions as much on a historical as a
personal level. Smith relies on her readership's memory to contextualize
her speaker's unhappiness, but she also conveys a sense of weariness with
her own situation, a desire to be and not to be where she is: both Selfed
and Selfless. This is conveyed initially through the poem's stylized
opening:

> On thy stupendous summit, rock sublime!
> That o'er the channel rear'd, half way at sea
> The mariner at early morning hails,*
> I would recline; while Fancy should go forth,
> And represent the strange and awful hour
> Of vast concussion;† when the Omnipotent
> Stretch'd forth his arm, and rent the solid hills,
> Bidding the impetuous main flood rush between
> The rifted shores, and from the continent
> Eternally divided this green isle.
> Imperial lord of the high southern coast!
> From thy projecting head-land I would mark
> Far in the east the shades of night disperse,
> Melting and thinned, as from the dark blue wave
> Emerging, brilliant rays of arrowy light
> Dart from the horizon; when the glorious sun
> Just lifts above it his resplendent orb.
>
>   (1–17)

I have argued elsewhere that Smith's subjunctive self-placement suggests
a certain hesitation about claiming the masculinized prospect view;[8] the
speaker's linguistic sidestep creates a double effect of absent presence that
the distinct physical details given belies. Whereas the 'I' is separated from
the 'summit' by 3 lines and 4 punctuation marks, the viewpoint attained
on the summit allows the speaker to see the Channel and visualize the
moment of 'vast concussion': effectively, to take the 'Omnipotent's' posi-
tion of overseeing the whole. Again, the speaker shelters behind grammar

---

* In crossing the Channel from the coast of France, Beachy-Head is the first land made.
† Alluding to the idea that this Island was once joined to the continent of Europe, and
torn from it by some convulsion of Nature. I confess I never could trace the resemblance
between the two countries. Yet the cliffs about Dieppe, resemble the chalk cliffs on the
Southern coast. But Normandy has no likeness whatever to the part of England opposite
to it.

when 'she' simultaneously watches the sunrise and tells us that is what
'she' 'would' do. Does 'would' function in the same conditional way? Or
is 'she' now moving towards a more intentional, directive meaning? Cer-
tainly, having revealed what 'she' 'would' have happen, the speaker goes
on to build on this: the sun rises, by line 29 reaches its 'high meridian',
and by line 72 'declines', allowing the 'early moon distinctly' to 'ris[e]'
(98). By line 99, then, a full day has passed, with the speaker apparently
still 'reclining' on the headland. If we return to the opening lines, we see
that as well as maintaining 'her' absent presence on the headland, the
speaker also appropriates the point of view of the mariner who 'hails' it,
another way of seeing all there is to see while not actually being there.
The prospect view, then, allows Smith a fluid approach to point of view;
she takes full advantage of its visual potential.[9]

Her upward movements have been unobtrusive and decorous, even
self-effacing, but the very fact that Smith achieves her eminence trans-
forms her subtle 'would' into an open claim to rightful access. Her
position translates as authority, especially linguistic; vales are invested
with vision, and fancy with sublimity: 'Fancy fondly soars, / Wandering
sublime thro' visionary vales' (85–86). This assumption of the prospect
should solidify the speaker's position as a coherent Self, but whereas in
her earlier poems Smith experimented with embodiment to create many
versions of the Self, here she seems curiously unconcerned: having taken
the trouble to manoeuvre her speaker to the eminence, and give 'her' vast
powers of observation, after line 12 the 'I' does not appear again until
line 282.[10] Instead, she gives visual power to the abstract Contemplation,
who takes over in line 117: 'Contemplation here, / High on her throne
of rock, aloof may sit' (117–118). This is, effectively, the speaker's first
sustained disguise in the poem; Contemplation, a subset of Reason,
assumes the speaker's physical placement and directive power, 'bid[ding]
recording Memory unfold / Her scroll voluminous' (119–120). In earlier
poems, when Smith turned to Memory it was to her own personal expe-
riences; here, Memory functions to usher in History in the form of the
Norman invaders (although the note attached to these lines goes back to
the Scandinavians of the eighth century; see chapter 1 for a discussion
of this note). The long history review of lines 117–166 is voiced, then,
by the speaker's proxy, Contemplation, who assumes her own form of
authority when she ignores the long note devoted to an account of
the Norman invasion and retells the story in lines 131–153. Either the
authority invested in the prospect view and putatively deposited with the
speaker is crumbling already, or Smith is investigating the very balance

of its power: although only about one-quarter of the way into the poem, Smith has already introduced at least three competing speakers: the initial 'I', Contemplation, and the note-speaker, all under the mantle of 'Mrs Smith' the author.

Contemplation is then herself replaced by the 'reflecting mind' (168), an even more evanescent persona whose confused take on 'peace and industry' dominates the next 114 lines until the reintroduction of the 'I'. The reflecting mind desires, that is, to see 'simple scenes of peace and industry', but it is able only to describe a rural life devoid of both. While the mind starts well enough, with a vision of a 'lone farm' (171) surrounded by outbuildings, it soon turns to 'the humble home / Of one, who sometimes watches on the heights' (175–176). Lest the reader begin to think of the initial speaker, who opens the poem by watching on the heights, the mind quickly distinguishes this figure as engaged in smuggling, 'quitting for this / Clandestine traffic his more honest toil' (182–183). The mind, as if realizing that this 'commerce of destruction' (190) cannot be called 'industry' in the accepted way, next presents a 'happy . . . hind', more conventionally industrious, but despite the mind's best efforts deprived of happiness. Even as the mind describes the hind and his family eking out a living 'but just remov'd from savage life' (207), it cannot envisage the hind as anything more than 'free . . . / [from] the dread that follows on illegal acts' (210–211).[11] Indeed, as this section proceeds the mind becomes increasingly desperate to find the very peace and industry it began by taking for granted, first characterizing the 'sturdy hind' as 'well content' despite the many lines of description of his deprivations (and thus coming perilously close to the very 'fabling dreams / Describing Arcady' it earlier eschewed), then asserting the 'secret care' of 'the child of Luxury', and finally giving in to despair: 'Ah! who *is* happy? Happiness! a word / That like false fire, from marsh effluvia born, / Misleads the wanderer, destin'd to contend / In the world's wilderness, with want or woe' (255–258). At this point the reader sees that the mind has been unable to find either peace or industry, and can only make a token gesture towards happiness by locating it in those too young to know 'what good or evil means' (260).

The poem's speaker has so far occupied three separate identities: a masculinized 'I', feminine Contemplation, and the gender-neutral 'mind'. Smith seems to be rehearsing personae while simultaneously exploring the possibilities available to variously gendered speakers. She is also experimenting with the notion of the Subject, the constituent parts of the Self, taking them apart so as to recombine them. This is a kind of

poetics of artifice, the baseline of which is being laid in the first third of
Beachy Head: even as Smith has made a career out of self-display while
also rigorously protecting the Self,[12] so too in this poem Smith seems to
be trying to figure out exactly what makes up the Self. Is it merely voice,
the speaking 'I'? Or is it something more to do with the act of poeticiz-
ing the 'I'? If the ' "Subject" remains in proximity to and possibly depends
upon a linguistic model, [and] the thought of literature provides the
Subject with its most immediate and exemplary self-image',[13] then it
would follow that Smith is using poetry to establish the very essence of
'Charlotte Smith' while also using poetry to question 'her' nature. Smith's
facility with language – her distinctive use of grammar in this poem, for
instance, and her reliance on the multiple meanings of words as seen in
previous chapters – constructs the linguistic model upon which she bases
the Subject, but the overall effect of the poetry is a deconstruction of the
Subject. The *Sonnets* offer multiple embodied 'I's, *The Emigrants* a
conflicted Self; *Beachy Head* builds on this to emphasize mutability and
disguise.

At this point in the poem Smith has offered personae who stand in for
each other at crucial junctures. The reintroduction of the 'I' functions in
this way, although the 'I' who now appears is less the continuation of the
masculinized prospect viewer of the poem's start than the familiar figure
of 'Charlotte Smith', sorrowful and needy. As if to make up for lost space,
this new 'I' dominates the next 100-odd lines, building a picture of the
poet nursed by Nature that has definite Wordsworthian overtones[14] even
as they continue the theme familiar to Smith's readers of a happy child-
hood followed by the 'guiltless exile' (288) of her married life. After the
'reflecting mind' has tried and failed to invoke peace and industry, and
found itself able only to lament lost happiness, the 'I' enters by focusing
attention on 'her' own childhood as the necessary link between the
mind's final images of happy but ignorant rural children. '*I* once was
happy', she begins, 'when while yet a child, / I learn'd to love these upland
solitudes, / And, when elastic as the mountain air, / To my light spirit,
care was yet unknown / And evil unforseen' (282–285). Memory as
deployed by Contemplation led to the exploration of Beachy Head's his-
torical past; now we see Memory as the personal backdrop of a persona
embodied as the Poet herself. Peace and industry finally make their
appearance as well, when the speaker reminisces about pleasant after-
noons spent watching 'the sturdy hind' (the same one as seen by the
reflecting mind?) toil with his 'panting team' up 'the hollow way' (307,
308, 305): that is, the speaker's younger self feels at peace while the hind

works industriously. The 'I' next reclaims the prospect, although indirectly; 'Advancing higher still / The prospect widens', recalls the speaker, but the 'I' has gone into temporary abeyance, and the next two stanzas fall back on describing the scene rather than inhabiting it. The prospect facilitates the visionary, but the embodied 'I' remains cautious in her self-placement, so while the reader looks down on scenes of pastoral beauty, the 'I' does not re-enter until it is safe to do so, when the speaker remembers receiving nosegays from the village women.

In this section of *Beachy Head* the landscape acts as a catalyst for the speaker, who relays her love of Nature – 'An early worshipper at Nature's shrine, / I loved her rudest scenes' (346–347) – and the benefit she derives from her memories – 'Ah! hills so early loved! in fancy still / I breathe your pure keen air' (367–368). Smith uses her speaker's enthusiasm to fill this section of the poem with detailed descriptions of the landscape (while the notes carry on supplying scientific detail and attesting to the note-speaker's reliance on personal observation for her information), but she also takes on the wider view allowed by the prospect to do two important things. First, she asserts her own power to represent 'those widely spreading views, mocking alike / The Poet and the Painter's utmost art' (370–371), in this way suggesting that her visual power somehow transcends that of mere poetry – in fact, becomes the basis for a Self-image derived from the literary process. In this way it is exactly the writing of the poetry that creates the Self who writes, even as the note-speaker conveys identity through tone and a distinct style of engagement with outside authority. Second, she springboards from detailed observation to a meditation on Science and Ambition, both represented as 'vain': Science for its self-defeating dissociation from real life, and Ambition for its inability to withstand 'the lapse of Time' (434).[15] What this suggests is that even as Smith's speaker(s) have appeared to follow a scientific regime of accurate description and historical veracity, this 'I' nonetheless believes more in personal experience than esoteric knowledge-gathering. The prospect view here serves to allow the speaker to reject its most typical intellectual stance: the disinterested, disengaged thinker. The speaker's memories, then, have reconfirmed her belief that a humane involvement with Nature encourages a more intimate understanding of the Self.

This is an attractive thought, and especially given Smith's overall rather pessimistic view of humanity and her own place within society, on its own acts as a healing metaphor for the rifts her other poetry presents. However, as with her other speakers, this 'I' now bows out. From line 369 to the poem's end, the 'I' is almost entirely absent and never again functions as an indicator of the embodied Self.[16] Instead, a disembodied descriptive narrator takes over, who offers vignettes of two hermit figures before the poem ends with the death of the second hermit. Given the intense personalism of the final poetic 'I' it is significant that Smith chooses to abandon a first-person speaker at this point. As this book has posited, Smith made a poetic career of embodying the 'I', of encouraging her readers to see the speaker as 'Charlotte Smith', and to react accordingly to the intimacy thus constructed, even when the poem itself would disavow such a close connection. But while her earlier poems have not been chary of personal details, this is the first time we have seen such an extended turn to memory. Even her invocation of memory in *The Emigrants* ushers in only twenty-five lines of reminiscing before turning to more recent woes. *Beachy Head* offers three substantial stanzas, and does not dilute their force with an ending emphasis on the present day. Smith keeps her speaking 'I' in the past – or rather, she maintains the dual perspective familiar to readers of Wordsworth: I am here, remembering, and I am there, being remembered. Her initial speaker's position on the eminence allows for a panoramic overview of her personal past, delivered in an appropriately personal way. This section of the poem has the feel of a climax. Why, then, does Smith choose to leave behind her 'I'? Why turn from an assertion of her 'Poet and . . . Painter's utmost art' (371) to a speculation as to the origin of 'the strange and foreign forms / Of sea-shells' (373–374) present as fossils on the headland?

We see that even though *Beachy Head* is written as if by a speaker highly familiar with her surroundings, the area still holds surprises, unexpected enough to startle the speaker from her memories to a consideration of what she 'observ[es]' around her (372). The 'strange and foreign' shells serve to remind the speaker of her own inherent strangeness; she has noticed them just at the point that she has found herself most deeply involved in her memory. Smith uses the word 'still', meaning 'even now', to link her speaker's memories with what she sees around her: 'in fancy still I breathe', 'and still behold', 'And still . . . wondering remark the strange and foreign forms' (368–369, 372–373). For a moment, past and present merge, and the speaker emerges from memory to find herself 'still' on the headland. Her subsequent loss of self represented by the lost 'I' indicates a poetic disenchantment with the notion of subjectivity, as if Smith is using subjectivity to critique itself. The idea that Smith may be playing with the idea of subjectivity – that she may be less concerned with establishing a speaking 'I' or exploring personal memories than with experimenting with poetic form and identity – is suggested not only by the multiple speakers she creates but also by the parallels she embeds in the poem. For even as the highly personal 'I' who has just spoken has revisited significant scenes from her past, so too the new disembodied narrator recreates those scenes while giving the starring role to figures distinctly other to 'Charlotte Smith'.

I have already noted that when Smith introduces Contemplation, she places this abstract figure in the same position her initial speaker occupied: reclining on the headland. This is the first example of a trope of parallels that runs through the poem: here, the initial speaker, then Contemplation, then the remembering 'I' described above take their successive positions atop Beachy Head, using the height thus gained to explore their chosen subjects in more depth. Each of these figures acts as an overt proxy for the author 'Mrs Smith', so that while it is interesting that the author splits her speaking self into parts, it could still be argued that those parts represent a coherent whole. But once we leave the remembering 'I' – and personal subjectivity itself – behind, we are still confronted with reclining figures. Indeed, in the middle of her reminisces, the remembering 'I' inserts a 'pensive lover of uncultur'd flowers' (359) who 'reclines' (358), albeit not on the headland itself, but in a version of the deep embowerment that the speaker of *The Emigrants* temporarily, though half-heartedly, longed for. This figure catches the eye[17] of the remembering speaker, who recounts her love of 'stroll[ing] among o'ershadowing woods of beech', the haunt, 'haply', of the 'pensive lover' (356, 358, 359). This partial parallel suggests the dramatic possibilities of multiplicity: the speaker both gazes and is the object of the gaze. The 'pensive lover' acts as a metonym for the speaker, who is thus able to fix a representation of herself even as she leaves behind her memories of the past. Thus this parallel figure occupies the same space as the speaker figuratively as well as literally, allowing the Self to expand. But since the speaker describes this figure so elliptically – it is unsexed and unbodied, and only 'haply' there at all – it also serves to emphasize the speaker's own ephemerality, and anticipates the 'strangeness' of a few lines later. Even, then, as the figure duplicates the speaker, it also indicates a loss of Self: it is both Self and Other.

Despite this figure's haziness, it does what the speaker does: luxuriates in Nature and gathers its flowers, just as the speaker devotes eight lines to describing the flowers thus collected. The next reclining figure seems much further removed from Smith or any of her speakers: 'the herdsman of the hill, / Who in some turfy knoll, idly reclined, / Watches his wether flock' (309–401). The herdsman is contrasted with the 'lone antiquary' (406) who functions as the representative of 'vain Science' (390), obsessed with the past at the expense of the present.[18] The herdsman is as unbothered by the history that underpins Beachy Head as the antiquary is excited by it; given that the poem spends most of its time uncovering the headland's various forms of history it is interesting that Smith seems to ally her speaker(s) more with the unreflecting herdsman than with the antiquary. Why spend most of the poem establishing the importance of history if, in the end, a kind of 'wise passiveness' is best after all? Smith exacerbates the confusion when she introduces her final reclining figure, the poem's first hermit: 'the tir'd hind / Pass'd him at nightfall, wondering he should sit / On the hill top so late' (514–516). Again, Smith proliferates her figures: the previous recliner *was* the hind, who now views another recliner clearly in the position of Smith's original speaker, out on the hilltop until all hours. A circle seems to have been closed, but somewhere an identity has been lost, or at least called into question. These three reclining figures have replicated the initial speaker's position, each successively higher up the hill: the pensive lover of flowers in the woods, then the herdsman on the knoll, and now the hermit on the hilltop. The higher we have climbed the closer the identification between the recliner and the first speaker, to the point that the hermit is also viewed by the same smugglers the initial speaker described at the poem's start (316–319). And yet the hermit is not a sympathetic figure; he is viewed with 'suspicious doubt' by the smugglers and even the sympathetic 'village maidens' consider 'his senses injur'd' (318, 320).

Smith seems to be playing with the notion of identity and selfhood with these parallel reclining figures, but more than that she seems to be undermining her own self-construction. While it is one thing to devolve the Self into Contemplation and a reflecting mind, it is quite another subsequently to take on the personae of an unreflecting herdsman[19] and an at best lunatic / at worst sinister hermit. She does something similar when she rewrites Contemplation ('high on her throne of rock') as Ambition, by inference also high enough to 'behold the nothingness of all / For which you carry thro' the oppressed Earth, / War, and its train of horrors' (420–422). This parallel is established less through placement than through Smith's association of images with each abstract: both Contemplation and Ambition survey a martial history beginning with the Danes, but where Contemplation oversaw a triumphal march from antiquity through to present-day Britain, Ambition presides over a dark landscape of savage war. The speaker goes so far as to ignore her earlier incarnation's display of knowledge when she states that the savages of history 'slee[p] unremember'd here' and that 'All, with the lapse of Time, have passed away' (428, 434) – another reminder of the differences between this disembodied speaker and the embodied 'I' who opened the poem. The very knowledge that one speaker displays with pride, another rejects with disgust.[20] Even the ability to engage imaginatively with faraway lands and draw moral conclusions, as the initial speaker displays when she looks more closely at the contents of the 'ship of commerce' (40 passim), is called into question when we note that the hermit 'nurs[es] dreams' and 'follows them in thought' to the same faraway lands – but uncritically and unreflectively. Given the parallels of placement, and the unsettling association of Contemplation and Ambition, Smith seems to be problematizing both the putative gains represented by the prospect view, and the high moral ground her first speaker staked out.

Smith's parade of speakers in *Beachy Head* work to call into question the viability of an authoritative, disengaged 'I'. The fact that she disembodies her speaker after the retreat to memory suggests that the act of remembering – that is, putting together – a version of the Self acts more to destabilize than to establish Selfhood. Her devolution of the Self into myriad constructed selves dramatizes the difficulty of sustaining the Self through poetry. But it is more than mere Selfhood; it is also the social self that is being investigated. Smith's first speaker situates 'herself' on the 'stupendous summit' of Beachy Head, a claiming of the prospect view with subversive undertones if we sex the speaker as female. Smith encourages this with her subsequent turn to a feminized Contemplation, but deconstructs this gendered edifice with all her following speakers, none of whom are overtly sexed – not even the remembering 'I', who takes on an identity only because of Smith's public, personal history. So is the speaker a female body challenging the cultural association of women with humility and 'lowliness'? Or is the speaker a male body assuming his usual place on the eminence? Or, is Smith relying on the fluidity of her speakers, their interchangeable positions and the suggestive nature of their parallel placements and images, to play with social identity and escape a fixed definition of the self? In this way, the point becomes the possibilities that poetry affords Subjectivity. Although Smith writes *Beachy Head* so as to avoid the assignment of an ultimate subjective 'I', she also builds into the poem an engagement with poetry as a public form of expression, and an awareness that to be read is to be, on one level at least, assimilated. When she mocks the lone antiquary, then, or portrays her hermit as an ineffectual dreamer, she is both undercutting the poetic authority her initial speaker claimed and offering a public critique of a certain kind of poetic disengagement.

Up to now I have emphasized how Smith's parallels work to call into question her own speakers: that is, Smith writes speakers whose pretensions are punctured by the poetry itself. But these images also work extramurally, furthering in *Beachy Head* conversations and scenarios that began in the 1790s. I noted in the last chapter that when Wordsworth writes of the 'five long years' that have passed between his visits to the Wye Valley, he echoes Smith's language of the passage of time in the opening to Book II of *The Emigrants*. In this section of the chapter I want to look at how Smith, in *Beachy Head*, seems to answer Wordsworth's appropriation of her imagery, creating personae that echo those offered by Wordsworth in, especially, *Lyrical Ballads*. But first it is worth repeating how 'Wordsworthian' the 'remembering I' is; her description of herself as 'an early worshipper at Nature's shrine' (346) and the general trajectory of this section of the poem have a strong flavour of 'Tintern Abbey'. The 'remembering I' revisits the scenes of her youth, engaging in a 'Tintern'-like application of the past to the present, allowing Memory to lead her through a version of Wordsworth's 'glad animal movements' ('elastic as the mountain air' 'I loved her rudest scenes', 284, 347), the language of the sense ('I loved to trace the brooks . . .', 354), and finally the 'deep interfusion' that occurs when the speaker momentarily merges the past and the present (the layers of observation linked by 'still', 368–374). But she is not merely replicating Wordsworth's creative trajectory; where Wordsworth constructs a speaker who clearly prefers his present state of being to his past incarnations, Smith's speaker compresses her past stages so that no one is privileged over the other, although any seems better than the 'now'. Smith's speaker chooses a loss of subjectivity (the loss of the 'I' discussed above) over the painful existence of the present day: she is unable to accept that intellectual power is 'abundant recompense' for what has been destroyed.[21] Just as tellingly, she is unable to sustain a belief in memory at all; where Wordsworth's speaker infuses his surroundings with his own enthusiasm and thereby enlivens and recreates it, Smith's can only retreat to an observational appreciation of her surroundings. It is hard to know if Smith is responding to Wordsworth with this section, but it is suggestive given their twinned approach to imagery and the language of the Self in

Nature, their certain knowledge of each other's work, and the homage
'Tintern' had already paid to *The Emigrants*.[22] For Smith's speaker, unlike
Wordsworth's, it is her attachment to vision and sensation that allows
her to recreate her past in poetry; she feels no need to subordinate or
demonize the 'tyranny of the eye' and substitute 'something far more
deeply interfused' ('Tintern Abbey' 96). Wordsworth's famous inexact-
ness becomes, in the 'remembering I''s rubric, as much an indication of
uncertainty and confusion as a sign of completed poetic maturation.

But Smith goes further in her engagement with Wordsworth. In delin-
eating her speakers' reactions to nature and culture, she often rewrites
Wordsworth's, challenging his creation of a hierarchy of perception with
her own description of a spectrum of experience. Throughout the poem-
proper, she alludes to a variety of Wordsworth's poems in a way that is
both restrained and oblique: she never names names but relies on her
readers' knowledge of his poems to make her point (even as she relies on
her readers' memories of her own past oeuvre). Smith's speakers depend
on indirection and hints, and because Smith openly concentrates on
building a poetic version of Beachy Head from its bottommost layers up
to 'herself' reclining on its headland, images of Wordsworth take their
place among the other aspects of the headland's history that she draws
in: fossils, its importance to past invaders, its security for present smug-
glers, its natural beauty. The result is that Wordsworth, too, is buried in
Beachy Head. But, as with her fossils, botany, geology and history, Smith
uncovers enough of her fellow poet to allow her readers a glimpse of his
work, especially that from 1798. There are several brief allusions: the
'fleet of fishing vessels' and the 'dubious spot' of the 'ship of commerce'
recall 'With Ships the Sea was Sprinkled' (36–44), while 'The Last of the
Flock' crops up when the initial speaker describes the hind whose 'few
sheep, / His best possession, with his children share / The rugged shed
when wintry tempests blow' (197–199).[23]

Later in the poem, and more to the point, Smith's by now disembod-
ied speaker invokes 'Lines left upon a Seat in a Yew-Tree' when recount-
ing the story of the first hermit: 'But near one ancient tree, whose
wreathed roots / Form'd a rude couch, love-songs and scatter'd rhymes,
/ Unfinish'd sentences, or half erased, / and rhapsodies like this, were
sometimes found' (573–577). The rhapsody then presented contains
imagery reminiscent of 'To My Sister': 'Oh! Could I hear your soft voice
there, / And see you in the forest green / All beauteous as you are, more
fair / You'd look, amid the sylvan scene, / And in a wood-girl's simple
guise, / Be still more lovely in mine eyes' (643–648). This song is

'composed' not by the disembodied speaker, but by a pastiche version of Wordsworth's solitary, introspective country hermits, echoing both his speakers and the persona he offers to his readers as genuine and sincere. This hermit, who leaves lines of poetry 'scatter'd' about 'one ancient tree' (574, 573) and who wanders the public way alone at night (566–572), is identical to the subjects of many of Wordsworth's poems. The second hermit, based, Smith's note tells us, on 'Parson Darby' who lived for many years in a cave under the cliff of Beachy Head, has rejected society because 'his heart / Was feelingly alive to all that breath'd' but who 'still acutely felt / For human misery' (687–691). Again, we recognize a portrait first painted by Wordsworth in 'Lines': where the first hermit does what Wordsworth's subject does, the second hermit acts from the same motives. Even as Smith celebrates these hermits for their piety and their model behaviour, she reproaches them too: the one through a subtle dissection of his naive idealism, the other through death. It would seem that being a Wordsworthian solipsist cannot be sustained.

However, even though the allusions to Wordsworth's work and his poetic preoccupations suggests that Smith to a certain extent reacts to what is becoming his poetic prominence, he is only one of the poem's targets. In its deconstruction of the logic of subjectivity, *Beachy Head* follows a poetics of self-critique. The hermits may well refer to outside examples, but they also carry on the parallels discussed earlier and so implicate Smith's speakers as well. I have already noted that both Smith's initial speaker and the first hermit visit 'distant climes' 'in thought' (albeit for different reasons); Smith also connects her remembering I to this hermit when they both lounge on the hilltop, viewed by passing hinds ('sturdy' to the I, and 'tir'd' to the hermit). And although her embodied personae never rescue stray sheep and drowning men as does the 'hermit of the rocks', both the hermit and the 'remembering I' are 'feelingly alive' to 'human crimes' (the phrase is used in both lines 440 and 690), a phrasing that suggests a close link in outlook. This trope of duplication effectively links all of Smith's speakers even as the poem equally effectively separates them; what is being highlighted through parallels is, again, disengagement and separation from the social world, and whereas in her earlier poetry Smith seemed to prefer, even require, such disengagement, in *Beachy Head* it comes under subtle critique. The Wordsworthian hermit, the prospect viewer, the speaker lost in the past, all inhabit a world the solitary nature of which militates against self-knowledge and self-improvement. It would seem that in her last major poem Smith advances a poetics of engagement – or at least she begins to disavow her earlier emphases on alienation, isolation and marginalization. By devolving her speakers into personae whose constructedness is clear, and by overtly inhabiting differently sexed bodies, Smith clarifies the theatricality that has been an element of her poetry all along, and she does so in order to illuminate the potential use-value poetry can have. It can be used merely to aid introspection; on the other hand, it can go even further than *The Emigrants* did and begin to offer instruction not only on a political level via the personal, but a personal level via the social.

It is not only her *Beachy Head* personae that Smith critiques. The poem seems to offer Smith the opportunity to revisit many of her previous poetic positions, most especially those dramatized in the *Sonnets*. As chapters 2 and 3 established, Smith uses the sonnets to construct mannered speakers whose identity rests on the public recognition of who 'Charlotte Smith' is, but who also escape definition through a theatrical reliance on disguise and ventriloquism. No matter how firmly Smith embodies her speakers, she also writes sonnets that problematize the very nature of that embodying – that cross-dress, for instance, or 'pass'. In the end, the sonnets posit a world in which identity just slips away at the moment of seeming fixedness, so the mother can be a lover, or the speaker the addressee. This creates a poetics of the liminal, the unknowable, that Smith seems to privilege; her speakers 'stray' and do so without admonishment. But in *Beachy Head*, as I have been suggesting, such straying seems more by habit than supported by the author; even as her personae exile themselves from an uncaring and criminal society, they are also subtly critiqued through the very vehicle of poetry: and so parallels and duplications call into question the viability of deliberate alienation and isolation.[24] It is not difficult to call to mind sonnet situations that anticipate the variety of positions taken by *Beachy Head* speakers: the initial 'I', for instance, who explores a headland not unlike that in Sonnet LXX, 'On being cautioned against walking on an headland'. Or the 'remembering I' and 'her' counterparts the hermits, wandering 'cheerless and unblest' as does the speaker in Sonnet LXII, 'Written on passing by moonlight through a village'. Or the second hermit, spending his time 'on some rude fragment of the rocky shore' as does the speaker in Sonnet XII, 'Written on the sea shore'. The situations the *Beachy Head* personae find themselves in resonate with earlier Smithian self-placements, but without the implicit approval given by the earlier Smith. Because so much of *Beachy Head* seems to call into question the use-value of the wandering which has been the *raison d'être* of her previous incarnations, the poem's inherent questioning of the nature of subjectivity begins to resemble a trial wherein Smith begins to judge, not society, but her own poetic output.

As I discussed above, Smith's use of authoritative positions in the poem, such as the prospect view, are undermined when she juxtaposes speakers to an almost satirical effect. Similarly, she seems to set up such situations only so that they may be undercut by a poet whose patience with her own unhappiness has run out. The personal nature of the memories in the poem's middle section, and the return to an 'I' whose sorrows need now only a kind of shorthand redaction to be wholly familiar, colour the entire poem with a personalized tone, so that an I is an eye is an I. But as I hope to have made clear, the competing personae that Smith constructs loosen the hold the personal has on the poem, allowing a space for authorial critique to emerge. In revisiting the main aspects of a poetic personality maintained over more than twenty years, Smith reconstructs her own canon, condensing her poetic selves to their most recognizable aspects. This kind of representation effectively emphasizes how much of Smith's personal tone has been dramatized, something the sonnets with their role-playing hinted at but kept at least as an open secret due to Smith's intense efforts at embodiment. But the subterranean irony in *Beachy Head* is the literal death of the author – embodiment is rendered a useless exercise and, as if Smith anticipates this, she writes her speakers out of existence, concentrating on their theatrical assumptions of each others' characteristics, roles, placements and back stories. If the speakers in *Beachy Head* are reincarnations of all Smith's previous personae, and if their viability is undermined by the writer herself, then a reappraisal of such personae is inevitable. What emerges is a stronger sense of performance than ever before, as the speakers play not only themselves, but each other, and the previous generation as well.

All along Smith's poetry has had a strong flavour of the theatrical, even when the figure 'Charlotte Smith' has seemed at her most sincere. But the techniques at work in *Beachy Head* extrapolate this theatricality to another level: it becomes a kind of self-critique. The 'dress' of the personae is made obvious, which in turn allows both the assumption of different forms of dress and the inference that dress itself must have a purpose. To return briefly to the prospect view: I suggested earlier that Smith's initial persona assumes the prospect view, and that this could be seen both as a female act of subversion and a male act of right. That the prospect does not lend its usual aid in achieving far sight and wisdom begins to deconstruct the value of the eminence. But in light of the poem's overall reliance on performance, this initial claim also situates the prospect as just another form of costume. This extends to the cross-sexing her personae engage in; speaking as a feminine 'remembering I' or through the portrayal of a Wordsworthian hermit are less political acts than poetic ones. Smith demonstrates for her readers the absolute fluidity of identity, as well as its artificiality, when she builds into the poem such an array of proliferating personalities. And this may be the most important aspect of her newly social mission: whereas in earlier poems her manipulations of identities and genders seemed mainly to critique, in this poem they seem more geared towards an attempt to understand how and why the social – the multiple – self exists.

This brings us back to the necessity of authority, for although the poem refuses to endorse the kind of disengaged authority that characterizes the reflecting mind, for instance, it nonetheless relies on two distinct forms: the amassed authority that supports the various images of the speakers contained in the Notes, and the overarching authority of the poem's architect, Smith herself. The latter keeps the poem under control, maintains the integrity of the parallels, even feels confident enough to mock her own poetic pretensions when she builds into the first hermit's song a quaint self-reflexivity that metonymically reproduces *Beachy Head* itself: 'Let us to woodland wilds repair / While yet the glittering night-dews seem / To wait the freshly-breathing air, / Precursive of the morning beam, / That rising with advancing day, / Scatters the silver drops away' (577–582). The hermit's rhapsody parodies the tone and substance of *Beachy Head*, especially in its use of common botanical details that are then illuminated in the Notes' precise style. Keeping in mind how the hermit also reproduces aspects of the 'remembering I', he seems to function both as emblem and distortion of the Poet. His problematic duality is not resolved in the poem; Smith merely leaves him behind to 'cherish his ideal bliss – / For what is life, when Hope has ceas'd to strew / Her fragile flowers along its thorny way? / And sad and gloomy are his days, who lives, / Of Hope abandon'd!' (667–671). Given that Smith has written most of her sonnets and other poetry from the point of view of one who 'lives of Hope abandon'd', the hermit's position as proxy 'Charlotte Smith' grows more complex. Indeed, as this chapter has discussed, within the body of the poem Smith actively disallows closure and resolution, introducing new speakers on the heels of old ones, practically mid-sentence. Her desire to destabilize a unified subjectivity means that in the poem, authority is ceded to variety.

However, as argued in chapter 1, the notes to this poem offer a consistent, confident speaker whose character is all the more significant where the poem's speakers are so fragmented.[25] While the poem explores the very nature of subjectivity and playfully cross-sexes speakers and vantage points, the notes maintain integrity; even the gradual style of the earlier poems' notes (increasing confidence as the poem goes on) is here dispensed with. Their combination of botanical, historical, geological and personal history is delivered throughout so as to establish the note-speaker's knowledge in the face of the poem-speakers' disintegration. In a letter to Joseph Johnson, who published her last volume, Smith acknowledges the current 'fashion of the day, to print the notes at the end', and tells Johnson that 'In this instance they would be rather numerous, because of historical biographal [sic] & local facts relative to Beachy, & and the Coast'.[26] Her turn towards 'facts' suggests that for her, the notes provide essentially unimpeachable information; printing them at the end of the volume allows her poetry to conclude forcefully and authoritatively.[27] The 'real' speaker of *Beachy Head*, then, resides 'behind' it, or even 'in' it: the voice whose knowledge cannot be challenged and whose personality does not change. It is striking that although the 'I' appears in many of the notes, which suggests personal knowledge and experience as well as a genuine writing Self, Smith does not offer any personal information in any of these notes. The 'I' only exists to attest to something that is known or unknown: 'I can find no species of sea bird of which this is the vulgar name' (n. to 113); 'I imagine that not even [the orchards] of Herefordshire, or Worcestershire, exhibit a more beautiful prospect' (n. to 314); 'It is now many years since I made these observations' (n. to 375); 'I had often heard of the elephant's bones at Burton, but never saw them' (n. to 412); '[The Night Hawk] was intended to be described in the Forty-Second Sonnet. I was mistaken in supposing it as visible in November . . .' (n. to 514). Even the last reference to the *Sonnets* is made passively, as if the speaker divorces herself from authorship of the poems. While in the notes to her earlier poems Smith had allowed personal information to be conveyed – about her politics, for instance, in *The Emigrants*[28] – the note-speaker in *Beachy Head* is concerned only with information, with facts.

Her dispassionate tone, matched with the poem's implicit critique of the 'remembering I', suggests that in her last poem Smith is attempting to create a new persona, one who is impatient with the vagaries of poetic emotion, who is unconcerned with the personal – who desires to narrate the stories of others for the edification of her readers rather than return-

ing compulsively to her own. This signals the new turn to the social mentioned earlier in the chapter, what Zimmerman calls her 'new role' as 'a
mediating figure'.[29] No longer basing her subjectivity on the Self, Smith
can open up subjectivity as a construct in her poem, and even critique
poetic subjectivity and its pretensions in her prosaic notes: 'poets have
never been botanists' (n. to 591), an aside that as easily plays against the
Poet as for her.[30] In this way, in *Beachy Head* Smith can be both Self and
Other (and, in her partial incarnation as the second hermit, both alive
and dead): a poetic freeing of the Self and a letting go, through reassignments both voice- and gender-based, of poetic concerns and identities. Gender operates here as a mask or a costume for the body that is
itself ceded to pure voice, the final disembodied 'I' of the notes. In *Beachy
Head*, the profusion of voices that allow Smith to gently mock the
hermits who are also versions of her previous selves, both in this and her
earlier poems, undoes the apparent sincerity with which she maintained
her embodied identity throughout her poetic career and makes plain the
performative nature of her self-presentation.

　　Beachy Head thus represents a compilation of Smith's multivocal self-
presentations. Poetry and a variety of histories intermix, even as she also
keeps them separate. *Beachy Head* embodies a hybrid poetry, where facts
are grafted onto verse, where history takes on different guises depending
on its placement. Smith is not content to speak in only one voice; after
a twenty-year career and a public reputation as poet and novelist and
children's writer and possibly even playwright, she seems to propose, in
Beachy Head, the creation of a composite poem based on and around an
experimental self-questioning, self-supporting chorus of voices. Beachy
Head juts out to sea; the poet reclines on its edge; the poem recreates its
surface, its depth, its inhabitants; the notes embody the knowledge
necessary to comprehend all the facets of Beachy and its composition
(and I use the word in all its meanings). Smith constructs her voices
according to the space they inhabit in the text, and she ends her poem
by metaphorically joining the margin and its enclosed centre. Her
vignette of the second hermit allows her to situate the text of *Beachy
Head on,* or even *in* Beachy Head: the poem ends 'Those who read / Chisel'd within the rock, these mournful lines, / Memorials of his sufferings,
did not grieve, / That dying in the cause of charity / His spirit, from its
earthly bondage freed, / Had to some better region fled for ever'
(726–731). *Beachy Head*, we are told in its Advertisement and as I noted
at the beginning of this chapter, 'is not completed to the original design.
That the increasing debility of its author has been the cause of its being

left in an imperfect state, will it is hoped be a sufficient apology' (*Poems* 215). And yet the poem's coherence and its deliberate plotting of structure, its inhabitants as well as its habitability, suggest otherwise. Smith's final lines may well refer to some part of the poem she did not complete, but their significance redounds onto the poet herself, and her poem. The text is 'chisel'd within the rock', and as such joins the poem and its speakers inside the landmass of Beachy.[31]

Beachy Head was unfinished because the 'increasing debility' of the author led to her death, and as such it is a posthumous statement of her self-placement in the landscape, of poetry, history and authority. Smith's final statement of self and poetry protrudes into unfinished space, and her last footnote retreats to the impersonal, identifying the 'dark porpoise' as, properly, '*Delphinus phocoena*'. Smith's own 'dark purpose' remains in shadow, but her persona reaches out to encompass the poem and its environs. She occupies Beachy Head, claiming squatter's rights and asserting her creative ownership. Having spent her poetic career in search of suitable accommodation, Smith portrays in *Beachy Head* speakers who reject culture, history and society: versions of herself, given finally a resting place by a poet who joins her hermits in creating Beachy Head as private property. She begins the poem on the headland, devotes much of its body to exploring Beachy's innards, and concludes her investigation under its overhanging cliff. We have gone in search of a poet, and have found instead a most appropriate memorial: one that dramatizes disguise, infiltrates and fragments subjectivity, and assumes and discards aspects of identity as easily as the costuming they are. In her very willingness to speak in different voices, Smith demonstrates the loose association of voice and body in a culture only too eager to tighten it.

Notes

1 See *The Poems of Charlotte Smith*, ed. Stuark Curran (Oxford: Oxford University Press, 1993), xxvii.

2 Letter to Mr Shirly, 22 August 1789, quoted in Rufus Paul Turner, Charlotte Smith (1749–1806): New Light on her Life and Literary Career (unpub. PhD diss., University of Southern California, 1966), 161.

3 For an excellent discussion of the Romantic wanderer, see Celeste Langan, *Romantic Vagrancy: Wordsworth and the Simulation of Freedom* (Cambridge: Cambridge University Press, 1995).

4 See Judith Pascoe, 'Female Botanists and the Poetry of Charlotte Smith',

Re-Visioning Romanticism: British Women Writers 1776–1837, eds. Carol Shiner Wilson and Joel Haefner (Philadelphia: University of Pennsylvania Press, 1994), 193–209; and Donelle Ruwe, 'Charlotte Smith's Sublime: Feminine Poetics, Botany, and *Beachy Head*', *Prism(s)* 7 (1999), 117–132.

5 Given the poem's fragment status, however, this may be a structural requirement; see below. I use quotation marks when referring to the poem's speaker since, as in many of the *Sonnets*, the sexed identity of the speaker is continually called into question.

6 'Tintern Abbey', 15–16.

7 This is enhanced, of course, by the 'Advertisement', which asserts Smith's presence by describing her absence: 'the admired author is now unconscious of . . . praise or censure' but her last poems 'bear the most unquestionable evidence of the same undiminished genius, spirit, and imagination, which so imminently distinguished her former productions' (*Poems* 215). The poems, then, act as representatives of the poet's intellectual qualities; they are the ultimate stand-in.

8 See Jacqueline M. Labbe, *Romantic Visualities: Landscape, Gender and Romanticism* (Basingstoke: Macmillan, 1998), 29–30.

9 By contrast, when Smith uses the prospect in *The Emigrants* she emphasizes more its affiliation with margins and edges; she overlooks the emigrants but is also one with them.

10 That is, in the poem-proper. In the notes, the 'I' reappears as early as the note to line 113, in referencing the sea snipe. In this note Smith begins to challenge authority, but here it is only that of 'sailors', whose use of the phrase Smith's note-self cannot justify: 'I can find no species of sea bird of which this is the vulgar name' (221). Interestingly, however, the poem's speaker blithely uses the term regardless of the note-speaker's unease.

11 In a parenthesis, the mind calls this 'scenes all unlike the poet's fabling dreams / Describing Arcady' (209–210). In fact, the mind attempts to speak with the real language of men.

12 To this end, Smith seems to have desired to hide her authorial identity in life, even though she used so many personal incidents in her poetry. Turner notes that 'Mrs Smith very often preferred to conceal her identity as a writer', asking her publishers Cadell and Davies to withhold her address from enquirers and requesting her friends to address letters to plain 'Mrs Smith' (167). This supports my argument that Smith's construction of the Self in her poetry was based on a strategy of artifice rather than on undisciplined revelations.

13 Marc Redfield, 'Romanticism, *Bildung*, and the Literary Absolute', *Lessons of Romanticism*, eds. Thomas Pfau and Robert F. Gleckner (Durham: Duke University Press, 1998), 41–54: 45.

14 Indeed, so strong is the Wordsworthian flavour that a student recently identified with great confidence a passage from this section of *Beachy Head* as coming from Wordsworth's *Two-Part Prelude*.

15 Sarah Zimmerman suggests that the 'lone antiquary' who makes a brief appearance as a representative of vain Science acts as 'Smith's alter-ego in the poem, a figure who collects artefacts . . . as the poet recalls the natural historical events such evidence indicates' (*Romanticism, Lyricism and History* (Buffalo: SUNY Press, 1999), 65). However, Zimmerman overlooks Smith's multiple speakers in the poem and overestimates the importance of the antiquary, who does not appear again. Rather, the antiquary functions as the antitype to the 'I' who speaks these lines, and who is concerned with connecting the past and the present rather than simply cataloguing the past.

16 The notes, however, continue to use the 'I' frequently and forcefully almost until the poem's end.

17 Given the parallel self-placements, of course, it could also be said that this figure catches the 'I' as well.

18 Although the entire poem of *Beachy Head* is itself dependent upon an exploration of the headland's past functions, nonetheless Smith seems to suggest a difference between her approach and the antiquary's: he 'loves to contemplate' 'times remote' (408, 406) only, without reference to the present day: a useless and esoteric enterprise. Smith uses words like 'doubtfully', 'perhaps' and 'fancy' (that is, dream or imagine) to emphasize his ineffectualness. See note 15.

19 Although at one point in her poem Smith attempts to show the hardships of the rustic life, and to portray with sympathy its impoverishment, she nonetheless also follows the common literary shorthand that rustic equals a kind of simplemindedness. And yet her approach to class is not always unreconstructed, as the character of Monimia in her 1793 novel *The Old Manor House* makes clear: the illegitimate Monimia is never given a noble parent, and spends the novel pure, good, resourceful and intelligent – and of working-class origin (although her marriage to Orlando gives her honorary membership in the gentry). See Charlotte Smith, *The Old Manor House*, ed. Labbe (Peterborough: Broadview Press, 2002).

20 As ever, the footnote speaker does not conform to this development; indeed, even the suspect lone antiquary is supported by a very long note detailing the excavation of elephant's bones, concluding with the note-speaker's usual turn to her own authoritative experience.

21 It is possible that Wordsworth's speaker also feels ambivalent about his choice; the subjunctive 'I would believe' that modifies his declaration of 'abundant recompense' carries with it as much doubt as conviction (87, 88).

22 It is my contention that between them, Smith and Wordsworth created what we now describe as 'Romantic' poetry; their similarities of approach, style, imagery and subjectivities go beyond the coincidental. It is, however, beyond the scope of this book to do more than assert their joint responsibility for Romanticism.

23 An intriguing clue that Wordsworth read and absorbed *Beachy Head* lies in line 649, in the middle of the first hermit's song to his beloved: 'Ye phantoms

of unreal delight / Visions of fond delirium born!' he laments. One notes that
Beachy Head was published in 1807, the same year as Wordsworth's 'She was
a phantom of delight'.

24 The flip side is that Smith's technique also calls into question the very nature
of poetic interpretation, as I have hinted when speculating on the double-
gendering going on in her use of the prospect view.

25 That Smith writes fragmented personae in a poem itself deemed 'incomplete'
allows an interesting interaction between structure and content and suggests
another way in which the poem is more 'finished' than it may seem.

26 Letter to Johnson, 12 July 1806, in Turner, 'Charlotte Smith (1749–1806)',
159–160.

27 Smith's wording suggests that she may have been in favour of printing the
notes as footnotes rather than endnotes. Doing so would have created a firm
foundation for the edifice of *Beachy Head* and would have allowed her know-
ledge to stand as its deepest layer.

28 See the note to Book I: 346.

29 Sarah Zimmerman, 'Charlotte Smith's Letters and the Practice of Self-
Presentation', *Princeton University Library Chronicle* 53 (1991), 50–77: 77.

30 In chapter 1, of course, I argue that in this note in particular Smith estab-
lishes herself as an authority against those more established, and male, such
as Shakespeare.

31 As Loraine Fletcher phrases it, 'the sense is that the whole poem is inscribed
inside the empty cave'. See *Charlotte Smith: A Critical Biography* (Basingstoke:
Macmillan, 1998): 335.

Coda

Smith, poetry, Romanticism

Smith's poetic career began in what has traditionally been identified as the 'pre-Romantic' period[1] and ended as Wordsworth was securing his reputation as an experimental poet of a new kind of poetry, one that privileged the personal voice and encouraged the development of subjectivity through poetry. But Smith is more than simply a peripheral voice to Wordsworth's, or a sidenote in the development of Romanticism, or even one of the most important women writers of her time. In her ongoing poetic project she explores the ways in which poetry can be used to establish notions of the self and cultural identity, especially the culture of gender that insists that women and men are best distinguished by a set of behavioural norms. In her poetry she capitalizes on this expectation by creating idealized versions of feminine selves, most especially the mother and the woman in need, but she also allows her speakers to take on aspects of masculinity as well: the prospect viewer, or the solitary. In doing so, she increasingly shows the transparency of such roles, and their status *as* roles: the performative nature of gender constructions becomes more and more apparent, until, by the end of her career, her poetry depends on both the familiarity and artificiality of her previous poetic self-constructions. Underlying her poetic corpus is the embodied author that she devoted much energy to building up; through images, prefaces, marginal matter, and above all with the revelation of personal details that reassured readers that the 'I' they read was indeed a real person rather than the poetic manifestation of a skilled and imaginative writer. Because of the strength and persistence of this embodied 'I', even modern readers, myself included, have been prone to see Smith's poetic speaker(s) as more or less unmediated versions of Charlotte Smith herself. And once this has happened, then poems in which the 'I' acts within an engendered character become kinds of manifestos of feminist resistance. In this book, I have tried to negotiate what I recognize is a tricky terrain, because while I believe that Smith is a highly politicized writer, and well aware of the limitations her culture places on women, and women writers in particular, I also want to avoid pigeonholing her as a 'woman writer'. To do so suggests that everything that Smith writes emanates from her position as an embodied female, in thrall to her own cultural positioning. And yet, Smith's poetry shows instead a writer able to play with gender as simply another aspect of identity, and by extension suggests a more self-conscious society than we have often wanted to admit.

While much of Smith's poetry can be read, then, as exemplifying a certain kind of female style and content, much can also be read as eminently, traditionally Romantic – which is another way of saying that it conveys nothing so much as the voice of the masculine. That voice, derived as it is mainly from the work of Wordsworth, has gained its gendering from that derivation – and hence Wordsworth has, for instance, colonized or co-opted the feminine at those poetic points when his cultural masculinity has seemed in abeyance.[2] But the coherence of the edifice of gendered poetics becomes shaky at best if we reinsert Smith as, at the least, Wordsworth's co-creator of a familiar Romantic poetics of subjectivity, nature, the imagination, and the formation of identity, for if they are both speaking the same language, then attempts to gender it according to the sex of the speaker become as artificial and imposed as gender itself. Wordsworth does not work nearly as hard as Smith to embody his poetic speaker, beyond suggesting frequently that the I who speaks, the I who writes, and the eye that sees are interchangeable. But his strategy of *suggestion* as effectively as Smith's more overt designations attaches his poetry to his real body, so that the growth of the poet's mind is taken at face value, even though Wordsworth plays with subjectivities every bit as much as Smith.[3] If we accord Smith the significance in Romantic studies that she deserves – not simply as a 'woman writer', but as a central figure – then we must also reexamine our critical responses to the workings of gender in the Romantic period, and question the binaries that have grown up in the formative stages of gender criticism.

Smith's own playfulness over her public persona as the sorrowful, needy, maternal figure is not confined to her 'serious' poetry. Her poetry for children acts as a kind of pantomime version, offering the familiar storylines in a didactic setting that is simultaneously pedantic and tongue-in-cheek. In *Conversations Introducing Poetry, Chiefly on Subjects of Natural History for the Use of Children and Young Persons* (1804), Smith redirects the botanical and historical knowledge already apparent in the sonnets and *The Emigrants* towards a putatively more impressionable audience; as Stuart Curran points out, the poems 'are very much directed to child's needs and levels of comprehension, with the poems serving as mnemonic devices for retaining information and as instruments of moral and ecological education'.[4] But such is the style of the poems that the well-versed Smith reader may also wonder for what else the poems serve as mnemonic devices. The very first poem, 'To a green-chafer, on a white rose', introduces the insect as a kind of fairy-tale princess: 'You dwell within a lovely bower, / Little chafer, gold and green, / Nestling in the fairest flower, / The rose of snow, the garden's queen' (1–4). The images of feminine purity, however, are not sustained through the poem; by line 7 the insect's body is called a 'corselet', glossed by the text's narrator Mrs Talbot as 'taken from the French word for armour, which was worn to cover the body in battle' (Curran, 179, n. to line 7). This inevitably introduces the masculine – or at least compromises the frailty and fragility of the opening images – which is then made overt when the narrator chastizes the insect: 'But do not wound the flower so fair / That shelters you in sweet repose. / Insect! be not like him who dares / On pity's bosom to intrude, / And then that gentle bosom tears / With baseness and ingratitude' (11–16). The calm, fairytale opening has given way to a typical Smithian outburst, conveyed via a typically fluid application of gendered characteristics and costuming.

It is interesting how consistently the simplest poems in *Conversations* conclude with negative and violent imagery. 'A walk by the water' directs the child-reader's attention to the myriad movements of fish; the first four stanzas are almost wholly descriptive, until the last line of stanza four: the fish 'shun with fear our near approach. / Do not dread us, timid fishes, / We have neither net nor hook; / Wanderers we, whose only wishes / Are to read in nature's book' (16–20). Similarly, 'Invitation to the bee' has a Blake-like tone of innocence, with a child-speaker who admires the bee's industry, but even Blake does not shift to Experience as jarringly: 'Yet fear not when the tempests come, / And drive thee to thy waxen home, / That I shall then most treacherously / For thy honey murder thee' (37–40). 'The hedgehog seen in a frequented path' is warned against 'man or thoughtless boy' who would 'thy quiet harmless life destroy' and advised to 'fly from the cruel; know than they / Less fierce are ravenous beasts of prey' (1, 2, 19–20). 'The early butterfly' is mourned for its 'unexperienc'd rashness' that leads to its death, while 'The moth' is called an 'insect suicide' and its death dwelt on with explicit imagery:

Round [the flame] he darts in dizzy rings,
And soon his soft and powder'd wings
Are singed; and dimmer grow his pearly eyes,
And now his struggling feet are foil'd,
And scorch'd, entangled, burnt, and soil'd,
His fragile form is lost – the wretched insect dies!
(25–30)[5]

'To the snow-drop' and 'Violets' are treated as opportunities to mourn the loss of childhood pleasures and the short shrift given to 'real merit' in the world ('Violets', 17). And as the poems become more complex, so too the messages of sorrow, and we once again encounter the speakers of the *Sonnets* and *The Emigrants*: by turns victimized, jaded, defensive and politically daring. Hence 'The wheat-ear' ends by comparing the 'simple bird' to 'those, that with distorted view / Thro' life some selfish end pursue, / With low inglorious aim; / *They* sink in blank oblivious night, / While minds superior dare the light, / And high on honor's glorious height / Aspire to endless fame!' (41–48). 'An evening walk by the sea-side' foreshadows trouble: 'And here on a rock that the tide will soon cover, / We'll find us a seat that is tapestried with weed', although it allows a last-minute escape: 'But now to retire from the rock we have warning, / Already the water encircles our seat' (7–8, 21–22). And despite the criticism she received in the 1790s for her political sensitivities, 'Ode to the olive tree' concentrates on the olive as an 'emble[m] of Peace!' and ends by declaring that 'genuine worth belongs to thee; / And Peace and Wisdom, powers divine, / Shall plant thee round the holy shrine / Of Liberty!' (36, 39–42).

It is common to argue that socially aware authors who write children's literature often embed in their writings the messages that they want children to imbibe without, perhaps, fully realizing it; the overt morality of late eighteenth and early nineteenth-century children's literature can mask a more challenging agenda. Smith's poems for children use genre to, as Curran notes, 'instruct' children 'in natural lore and poetic forms and usage' (177, note) by concentrating on birds, animals, insects and plants, and by gradually increasing the level of complexity of the poems as the text progresses. The child-reader thus advances from the simple iambic quatrameter, *abab* pattern of the first few poems through to rhyming iambic pentameter and the internal structural and rhyme variety of the later poems. As they read, they learn, and subsequent poems capitalize on that learning. Likewise, the later poems' emphasis on personal danger and unappreciated personal worth in place of the, by contrast, simple risks of the earlier poems suggest that, for Smith, the poetic project does not change despite the change in audience; as with the sonnets and her longer poems, content and structure still work together, and anxiety and trials still feature prominently in the formation of the speakers' subjectivity. Do the children's poems merely exist to convey the same message of sorrow and woe? Or are they, like Smith's other poems, more complex than superficial readings allow?

The didactic force of the poems is evident, but if the poems are read in their poetic context, as part of Smith's overall output, then their content needs to be more closely scrutinized. Of all her potential audiences, the juvenile one is least positioned to respond materially to the need implicit in these poems, and yet Smith follows its marked path regardless. Likewise, she re-presents the outspokenly critical speakers in only slightly changed settings. Perhaps it has become second nature, but as the sonnets show repeatedly, Smith's speakers 'delight to stray', and it is unlikely that here she would passively stick to her own formula, especially given the children's literature format. Certainly, moral warnings and images of violence are staples of the didactic children's texts of the time, but usually the violence is pointed to explicate the moral; that is, the naughty are punished while the good are rewarded. The almost casual violence and threats of violence of these poems does not fit the children's literature pattern, but it does illustrate a playful cynicism on the part of Smith. The imagery of the innocent victim that has suffused her poetry for adults is itself undermined once attached to fish, bees, hedgehogs and snowdrops; Smith mocks her own speakers' propensity for anguish when she portrays insects and flowers as sharing it – especially since these creatures are represented as fearing potential harm rather than actually experiencing it. Are her embodied speakers, then, also more victims of their own anxieties than of the perfidies of others? Even if Smith only floats the suggestion, its effect is deflating. The doom-laden narrator of these poems, who brings to her tales of insects and animals the gloomy anxiety of the *Sonnets*, may well teach her charges about the need to be kind to the helpless and avoid murdering bees, but she compromises the gravity of Smith's 'adult' speakers in so doing. The effect of reproducing the more socially responsible voice, however, is to insert in the children's poems a sense that it is never too early to point out the risks of social interaction, as well as social *in*action. Revelations of casual cruelty simultaneously sensitize, warn, and re-educate young readers; as she will do in *Beachy Head*, Smith destabilizes the force of fruitless moaning while pushing a new message of social responsibility.

The children's poems, then, operate on a level of simultaneous self-critique and self-justification. Merely reacting to perceived sorrows, or indeed anticipating the continuation of sorrows, comes to seem as fruitless as the moth's suicide. By designating the moth's instinctive action as 'suicide', by definition a planned act, and then holding up the moth as an object lesson for young readers, Smith embeds in this and the other poems a sense that passivity in the face of dangers is unacceptable, just as the fates of her *Beachy Head* hermits will suggest her disenchantment with deliberate self-isolation. And this takes us back to Romanticism, and its social consciousness, the Wordsworthian concern with the 'real language of men' and with elevating the lowly to prominence, subscribing to values of simplicity and naiveté.[6] Smith's poems for children, like Wordsworth's poems about children, situate childhood as both the ideal site for learning, and the ideal space for the creative imagination. For both poets, the simple and the childlike function as code for a renewal of subjectivity. And for both poets, a dedication to self-discovery underlies the turn to the other. For Smith, as I have argued in this book, self-discovery is in many ways an active process – that is, she reveals herself to her readers while also manifesting a variety of selves that both are and cannot be herself. Smith exposes to her readers' view her culture's open secret by acting it out.

When we read her poetry, then, we read a kind of primer or how-to guide on gender and identity in the late eighteenth century – but we must also re-examine our own assumptions as we do so. Smith's poetry yields easily to theories of gender and sexed identity; as this book has shown, a variety of competing approaches can be fruitfully followed. In each, the notion of identity and subjectivity becomes paramount. A thorough reading of Smith shows that as much as she was concerned to investigate and interrogate her place as a woman in her society, she was also fascinated by something more basic: her place as a human being, and the construction of an identity recognizable to her readers. Smith's Romanticism is about subjectivity and the creation and maintenance of the Self, and it is also about the trappings and dress that allow that Self a place within – or outside of – society. Poetry became the vehicle by which identity (as woman, mother, lover, human being, ultimately communicator) could be explored, established, and ultimately reconstructed. Smith's poetry exemplifies the main tenets of 'traditional' Romanticism, and this is because Smith is one of the creators of it. *Elegiac Sonnets, The Emigrants,* and *Beachy Head* show that the culture of gender, poetry and Romanticism is a web, intricate and self-sustaining, 'the golden thread that Fancy weaves / . . . / . . . while sevenfold wreaths / Of rainbow-light around [the Poet's] head revolve'.[7] By writing poetry of the Self, Smith produces, directs and enacts Romanticism.

Notes

1 See Marshall Brown, *Preromanticism* (Stanford: Stanford University Press, 1991); see also *Early Romantics: Perspectives in British Poetry from Pope to Wordsworth*, ed. Thomas Woodman (Basingstoke: Macmillan, 1998). A major conference, 'Early Romantic Poetry Revisited' (St Mary's University College Strawberry Hill, September 2000), began to question the formulation of 'preromanticism'.

2 Alan Richardson provides a strong argument in 'Romanticism and the Colonization of the Feminine', *Romanticism and Feminism*, ed. Anne Mellor (Bloomington: Indiana University Press, 1988), 13–25.

3 See Judith Pascoe's chapter on Wordsworth, 'Performing Wordsworth', *Romantic Theatricality: Gender, Poetry and Spectatorship* (Ithaca: Cornell University Press, 1997), for an especially trenchant exploration of Wordsworth's theatricality.

4 See *The Poems of Charlotte Smith*, ed. S. Curran (Oxford: Oxford University Press, 1993) 177, note.

5 For both 'The early butterfly' and 'The moth' the text's narrator, Mrs Talbot, notes the 'trite' and clichéd subject matter and the difficulty of finding something new to say 'on so obvious and hackneyed a subject'. Smith's relish in depicting the insects' death seems to be her route away from the 'mere commonplace' (quotes from *The Poems of Charlotte Smith*, ed. Curran, 184, 185, notes to the two poems).

6 Of course, neither Smith nor Wordsworth can be said to advocate true class mixture; instead, both see virtues in rusticity while also betraying unease with the actuality of the rustic (Smith perhaps more so than Wordsworth in this instance).

7 'Sonnet LXXVII: To the insect of the gossamer', 9, 12–13. The similarities to the last few lines of Coleridge's 'Kubla Khan' are suggestive.

Select bibliography

Ashfield, Anthony. *Romantic Women Poets, 1770–1838*. Manchester: Manchester University Press, 1995.

Behrendt, Stephen. '"A Few Harmless Numbers": British Women Poets and the Climate of War, 1793–1815'. *Romantic Wars: Studies in Culture and Conflict, 1793–1822*. Ed. Philip Shaw. Aldershot: Ashgate, 2000, 13–36.

Benstock, Shari. 'At the Margin of Discourse: Footnotes in the Fictional Text'. *PMLA* 98 (1983): 204–225.

Bray, Matthew. 'Removing the Anglo-Saxon Yoke: The Francocentric Vision of Charlotte Smith's Later Works'. *The Wordsworth Circle* 24 (1993): 155–158.

Brooks, Stella. 'The Sonnets of Charlotte Smith'. *Critical Survey* 4 (1992): 9–21.

Brown, Marshall. *Preromanticism*. Stanford: Stanford University Press, 1991.

Burns, Elizabeth. *Theatricality: A Study of Convention in the Theatre and in Social Life*. London: Longman, 1972.

Burroughs, Catherine. *Closet Stages: Joanna Baillie and the Theater Theory of British Romantic Women Writers*. Philadelphia: University of Pennsylvania Press, 1997.

Butler, Judith. *Gender Trouble: Feminism and the Subversion of Identity*. New York: Routledge, 1990.

Carlson, Julie. *In the Theatre of Romanticism: Coleridge, Nationalism, Women*. Cambridge: Cambridge University Press, 1994.

Chu, Patricia. '"The Invisible World the Emigrants Built": Cultural Self-Inscription and the Antiromantic Plots of *The Woman Warrior*'. *Diaspora* 2 (1992): 95–115.

The Critical Review 9 (October 1793): 299–302.

Crochunis, Thomas. 'Authorial Performances: Romantic Women Playwrights'. *Women in British Romantic Theatre: Drama, Performance, and Society, 1790–1840*. Ed. Catherine Burroughs. Cambridge: Cambridge University Press, 2000, 223–254.

Crossley, Ceri and Ian Small. Eds. *The French Revolution and British Culture*. Oxford: Oxford University Press, 1989.

Curran, Stuart. 'Romantic Poetry: The "I" Altered'. *Romanticism and Feminism.* Ed. Anne K. Mellor. Bloomington: Indiana University Press, 1988, 186–207.

Dallery, Arleen. 'The Politics of Writing (the) Body: *Ecriture Feminine*'. *Gender/Body/Knowledge: Feminist Reconstructions of Being and Knowing.* Eds. Alison M. Jaggar and Susan R. Bordo. New Brunswick: Rutgers University Press, 1989, 52–67.

Desan, Suzanne (1994). 'Women's Experience of the French Revolution: An Historical Overview'. *Literate Women and the French Revolution of 1789.* Ed. Catherine R. Montfort. Birmingham, AL: Summa Publications, Inc., 1994, 19–30.

Donohue, Jr, Joseph W. *Dramatic Character in the English Romantic Age.* Princeton: Princeton University Press, 1970.

Edholm, Felicity. 'Beyond the Mirror: Women's Self-Portraits'. *Imagining Women: Cultural Representations and Gender.* Eds. Frances Bonner, Lizbeth Goodman, Richard Allen, Linda Janes and Catherine King. Cambridge: Polity Press, 1992: 154–172.

Eger, Elizabeth, Charlotte Grant, Cliona Ò Gallchoir, and Penny Warburton. Eds. *Women, Writing and the Public Sphere, 1700–1830.* Cambridge: Cambridge University Press, 2001.

Ellis, Markman. *The Politics of Sensibility: Race, Gender and Commerce in the Sentimental Novel.* Cambridge: Cambridge University Press, 1996.

Epstein, Julia and Kristina Straub. Eds. *Body Guards: The Cultural Politics of Gender Ambiguity.* New York: Routledge, 1991.

European Magazine 24 (1793): 41–45.

Favret, Mary. 'Spectatrice as Spectacle: Helen Maria Williams at Home in the Revolution'. *Literate Women and the French Revolution of 1789.* Ed. Catherine R. Montfort. Birmingham, AL: Summa Publications, Inc., 1994, 151–172.

Fletcher, Loraine. *Charlotte Smith: A Critical Biography.* Basingstoke: Macmillan, 1998.

Gelpi, Barbara. *Shelley's Goddess: Maternity, Language, and Subjectivity.* Oxford: Oxford University Press, 1992.

Gilroy, Amanda. ' "Candid Advice to the Fair Sex": Or, the Politics of Maternity in Late Eighteenth-Century Britain'. *Body Matters: Feminism, Textuality, Corporeality.* Eds. Avril Horner and Angela Keane. Manchester: Manchester University Press, 2000, 17–29.

Gonda, Caroline. *Reading Daughters' Fictions.* Cambridge: Cambridge University Press, 1998.

Goodwin, Albert. *The Friends of Liberty: The English Democratic Movement in the Age of the French Revolution.* London: Hutchinson, 1979.

Grafton, Anthony. *The Footnote.* London: Faber and Faber, 1997.

Guest, Harriet. 'Eighteenth-Century Femininity: "A Supposed Sexual Character" '. *Women and Literature in Britain 1700–1800.* Ed. Vivien Jones. Cambridge: Cambridge University Press, 2000, 46–68.

Harries, Elizabeth W. ' "Out in Left Field": Charlotte Smith's Prefaces, Bourdieu's Categories, and the Public Sphere'. *Modern Language Quarterly* 58 (1997): 457–473.

Harris, Geraldine. *Staging Femininities: Performance and Performativity.* Manchester: Manchester University Press, 1999.

Hawley, Judith. 'Charlotte Smith's *Elegiac Sonnets:* Losses and Gains'. *Women's Poetry in the Enlightenment: The Making of a Canon, 1730–1820.* Eds. Isobel Armstrong and Virginia Blain. Basingstoke: Macmillan, 1999, 184–198.

Hess, Jonathan. 'Wordsworth's Aesthetic State: The Poetics of Liberty'. *Studies in Romanticism* 33 (1994): 3–29.

Hind, Arthur. *A History of Engraving and Etching.* New York: Dover, 1963.

Hoeveler, Diane Long. *Gothic Feminism: The Professionalization of Gender from Charlotte Smith to the Brontes.* Liverpool: Liverpool University Press, 1998.

Hunnisett, Basil. *Steel-Engraved Book Illustration in England.* London: Scolar Press, 1980.

Hunt, Jr, Bishop C. 'Wordsworth and Charlotte Smith'. *The Wordsworth Circle* 1 (1971): 85–103.

Jacobus, Mary. *First Things: The Maternal Imaginary in Literature, Art, and Psychoanalysis.* London: Routledge, 1995.

Johnson, Claudia. *Equivocal Beings: Politics, Gender, and Sentimentality in the 1790s. Wollstonecraft, Radcliffe, Burney, Austen.* Chicago: The University of Chicago Press, 1995.

——'Mary Wollstonecraft: Styles of Radical Maternity'. *Inventing Maternity: Politics, Science and Literature, 1650–1865.* Eds. Susan C. Greenfield and Carol Barash. Lexington: The University of Kentucky Press, 1999, 159–172.

Jones, Vivien. 'Femininity, Nationalism and Romanticism: The Politics of Gender in the Revolution Controversy'. *History of European Ideas* 16 (1993), 299–305.

Kennedy, Deborah. 'Thorns and Roses: The *Sonnets* of Charlotte Smith'. *Women's Writing* 2 (1995): 43–53.

Kristeva, Julia, *The Kristeva Reader.* Ed. Toril Moi. New York: Columbia University Press, 1986.

Labbe, Jacqueline M. 'Selling One's Sorrows: Charlotte Smith, Mary Robinson, and the Marketing of Poetry'. *The Wordsworth Circle* 25 (1994), 68–71.

——*Romantic Visualities: Landscape, Gender and Romanticism.* Basingstoke: Macmillan, 1998.

——'Charlotte Smith: "Beachy Head" '. *A Companion to Romanticism.* Ed. Duncan Wu. Oxford: Blackwells, 1998, 204–210.

—— ' "Transplanted into More Congenial Soil": Footnoting the Self in the Poetry of Charlotte Smith'. *Ma(r)king the Text: The Presentation of Meaning on the Literary Page.* Eds. Joe Bray, Miriam Handley and Anne C. Henry. Aldershot: Ashgate, 2000, 71–86.

——'The Exiled Self: Images of War in Charlotte Smith's *The Emigrants*'.

Romantic Wars: Studies in Culture and Conflict, 1793–1822. Ed. Philip Shaw. Aldershot: Ashgate, 2000, 37–56.

—— 'The Romance of Motherhood: Generation and the Literary Text'. *Romanticism on the Net* 9 (May 2002).

Landes, Joan. *Women and the Public Sphere in the Age of the French Revolution.* Ithaca: Cornell University Press, 1988.

Litvak, Joseph. *Caught in the Act: Theatricality in the Nineteenth-Century English Novel.* Berkeley: University of California Press, 1992.

Livingston, Ira. 'The "No-Trump Bid" on Romanticism and Gender'. *Romanticism and Gender.* Ed. Anne Janowitz. Cambridge: D. S. Brewer, 1998, 161–173.

Lorraine, Tamsin E. *Gender, Identity and the Production of Meaning.* Oxford: Westview Press, 1990.

McGann, Jerome. *Romantic Period Verse.* Oxford: Oxford University Press, 1994.

Mellor, Anne. *Mothers of the Nation: Women's Political Writing in England, 1780–1830.* Bloomington: Indiana University Press, 2000.

Mermin, Dorothy. 'The Damsel, the Knight, and the Victorian Woman Poet'. *Critical Inquiry* 13 (1986): 64–80.

Montfort, Catherine R. and J. J. Allison. 'Women's Voices and the French Revolution'. *Literate Women and the French Revolution of 1789.* Ed. Catherine R. Montfort. Birmingham, AL: Summa Publications, Inc., 3–17.

Monthly Review 12 (1793): 375–376.

Miller, Christopher. 'The Postidentitarian Predicament in the Footnotes of *A Thousand Plateaus*: Nomadology, Anthropology, and Authority'. *Diacritics* 23 (1993), 6–35.

Nussbaum, Felicity. *Torrid Zones: Maternity, Sexuality, and Empire in Eighteenth-Century English Narratives.* Baltimore: Johns Hopkins University Press, 1995.

Ostriker, Alicia. 'A Wild Surmise: Motherhood and Poetry'. *Imagining Women: Cultural Representations and Gender.* Eds. Frances Bonner, Lizbeth Goodman, Richard Allen, Linda Janes and Catherine King. Cambridge: Polity Press, 1992: 103–107.

Outram, Dorinda. '*Le Langage Male de la Vertu*: Women and the Discourse of the French Revolution'. *The Social History of Language.* Eds. Peter Burke and Roy Porter. Cambridge: Cambridge University Press, 1987.

Newlyn, Lucy. *Reading, Writing, and Romanticism: The Anxiety of Reception.* Oxford: Oxford University Press, 2000.

Pascoe, Judith. 'Female Botanists and the Poetry of Charlotte Smith'. *Re-Visioning Romanticism: British Women Writers, 1776–1837.* Eds. Carol Shiner Wilson and Joel Haefner. Philadelphia: University of Pennsylvania Press, 1994, 193–209.

—— *Romantic Theatricality: Gender, Poetry, and Spectatorship.* Ithaca: Cornell University Press, 1997.

—— '"Unsex'd Females": Barbauld, Robinson and Smith'. *The Cambridge*

Companion to English Literature 1740–1830. Eds. Jon Mee and Tom Keymer. Cambridge: Cambridge University Press, forthcoming 2003.

Pinch, Adela. *Strange Fits of Passion: Epistemologies of Emotion, Hume to Austen*. Stanford: Stanford University Press, 1996.

Poovey, Mary. *The Proper Lady and the Woman Writer*. Chicago: Chicago University Press, 1984.

Redfield, Marc. 'Romanticism, *Bildung*, and the Literary Absolute'. *Lessons of Romanticism: A Critical Companion*. Eds. Thomas Pfau and Robert Gleckner. Durham: Duke University Press, 1998, 41–54.

Richardson, Alan. *Literature, Education, and Romanticism*. Cambridge: Cambridge University Press, 1994.

Ruwe, Donelle. 'Charlotte Smith's Sublime: Feminine Poetics, Botany, and *Beachy Head*'. *Prism(s)* 7 (1999): 117–132.

St Cyres, Viscount de. 'The Sorrows of Mrs. Charlotte Smith'. *The Cornhill Magazine* 15 (1903): 683–96.

Scott, Walter. 'Charlotte Smith'. *Miscellaneous Prose Works*. 4 vols. Edinburgh: Cadell, 1834.

Shapiro, Judith. 'Transsexualism: Reflections on the Persistence of Gender and the Mutability of Sex'. *Body Guards: The Cultural Politics of Gender Ambiguity*. Eds. Julia Epstein and Kristina Straub. New York: Routledge, 1991, 248–279.

Smith, Charlotte. *Elegiac Sonnets*. Vol. I: London: T. Cadell, Junior and W. Davies, 1797; Vol. II: London: T. Cadell, Junior and W. Davies. 1800.

—— *The Poems of Charlotte Smith*. Ed. Stuart Curran. Oxford: Oxford University Press, 1993.

—— *The Old Manor House*. Ed. Jacqueline M. Labbe. Peterborough: Broadview Literary Texts, 2002.

Sutherland, Kathryn 'Writing on Education and Conduct: Arguments for Female Improvement'. *Women and Literature in Britain, 1700–1800*. Ed. Vivien Jones. Cambridge: Cambridge University Press, 2000, 25–45.

Turner, Rufus Paul. 'Charlotte Smith (1749–1806): New Light on her Life and Literary Career'. Unpub. PhD diss. University of Southern California, 1966.

Walker, Michelle Boulous. *Philosophy and the Maternal Body: Reading Silence*. London: Routledge, 1998.

Wallace, Anne D. 'Picturesque Fossils, Sublime Geology? The Crisis of Authority in Charlotte Smith's *Beachy Head*'. *European Romantic Review* 13 (2002): 77–96.

Wittig, Monica. 'The Mark of Gender'. *The Poetics of Gender*. Ed. Nancy K. Miller. New York: Columbia University Press, 1986, 63–73.

Wolfson, Susan. 'A Lesson in Romanticism: Gendering the Soul'. *Lessons of Romanticism: A Critical Companion*. Eds. Thomas Pfau and Robert F. Gleckner. Durham: Duke University Press, 1998, 349–375.

Woodman, Thomas. Ed. *Early Romantics: Perspectives in British Poetry from Pope to Wordsworth*. Basingstoke: Macmillan, 1998.

The Works of Sir William Jones. 13 vols. Delhi: Agam Prakashan, 1976–80.

Wu, Duncan. *Romantic Women Poets: An Anthology*. Oxford: Blackwells, 1997.

Zerilli, Linda. 'Text/Woman as Spectacle: Edmund Burke's "French Revolution"'. *The Eighteenth Century* 33 (1992), 47–72.

Zimmerman, Sarah. 'Charlotte Smith's Letters and the Practice of Self-Presentation'. *Princeton University Library Chronicle* 53 (1991): 50–77.

——*Romanticism, Lyricism and History.* State University of New York Press, 1999.

Index

abject 55, 121–123, 126, 131, 137

Beachy Head 8, 9, 12, 19, 53–59, 142–162
Benstock, Shari 54–57 *passim*
Butler, Judith 5, 94, 95

chivalry 9, 18, 27, 48, 91, 94, 98
chora 54–55, 58–59
Conversations Introducing Poetry 167–170
Crochunis, Thomas 94, 97
Curran, Stuart 7, 139n.13, 141n.35, 142, 168

dedications 12, 18, 24–32, 60n.9
Derrida, Jacques 55, 58
Desmond 118, 139n.5

Elegiac Sonnets 1, 3, 8–9, 15, 18–19, 45–49, 70–81, 91–97, 112, 157
Ellis, Markman 93–94, 113n.7
Emigrants, The 8–12 *passim*, 18–19, 49–53, 81–86, 118–138
Emmeline 106
engravings 15, 32–44
exile 117–118, 121, 123, 126–128, 132–135

Favret, Mary 127
femininity 7–8, 12, 20, 24, 26, 55, 57, 59, 92–95, 104, 112, 124, 127
French Revolution 51–53, 117–129 *passim*
Freud, Sigmund 120–121
frontispiece 1–6 *passim*

Gelpi, Barbara 67–68, 70, 74
Guest, Harriet 4

Harris, Geraldine 94–95
Hawley, Judith 74
heimlich/unheimlich 120–121, 132, 137

Johnson, Claudia 82, 107

Kristeva, Julia 23, 45, 53–55 *passim*, 66, 71, 73, 76, 80, 121, 124

Landes, Joan 122–123
legality 28, 60n.7, 121
Long Hoeveler, Diane 8, 17

margins 23, 44–45, 49–59, 82, 86, 120–124 *passim*, 128, 131, 133, 136
Marie Antoinette 83–85
masculinity 3, 6, 14–15, 109, 124, 127, 133, 167

Lightning Source UK Ltd.
Milton Keynes UK

172383UK00001B/30/P